Sexual Abuse of Girl Children

Sexual Abuse of Girl Children

Some Hidden Facts

Rama Achyut Pande

RAWAT PUBLICATIONS

Jaipur • New Delhi • Bangalore • Guwahati • Kolkata

ISBN 978-81-316-0789-3

The publication of this book was financially supported by the ICSSR. The responsibility for the facts stated, opinions expressed, or conclusions reached, is entirely that of the author and that the ICSSR accepts no responsibility for them.

ICSSR Consultant: Professor C.P. Singh, Department of Social Work, Kurukshetra University, Kurukshetra, Haryana.

Published by
Prem Rawat for **Rawat Publications**
Satyam Apts, Sector 3, Jawahar Nagar, Jaipur 302 004 (India)
Phone: 0141 265 1748 / 7006 Fax: 0141 265 1748
E-mail: info@rawatbooks.com
Website: www.rawatbooks.com

New Delhi Office
4858/24, Ansari Road, Daryaganj, New Delhi 110 002
Phone: 011 2326 3290

Also at *Bangalore, Guwahati* and *Kolkata*

Typeset by Rawat Computers, Jaipur
Printed and bound in India

Dedicated to

All those girl children

who are victims of 'culture of silence'

Contents

Preface

Girl child sexual abuse is not the problem of any particular country, but is a rapidly increasing global problem. Exploitation and sexual abuse of girl children is of serious consequences to the society in general, and girl child in particular. The future of a nation cannot be secure if it does not build the capacity to assure good psychological and physical development of girl children. Unfortunately, in India, girl children are not only neglected but are also sexually abused and exploited even in their own families, by their near and dear ones. Most of these girl children have had painful experiences emotionally, psychologically and socially.

The present book is an outcome of my Ph.D. thesis on 'A Study of Sexual Abuse of Girl Children with Special Reference to Beed District'. This was based on empirical study conducted in two tahasils, Ambajogai and Kaij, of Beed District. The information has been collected through focus group discussion, one-on-one interaction, interview schedule and interviews with key informants.

This book would be useful for parents of girl children, social workers, teachers, students, policy-makers in the field of social work, home affairs, women and child welfare, women studies, researchers and all those NGOs who are working on the issue of girl children sexual abuse. Moreover, this book will help policy-makers and the government for intervention in strategies and rehabilitative programme.

I am obliged to express my deep sense of gratitude to Professor Shubhangi Gavhane who guided me during the entire process of writing this book. I am thankful to Dr E.N. Ashok Kumar, Director, Department of Sociology, Solapur University, Solapur and my colleague Dr Shaik Nazir for their valuable guidance and suggestions to make this book more readable. I have special thanks for G.V. Kulkarni (my brother-in-law) for his scholarly scrutiny and valuable suggestions. I am thankful to Ashok Tanksale, Arohi, Kalpana, Sachin and Tejas for their help during this entire process.

I have no words to express my thanks to my life partner, Mr Achyut Pande and my son, Aditya Pande who helped me during the process. I am also thankful to all my family members for their constant support and encouragement.

I am grateful to my college principal Dr Prakash Jadhav, my colleague Dr Arundhati Patil, Assistant Professor; Sukeshi Ramteke, Librarian and all other staff members for their inspiration and constant support.

Rama Achyut Pande

1

Introduction

'The child is father of the man' said Willam Wordsworth. What he obviously meant was that the productiveness of an adult depends on the opportunities he has had to grow and develop as a child. From this follows that ultimately the quality of a nation depends on the attention it pays to its children.[1]

This was rightly focused by Dr A.P.J. Abdul Kalam (2007), former President of India, in his address to the joint session of the Parliament. He reiterated the government's commitment towards women and children. 'The rights of women and children and their aspirations are of paramount importance in our march towards an inclusive and equitable society. Keeping in view the constitutional provisions and in order to give greater focus to issues relating to women and children, an independent ministry of women and child development has been created. Investment in the well-being of children is an investment in the future of the country. At the same time issues relating to child protection are high on my Government's agenda'.[2]

India's children are India's future as the strength of the nation lies in a healthy, protected, educated and well-developed child population that will grow up to be productive citizens of the country. Protecting the physical and mental development of children is the most important of all investments in the social and economic development of our society.

Children are the wealth of the nation. They are real social capital of our future and they are the citizens of tomorrow. They are the pillars of tomorrow's healthy society. A society can be accessed on the basis of how it treats its children and women.

It is the right of all children to be protected wherever they are, be it at home, in school, on the streets and at all times, be they of peace or conflicts or calamity. Their right to protection is as intrinsic to their well-being as is the right to survival, development and participation. Children deserve to live in an environment where good governance and full enjoyment of human rights are mutually reinforcing.[3]

Before going to further details of children's development, it is important to know who is a child.

Definition of Child

The child, internationally, is defined as any person aged up to 18 years. With the adoption of the Juvenile Justice Act (1986, amended in 2000), the National Plan of Action for Children 2005, and the Commissions for the Protection of Children's Rights Act 2005, the Government of India has now recognized that childhood legally extends to the age of 18 years.[4]

In India, the law considers any one less than 18 years of age to be a child/minor.[5]

The Protection of Children from Sexual Offences Bill 2012, defines a 'child' as any person below the age of 18 years and seeks to penalize anybody who commits a sexual offence against him or her. With more than a third of its population below the age of 18, India has the largest child population in the world. This background explores the levels of health, nutrition, education and social security of children, and government policy and action on child rights. In this context, it is essential to know the status of children in India.

Status of Children

Children are the citizens of tomorrow. They are the wealth, the real social capital, of the nation. The quality of a nation depends on physical and psychological development of its children. They are the pillars of tomorrow's healthy society. The strength and stability of the social edifice that society tries to erect depend upon how children are raised in the society. The quality of the life of a child determines the quality of a nation that citizens seek to build.

India is home to almost 19 per cent of the world's children. More than one-third of the country's population, around 440 million, is below 18 years, 40 per cent of these children are in need of care and protection, which indicates the extent of the problem. In a country like India, with its multicultural, multi-ethnic and multi-religious population, the problem of socially marginalized and economically backward groups are immense. Within such groups, the most vulnerable section is always that of the children. The challenge is to reach out to the most vulnerable and socially excluded child of this country and create an environment wherein not only is every child protected, but every child also has access to opportunities and education for all-round growth and development.

In India, nearly 90 per cent children suffer from malnutrition, about one lakh succumbing to it every month. India's infant mortality rate of 120 in 1,000 has put it in the 27th position from the top in a list of 130 countries.

The 2011 Indian Census reveals some shocking data about child (0–6 years) population. Child population in India has decreased whereas overall population has increased by about 17.64 per cent in last 10 years. Something that is alarming is that the sex ratio of children under 6 years has dropped to just 914 girl child per 1,000 boys. Both rural and urban India has the same negative changes. This negative change makes the girl face a number of problems like low educational status which results in school dropout and low health status which results in malnourished children. Her low status in family and society leads to female foeticide; early marriage further results in early maternal mortality, childhood neglect, physical, emotional and sexual abuse and overall social injustice. The lame explanation of son preference as a social bias or poverty can no longer be an excuse; the state must find a way to protect both the dignity and the lives of daughter.[6]

As India races towards achieving superpower stature, the status of child population is a serious problem. Without increasing the status of its child population, especially girl child, it cannot become a superpower. The development of a nation can be assessed with the progress of its children by ensuring them all their necessities, because children are the future of tomorrow. But India's children continue to face a huge backlog of deprivations, especially girl children are still lacking in terms of healthcare, education and other facilities. Let us see the educational and health status of children in India.

Educational Status

Education is the ultimate panacea for curing the ills of people; it is one of the important factors responsible for the development of a human personality. Right to education, therefore, is held as a very important human right. Right to Education Act (RTE), which was passed by the Indian Parliament on 4 August 2009, describes the modalities of the provision of free and compulsory education for children between 6 and 14 in India under Article 21 A of the Indian Constitution. India became one of the 135 countries to make education a fundamental right of every child when the Act came into force on 1 April 2010.[7]

The Act provides that no child shall be held back, expelled, or required to pass a board examination until the completion of elementary education. There is also a provision for special training of school dropouts, to bring them up at par with students of the same age.

Girl Child Literacy Updates in India

Education is the cornerstone of girl's empowerment because it enables her to respond to opportunities, to challenge their traditional roles and to change their future. This is true not only because education is an entry point to other opportunities, but also because it has a ripple effect within the family and across generations; investing in secondary school education, for girls yield high dividends.

Education strategy in primary and secondary schooling is the most important intervention for giving children their due right. The Government of India's National Plan of Action for Children 2005, comprehensively commits itself to ensure all rights to all children up to the age of 18 years.[8]

According to 2011 Census report, pre-primary school participation, gross enrolment ratio (%) of girl children in 2007–2010, is 54 per cent, primary school participation, net enrolment ratio (%), 2007–2010, of girl children is 94 per cent. Secondary school participation, net attendance ratio 2005–2010, of girl children is 49 per cent.

The Eleventh Five-Year Plan envisions reaching out to all categories of children. It includes children with disabilities who are discriminated against in the education system. Sarva Shiksha Abhiyan is the flagship programme of the Government of India to achieve universal elementary education, in a time bound manner. The 86th Amendment to the Constitution makes free and compulsory education to children in 6 to 14 years age group, a fundamental right.

Sarva Shiksha Abhiyan also seeks to provide quality elementary education, including life skills. It has a special focus on the education of the girl child and children with special needs. Another important component of the Abhiyan is to provide computer education to bridge the digital divide.

'Short-changing girls is not only a matter of gender discrimination: it is bad economics and bad social policy, experience has shown, over and over again, that investment in girls education translate directly and quickly into better nutrition for the whole family, better health care declining fertility, poverty reduction and better overall economic performance' (*Millennium Development Goals Report, 2011*, UN).

Education helps girls to know their rights and to gain confidence to claim them. Despite government efforts, education appears to be a distant dream for many a girl from rural area. This educational backwardness of girls has been the cause of the low status of girls in the country. Hence, parents have to change their attitude towards educational development of their daughters and encourage them for learning.[8]

Health Status

For a nation's progress, it is essential that the health of its population, including health and nutrition of women, children and especially girl children, mothers of the new generation, is adequately cared for. The health and nutritional status of women, children and adolescent girls leaves much scope for improvement, as anaemia affects 74 per cent of children under the age of 3 years, more than 90 per cent of adolescent girls and 50 per cent of women. Girls are more at risk of malnutrition than boys because of their lower social status. It has serious consequences because malnourished children are less likely to perform well in school and more likely to grow into malnourished adults at a greater risk of disease and early death.[9]

Facts of Health

Special Statistics on Girl Child

- 1 out of every 6 girls does not live to see her fifteenth birthday.
- Of the 12 million girls born in India, 1 million do not see their first birthday.
- Of the 12 million girls born in India, 3 million do not see their fifteenth birthday, and a million of them are unable to survive even their first birthday.
- One-third of these deaths take place at birth.
- Every sixth girl child's death is due to gender discrimination.
- Females are victimized far more than males during childhood.
- 3 lakh more girls than boys die every year.
- Female mortality exceeds male mortality in 224 out of 402 districts in India.
- Death rate among girls below the age of 4 years is higher than that of boys. Even if she escapes infanticide or foeticide, a girl child is less likely to receive immunization, nutrition or medical treatment compared to a male child.[10]

The above statistics show the lower health status of girl child. Indian girls are facing discrimination in the home and in society due to their lower status, they are treated as a burden not as an asset. A girl child in a family or outside in the world has to face double jeopardy, beside other deprivations she is discriminated against because of her sex. Her low status makes her feel inferior and to tolerate exploitation such conditions makes her silent even when she is sexually abused in her family by her near and dear ones. Hence, due to low educational status and low health status, she loses her confidence and she feels sad about herself being a girl

Status of Girl Child

Even in the 21st century, the girl children are suffering due to a secondary status in their families and in society. In such unfavourable situations in family and society, the girl child is double deprived. Besides common deprivations, she is discriminated because of her sex. The discrimination is confirmed by the skewed male-female ratio in our country; 913 females to 1,000 males, an imbalance causing many girls to suffer from malnutrition in comparison to boys. Morbidity is higher among the female children than among male and girls enter adolescence and motherhood in undernourished condition, in turn giving birth to underweight babies. Thus, girl children are neglected. As the institution of family is under stress and strain for various reasons and the child, specially girl child, is the victim of this breakdown of family structure, she is not only neglected in the society but she is neglected and abused in her own families. The future of a nation cannot be secured if it does not build the capacity to assure good health facilities, education facilities and insured and secured life for its future mothers, i.e. the girl children.

Although the Constitution of India guarantees equality to all citizens, the status of women and girls is not at par with that of males in some sections of society. The skewed sex ratio in the 0–6 year age group is an indicator of this fact. The Government of India has launched several schemes and programmes for the welfare of the girl child and is trying to reduce discrimination against the girl child. Some of these are:

Girl Child Scheme/Adolescent Girl Scheme

1. Sarva Shiksha Abhiyan (2002)
2. Balika Samriddhi Yojana (1997)
3. Kishori Shakti Yojana (2000)
4. Jan Shikshan Sansthan (1998)
5. District Primary Education Programme (1994)
6. Reproductive and Child Health Programme (1996)
7. Integrated Child Development Services (1975)
8. National Programme of Nutritional Support to Primary Education (Mid-Day Meal Scheme) (1995)
9. Integrated Child Protection Scheme (2009)
10. 'SABALA', scheme for Adolescent Girls (Launched in 2010)

Legislative Measures

Various legislations have been enacted for the protection of children. These are:

1. The Pre-conception and Pre-natal Diagnostic Techniques (Regulation and Prevention of Misuse) Act, 1994.
2. The Medical Termination of Pregnancy Act, 1971.
3. Child Marriage Restraint Act, 1929 (Amended in 1979, 2006 and 2008).
4. Child Labour (Regulation and Prohibition) Act, 1986 (Amended in 2006).
5. Infant Milk Substitutes, Feeding Bottles and Infant Food (Regulation of Production, Supply and Distribution) Act, 1992 (NIPCED, 2010).
6. The Protection of Children Against Sexual Assault Act, 2012.

Although the democratic Constitution and laws state that there have to be equal and full opportunities, the girl child, if she survives, barely gets to see her fifteenth birthday. Out of the 15 million baby girls born in the country, every year nearly 25 per cent of them do not reach their fifteenth birthday.

It is only a woman who understands that, whether a male or female child, it should be healthy and given equal status. A woman has the power to end the evil of dowry system also. As girls are given a chance to live, there will be control in population. Families will be small, healthy, better educated and happy. Today's woman has to be given the confidence to live. She will eventually be a balanced mother. The craving for the ubiquitous male heir has to vanish. Discrimination between the male and female child has to end forever. Educated Indians have to behave responsibly and set an example for one another.[11]

In many homes across the country, girls are treated with indifference. Daughters are considered as liabilities. Every 26 minutes, a woman is molested. Every 34 minutes, a rape takes place. Every 42 minutes, a sexual harassment incident occurs. Every 43 minutes, a woman is kidnapped. And every 93 minutes, a woman is burnt to death over dowry. One-quarter of the reported rapes involve girls under the age of 16. but they are never reported.[12]

Girl Child Education in India

The Constitution guarantees free primary school education for boys and girls up to 14 years of age. But till today, only 39 per cent of girls and 64 per cent of boys get education in Bihar, Rajasthan, Uttar Pradesh and Madhya Pradesh. If women teachers were increased, chances are that girls in rural areas would continue to study. As girls get enlightened, they will raise better families.[13]

These girls are also deprived of the right to education due to their domestic work like household chores, or they care for cattle, attend to younger children, collect firewood and work in fields. The status and action report of the Central Advisory Board of India states that at least 15 per cent of all sex workers in the country are girls under the age of 15.

The Millennium Report UNO Vital Statistics

- Of more than 110 million children not in school, approximately 60 per cent are girls.
- By age 18, girls have received an average on 4.4 years less education than boys.
- Worldwide, of more than 130 million primary school age children not enrolled in school, nearly 60 per cent are girls.

- In some countries in Sub-Saharan Africa, adolescent girls have HIV rates up to five times higher than adolescent boys.
- Pregnancies and childbirth-related health problems take the lives of nearly 146,000 teenage girls each year.
- At least one in three girls and women worldwide has been beaten or sexually abused in her lifetime.
- Two million girls and women are subjected to female genital mutilation every year.

Hence, many of these girl children have not got their needs satisfied by their parents. Most of these children have had painful experiences in their emotional, psychological fields and social coping. Stressful pattern in the families often impede opportunities to children to share their feelings in family life. Broken marriages, disintegrated families and single parent families, migrant families and addiction in the family, are leading to lack of interaction between parents and children and such families become weak in guiding and understanding the needs of children which create a vacuum in the life of girl children.

The situation of girl children in urban area is not different. In the nuclear families, in urban area, many children are left in the hands of professional caretakers and in daycare centres, in leisure clubs, sports clubs, residential institutions and boarding schools. A good number of children are abused by the caretakers, teachers and other persons.[14]

We forget that children have their own emotional, physical, psychological needs for which they are dependent on their parents but, most of the time, in the families, parents cannot fulfil the needs of their children. Now the structure of the family has changed and due to this, children feel isolated in their homes. They feel insecure in their own family as there is nobody to share their feelings and such situations are misused by the neighbours, family friends, caretakers, adults in the families and these people exploit the children sexually. The girl child who is victim of sexual abuse in the family stays silent in such situations, not disclosing the incidence due to shame and fear.

These girls are not only abused in their families, they are even abused outside the homes. The fact is that India is a home to around 440 million children, nearly 42 per cent of the country's population, the largest number of minors in any country in the world. Over 16 million children work in India, comprising 5 per cent of the workforce. Most of them are exploited and thousands of girl children are kidnapped every year.

Despite her ethos of non-violence, tolerance and spirituality, India hosts the world's largest number of sexually abused children, a far higher rate than in any other country. According to the World Health Organization (WHO), one in every four girls and one in every seven boys in the world is sexually abused. Among the countries where children are most vulnerable,

India ranks sixth. The fault is not only of the state, but the problem is so serious that any efforts made by the state are very limited when compared to the problem.

Thus, conditions are unfavourable to the girl children in their homes as well as in the society, due to deep rooted biases. Traditionally in India, the responsibility of care and protection of children has been with families and communities. A strong knit patriarchal family that is meant to look after its children well has seldom had the realization that children are individuals with their own rights. While the Constitution of India guarantees many fundamental rights to the children, the approach to ensure the fulfilment of these rights was more need-based rather than rights-based. The transition to the rights-based approach in the government and civil society is still evolving. The situation can only improve with a change in attitude (Chaudhary, 2007).

Indian society is facing various problems these days. There is a large child population in India and a large percentage of this population is vulnerable to sexual abuse and exploitation. They are facing various problems and one of the serious problems is of child abuse. Children have their own physical, psychological and emotional needs for which they are dependent on the family and the society around. If a child is insecure and feels isolated, the situation is misused by caretakers, family friends and neighbours to exploit and abuse the child sexually and the child suffers in silence, not speaking about the incidence due to shame and fear.

There was an enormous number of children needing care and protection, while on the other hand, there were not enough schemes or sufficient budgetary allocations to deal with them. It was also observed that to carry the issue of child protection forward there was a need to create an enabling environment through a legislation to address issues of child abuse, make a policy on child protection, formulate interventions and outreach services and create an information base on child protection.

The problem is that data on child sexual abuse is limited. The only source of data presently available was with the National Crime Records Bureau. Although this data was useful, it constituted a miniscule of the total crimes/violence committed against children. The reason for this is that very often crimes against children are either not reported or cognizance is not taken and also that some crimes against children are not covered under existing legislations. Though gaps in information were at all levels, child abuse, being an issue shrouded in secrecy, emerged as the most burning issue.

A nation's girl children are its future and India is no exception. A little amount of care, a handful of warmth and a heart full of love for a girl child can make a big difference. Close your eyes, free your thoughts and hear the voice of a girl, she is saying something to all of us, 'Save Me'.

In this concern it is necessary to understand the concept of child abuse and girl child sexual abuse which make the girl most vulnerable in home and in society. After discussing the children and their status in India, the need is to discuss the problem of girl sexual abuse, but before that, it is important to note that this particular problem is studied under the branch of criminology.

Criminology is that branch of 'sociology' which deals with the scientific study of crime as a social phenomenon. It includes within its scope the process of making laws, of violating laws and reaction towards the breaking of laws.[15]

It is also described as a study of the crime and its causes. In its broader perspective, criminology means the study of crime, the causes of crime, the prevention of crime, effects of punishment on criminals and society and the treatment of criminals.[16]

Definition of Criminology

According to Sutherland (1924), 'Criminology is the body of knowledge regarding crime as a social phenomenon'.

The knowledge of criminology will contribute to the development of other social sciences and, through these, other social studies will contribute to the efficiency in general social control of crimes. Besides theoretical knowledge, criminology is also important from its applied point of view. Its main aim is to give practical shape to all the measures of crime control.

Sex crime is such a crime which has been prevailing in almost all societies from ages. Modern mechanization and urbanization has brought about total disintegration of the 'family' institution which has created serious problems in human life. The control of parents over their children has weakened considerably. In fact, it is parental negligence which is responsible for growing problem of abuse of children. It has become a global problem. The problems of children are increasing in the form of unmarried motherhood, incest, rape, kidnapping, enticement, abduction, indecent assault, etc.

Like any other western country, India is also facing the problem of girl child sexual abuse. Despite repressive socio-legal measures to control sex-crimes, India is facing the problems aggravated by causing obstruction for prosecution and punishment for sexual offenders. These offences, therefore, have thrown a great challenge before the society.

In this context, the researcher in the present study studied the nature, extent, causes, consequences and rehabilitative measures of girl child sexual abuse, as a study under the branch of criminology.

Child Abuse

Child abuse is a state of emotional, physical, economic and sexual maltreatment meted out to a person below the age of 18 and is a globally prevalent phenomenon. However, in India, as in many other countries, there has been no understanding of the extent, magnitude and trends of the problem. The growing complexities of life and the dramatic changes brought about by socio-economic transitions in India have played a major role in increasing the vulnerability of children to various and newer forms of abuse.

Child abuse is a violation of the basic human rights of a child and is an outcome of a set of interrelated familial, social, psychological and economic factors. The problem of child abuse and human rights violations is one of the most critical matters on the international human rights agenda. In the Indian context, acceptance of child rights as primary inviolable rights is fairly recent, as is the universal understanding of it.

Child abuse in one form or another has occurred in almost all societies throughout history. However, its recognition as a social problem is of recent origin in developed countries like UK and the USA; the number of cases of child abuse may be equally enormous in developing countries (Rane, 1994).

Children are exploited or abused in the society, child labourers by employers, street children beggars, orphans by strangers, and child prostitute by elders, adults. Not only girl children are the victims of sexual abuse but male children are also the victims of sexual abuse in the world. Child abuse is not only limited to any one community or illiterate people but it has become a national problem. Unfortunately, the phenomenon in our country is not yet recognized.

The phenomenon of child abuse has not yet come to the forefront in India due to various reasons. Poffenberger (1981) rightly observed that punitive child rearing practices and authoritarian treatment of children by their parents in Indian society have been persisting for centuries and have become purposeful socio-cultural norms. Such behaviour of parents is, very often, justified because of widespread acceptance of corporal discipline as a part of child rearing and parental authority in disciplining their children.

According to Sharan (1990), child abuse in India is manifested to a great extent in the form of child neglect, child labour, child beggary, abandonment of children and child marriage. Several factors such as poverty and sex problems of adults, is cause of child sexual abuse in India (Rane, 1994). According to Rath (1991), the role of parenting behaviour in the dynamics of child abuse can be viewed under two major perspectives under Indian conditions, the essence of which is rare in other societies elsewhere in the world. The first perspective refers to the macro variables relating to social, economic, religious, educational and other demographic variables. The second perspective refers to the micro level variable, relating to parental attitude, child rearing history, emotional neglect, distinct motivational and personality typology within the individual (Rane, 1994).

Child abuse has serious physical and psycho-social consequences which adversely affect health. It refers to any act or failure to act that violates the rights of the child that endanger his or her optimum health, survival and development.

Human Touch Bureau Report (2004) defines 'Child Abuse' as causing or permitting any harmful or offensive contact with a child's body, and any communication or transaction of any kind which humiliates, shames or frightens the child. Some child development experts go a bit further and define child abuse as any act or omission, which fails to nurture or in the upbringing of the children.[17]

The Child Abuse Prevention and Treatment Act defines child abuse and neglect as, at minimum, any act or failure to act on the part of a parent or caretaker which results in death, serious physical or emotional harm, sexual abuse or exploitation or an act or failure to act which presents an imminent risk of serious harm to the child.

According to Burgess (1971), child abuse refers to any child who receives non-accidental physical and psychological injury as a result of an act and an omission on the part of his parents or guardians or employers.

The most common ways of defining child abuse has been in terms of physical injuries to the child. According to Gil (1970) abuse of children is the intentional, non-accidental use of force or intentional, non-accidental acts of omission on the part of parents or caretaker interacting with the child in his care aimed at hurting the child.

In the Indian context, the committee constituted at the national institute of public operation and child development, New Delhi, in June 1988 evolved the following definition of child abuse. 'Child Abuse and Neglect (CAN) is the intentional, non-accidental injury, maltreatment of children by parents, caretakers, employers or others including those individuals representing governmental, non-governmental bodies which may lead to temporary or permanent impairment of their physical, mental and psychosocial development, disability or death'. It is a broad definition involving abusive behaviour of all types of caretaker towards children in their care.[18]

Child abuse or maltreatment constitutes all forms of physical and/or emotional ill-treatment sexual abuse, neglect or negligent treatment or commercial or other exploitation resulting in actual or potential harm to the child's health, survival, development or dignity in the context of a relationship of responsibility, trust or power.[19]

This problem can be seen everywhere without discrimination of sex, religion, colour, social economic, background, age, etc. There are many factors that may contribute to the occurrence of child abuse and neglect.

Parents may be more likely to maltreat their children. Some parents may not be able cope with the stress resulting from the changes and may experience difficulty in caring for their children.

Major Types of Child Abuse

Neglect

The failure to provide for child's basic needs, neglect can be physical, educational or emotional Physical neglect can include not providing adequate food or clothing, appropriate medical care, supervision or proper weather protection; educational neglect includes failure to provide appropriate schooling or special educational needs. Emotional or psychological neglect includes the lack of any emotional support and love, never attending to the child, spousal abuse, and drug and alcohol abuse including allowing the child to participate in drug and alcohol use are some of the examples of emotional or psychological neglect of the child.

Emotional Abuse

Emotional abuse means verbal abuse, mental abuse and psychological maltreatment which includes act or the failure to act by parents or caretakers that cause or could cause serious behavioural, cognitive, emotional or mental disorders to the child.

Physical Abuse

Physical abuse is causing physical injury to a child. This may include burning, hitting, punching, shaking, kicking, beating or otherwise harming a child. The parent or caretaker may not have intended to hurt the child. The injuries caused may be the result of over discipline or physical punishment which is not proper.

Sexual Abuse

Sexual abuse means improper sexual behaviour with a child. It includes fondling a child's genitals, making the child fondle the adult genitals, intercourse, incest, rape, sodomy, exhibitionism and sexual exploitation.

Sexual abuse of girl children is taking place in our neighbourhood, friend's circle and even in our own family. It is more shocking that the persons who are supposed to be responsible for socialization of the children are the ones who are destroying their future. Childhood, which ideally should be a carefree time of life filled with love and joy, becomes a shameful experience for these abused children.

Definition of Child Sexual Abuse

According to Human Touch Bureau Report (2004): Sexual abuse is defined as 'the involvement of child in any sexual activity whether forced or consensual that occurs prior to the age of 18, the legal age of consent in India. It includes fondling a child's genitals, intercourse, incest, rape, sodomy, exhibitionism and sexual exploitation'.

Definition of child sexual abuse by the World Health Organization (WHO): Sexual abuse is inappropriate sexual behaviour with a child. It includes fondling a child's genitals, making the child fondle the adult's genitals, intercourse, incest, rape, sodomy, exhibitionism and sexual exploitation.

Girl Child Sexual Abuse: World Scenario

Girl child sexual abuse has gained public attention in the past few decades and has become one of the most high profile crimes since the 1970s. The sexual abuse of children and child molestation has increasingly been recognized as deeply damaging to children and not acceptable to society as a whole. While sexual use of children by adults has been present throughout history, it has only become the object of significant public attention in recent times.

Feminism has brought greater awareness of child sexual abuse and violence against women and made them public, political issues. Judith Lewis Herman, professor of psychiatry in Harvard University, wrote the first book ever on father-daughter incest when she discovered, during her medical residency, that a large number of women she was seeing had been victims of father-daughter incest. Herman notes that her approach to her clinical experience grew out of her involvement in the civil rights movement. Her second book, *Trauma and Recovery* (1992) is considered a classic and a ground breaking work.[20]

Anne Hastings (1998) described these changes in attitude towards child sexual abuse as 'the beginning of one of history's largest social revolution'.

A 2000 World Health Organization Geneva Report, *The World Report on Violence and Health* (Chapter 6, Sexual Violence) states, 'Action in schools is vital for reducing sexual and other forms of violence'.

On 11 October 2006, the United Nations (UN) released the first UN Secretary General study on violence against children within the schools, alternative care institutions and detention facilities, places where children work and communities. The study took years to complete and was supported by the United Nations Child Fund (UNICEF), the World Health Organization (WHO) and the Office of the High Commissioner Human Rights (OHCHC).

Girl Child Sexual Abuse at International Level

Girl child sexual abuse is not the problem of any particular country, but it is a rapidly increasing global problem. According to a study conducted by UN population fund, titled International Statistics on Child Sexual Abuse, at least two out of four girls are victims of sexual abuse.

A multi-country study by WHO, including both developed and developing countries, showed that between 1 and 21 per cent of women were reported to have been sexually abused before the age of 15, in most cases by male family members other that the father or stepfather (WHO, 2005).

Sexual abuse statistics vary between countries and reports, but are consistently alarming: Research indicates that 36 per cent of girls have suffered child sexual abuse and 46 per cent girls have experienced sexual coercion (The 57th Session of the UN Commission on Human Rights).

Girl Child Sexual Abuse in US and Europe

Child sexual abuse occurs frequently in western society. The rate of prevalence can be difficult to determine. There is great difference between the number of reported cases and the number also covered by retrospective surveys years after the events.

United Kingdom (UK)

In the UK, it is estimated at about 8 per cent for boys and 12 per cent for girls. In United Kingdom 0.3 per cent of children were reported as discovered cases of sexual abuse (Mrazek, et al., 1981); this postal survey revealed the gross under reporting of abuse at the time it was made referring to 18 months in 1977–78.

Girl children are used for pornography of every conceivable kind including the making, selling and buying of photographs, films and videos. Sex rings have come into practice in England (Wild and Wynne, 1986) in one area of Leeds; in such 11 sex rings, 175 girl children were engaged in 1984–85. A man who lived alone enticed a girl into a range of abuses, from looking, photographing or touching, to masturbation and intercourse.[21]

In the UK, it is estimated that about 8 per cent of boys and 12 per cent of girls have suffered sexual abuse in some form or the other. The most serious sexual crime encompasses rape, sexual assault, and sexual activity with children. From 2007 to 2008, 41,460 'most serious sexual offences' were recorded by the police within this 11,648 rape cases of girls and 20,534 cases of sexual assault of girl children were recorded.

According to NSPCC report (2007), 10 per cent of children aged under 16 experienced sexual abuse by father and 3 per cent by another relative, 11 per cent of children aged under 16 experienced sexual abuse by people known but unrelated to them.

Between the years 2004 and 2009, the annual number of children counselled by child line regarding sexual abuse rose from 8,637 to 12,268, giving an overall increase of 42 per cent; 17,727 sexual crimes against children under 16 were recorded in England and Wales in 2010–11.

United States of America (USA)

The estimates for the United States vary widely, a literature review of 23 studies found rates at 3 per cent to 37 per cent for males and 8 per cent to 71 per cent for females, which produced an average of 17 per cent for boys and 28 per cent for girls, while a statistical analysis based on 16 cross sectional studies estimated the rate to be 7.2 per cent for males and 14.5 per cent for female. The US Department of Health and Human services reported 83,600 sustained reports of sexually abused children in 2005, including incidents which were not reported would make the total number even larger.[22]

A study by Lawson and Chaffin (1992) indicated that many children who were sexually abused were 'identified solely by a physical complaint that was later diagnosed as large real disclosure of sexual abuse during the initial interview'.

In the United States, 19 per cent of women and 9 per cent of men had been abused, among 796 college students (Finkelhor, 1979).

In the United States, 28 per cent of girls were abused before 14 years, 38 per cent of girls were abused before 18 years (Russell, 1983). In the United States, 12 per cent of girls were abused under 14 years, 16.8 per cent of boys were abused under 16 years (Buchanan, 1986).

In the US schools, according to the US Department of Education, nearly 9.6 per cent of students are targets of educator sexual misconduct some time during their school career. In study of student sexual abuse by male and female educators, male students were reported as targets in ranges from 23 per cent to 44 per cent in US schools setting same sex (female/male) sexual misconduct against students by educators.

In the absence of public and government interest in the problem of child abuse in the United States, Gil (1970) estimated that there were between 2.5 and 4.1 million cases of child abuse per year.[23]

The estimates for the United States vary widely. A literature review of 23 studies found rates at 3 per cent to 37 per cent for males and 8 per cent to 71 per cent for females. In the United States, 28 per cent of girls are abused before 14 years and 38 per cent of girls are abused before 18 years.

The United States has the worst record in the industrialized nations – losing five children every day due to abuse related deaths; 78.3 per cent children were sexually abused in the USA in 2010–11 (Children's Bureau, 2011).

Africa

The prevalence of child sexual abuse in Africa is compounded by a belief that sexual intercourse with a virgin will cure a man of HIV or AIDS. This belief is especially common in South Africa which has the highest number of HIV positive citizens in the world.

Eastern Cape social worker Edith Kriel notes that 'children abusers are often relatives of their victims, even their fathers and providers. More than 67,000 cases of sexual assaults against children were reported in 2000 in South Africa'.

Researcher Leclerc-Madlala (2009) states that the myth that sex with a virgin is a cure for AIDS is not confined to South Africa: 'Fellow AIDS researchers in Zambia, Zimbabwe and Nigeria have told me that the myth also exists in these countries and that it is being blamed for the high rate of sexual abuse against young children'.

Zambia

On 30 June 2008, in the nation of Zambia, the issue of teacher-student sexual abuse and sexual assault was brought to the attention of High Court of Zambia where a landmark case decision, with presiding judge Philip Musonda, awarded a compensation of $45 million Zambian Kwacha ($13,000 USD) to the plaintiff, a 13-year-old girl student, for sexual abuse and rape by her school teacher.

The prevalence of physical and sexual violence against women and girls in Zambia is extremely high. A 2007 government survey reported that 47 per cent of Zambian women had been the victim of sexual violence at least once since the age of 15.

The Zambian Victim Support Unit (VSU), a unit of the Zambian police, recorded that there has been a sharp increase in cases of statuary rape, since 2008, when the rape cases were 1,237; and this number increased to 2,430 in 2010.

Canada

In Canada, national statistics on child abuse and neglect first became available in 2000–01 with the publication of the first *Canadian Incidence Study of Reported Child Abuse and Neglect (2001)*. Before that they had not been compiled largely due to the challenge posed by varying definitions of child abuse across the countries, provinces and territories.

Australia

Commonwealth Department of Family and Communal Services is working for prevention of child abuse and neglect in Australia.

It is estimated that less than 30 per cent of all sexual assaults on girl children are reported and that the reporting rate is even lower for aboriginal and Torres Strait Islander children (Stanley et al., 2003).

According to Robert Hini (2012), contemporary child sex abusers are much more likely to be male relatives than they are to be catholic priest. While more than 70 priests have been convicted of sex offences in Australia in 2010–11, there were 5,437 substantiated claims of sexual abuse throughout Australia, according to the Child Protection Australia 2010–11 report; 431 of those came from Western Australia.

Sexual abuse made up 13 per cent of all substantiated harm. In every state and territory, girls were more likely than boys to be sexually abused.

What these facts reveal is that we certainly do have a problem transforming into a horror that is the sexual abuse of children but it is 'our' problem, as a society, not just for 'those people' in the catholic church.[24]

Thus, sexual abuse against girl child is a global human rights violation of vast proportion with severe health and social consequences. In 2007, the World Health Organization estimated that 150 million girls under the age of 18 had experienced sexual abuse (WHO, 2007). Further, studies also indicate that 36 per cent – 62 per cent of reported sexual assaults are committed against girls aged 15 and younger. A survey conducted in Swaziland by UNICEF, the Centre for Disease Control and Prevention (CDC), and local partners in 2007 illustrated the scope of the problem, with approximately one in three girls a victim of sexual abuse prior to the age of 18, and three quarters of the perpetrators being men and boys (including boyfriends, husbands, and male relatives) from the neighbourhoods the victim reside in.[25]

Rodney (Director, Division of Violence Prevention, CDCs) says, 'while it is generally known that sexual violence against girls is a global problem, very limited data exist on the extent of this problem in the developing world. Obtaining valid data is a key step towards mobilizing policy and other positive interventions'.

In addition, girl sexual abuse has overarching consequences both over the short and long term. Girls who are victims of sexual violence are three times more likely to have an unwanted pregnancy, and girls younger than 15 years who are pregnant are five times more likely to die in childbirth than pregnant women aged 20 to 24 years. Sexual violence is often hidden and under reported due to the panic, shame, and disbelief associated with the act. Only an estimated 10–20 per cent of child sexual abuse cases are reported to authorities.

Girl sexual abuse is also connected to issues of social and economic injustice. The threat of sexual abuse can affect a survivor's chances of receiving an education. Girls who have experienced sexual abuse can find themselves pulled out from school by their families and care givers, or they choose to leave school because of their fear and depression. A lack of education hinders a girl's prospects of earning a sustainable income, perpetuating and deepening the cycle of vulnerability. Ultimately, societies pay a deep price for these outcomes because educated women are vital to the health and prosperity of the country.

Girl's sexual abuse can also increase the risk of infectious diseases and chronic disease later in life. Girls who are victims of sexual abuse are at increased biological risk of contracting HIV/AIDS and other sexually transmitted infections. Sexual abuse alters the life path of many girls, leading them down a road of depression, substance abuse, and high-risk behaviours. Ending sexual abuse will allow girls worldwide to live safer and healthier lives and fulfil their right to freedom from exploitation and abuse.

Health service providers need to understand the context of abuse, identify signs of abuse and provide sensitive and empathic care. Often the nature of injury helps doctors in their surmise. Appropriate documentation of cases with confidentiality will strengthen the evidence base and help provide redressal to the victims.

The health care system can help reduce the consequences of abuse by providing services to the survivors, training to providers to detect cases of injury arising from sexual violence, counselling for abused children, appropriate treatment and referral. A range of approaches including residential care, psycho-therapy and community-based programmes have been found useful. The capacity of the health sector to manage abused survivors needs to be strengthened. This may be done through appropriate integration of girl sexual abuse issues into health services.

Hence, girl child sexual abuse is identified as a priority issue for immediate action. The issue needs to be given special attention and the culprits should be given exemplary punishment so that examples are set for potential abusers.

Girl Child Sexual Abuse in Asia

Child abuse and neglect issues are common in all countries at the global level such as physical abuse, emotional and psychological abuse, abandonment and, increasingly, problems of street children. There are also many issues which are prevalent only in certain regions of the world. For instance, in Asia where population density is high, the issues of child labour and child sexual exploitation are also high.

Political instability and other internal disturbances including conditions of insurgency in many countries in Asia are also creating major problems, with increasing number of child soldier, refugee children, trafficked children and children on the streets.

The situation of girl child is very critical as she is doubly deprived. She is a silent sufferer of the problem. Girl child sexual abuse in the south-east region is largely under reported or 'hidden'. It occurs in various forms and is deeply rooted in the cultural, economic and socio-cultural environment. Rape is a frequently reported type of abuse in the region. Of the 5,738 cases of rape reported in Bangladesh from 1991 to 1996, almost 17 per cent of rape victims were minors.[26] In India, of all rape cases in 1997, children alone accounted for 28.8 per cent (NCRB, 2000). In Sri Lanka, a study among advanced secondary and university students reported that 12 per cent of girls had experienced sexual abuse as children. A report on injuries and deaths from assaults by the Epidemiology Division of the Ministry of Public Health, Thailand, in 2002 has stated that sexual assaults of girl children under 10 years was reported from every hospital in the surveillance system. Several cases of girl child rape reported from South-East Asia are attributed to the myth that intercourse with a virgin may be a cure for Sexually Transmitted Infections (STIs).[27]

In Nepal, a survey conducted in 1996 on domestic violence found that 13 per cent of the respondent girls knew about at least one case of child sexual abuse.[28] In Maharashtra, India, it is alleged that 500 girls under 16 years of age were sexually abused and then photographed for blackmail (UNICEF, 2003).

Prevention of child abuse and neglect is still an uncharted field in Asia. The largest population of these children lack access to proper health care, nutrition and education. This reflects the socio-economic reality of the developing countries of the Asian region. The main factors that contribute to the magnitude of the problem of child abuse are poverty, illiteracy, caste systems and landlessness, lack of economic opportunities, rural to urban migration, population growth, political instability and weak implementation of legal provisions.

Girl Child Sexual Abuse in India

Independent India has taken large strides in addressing issues like child education, health and development. However, child protection has remained largely unaddressed. There is now a realization that if issues of child abuse and neglect like female foeticide and infanticide, girl child discrimination, child marriage, trafficking of children, child sexual abuse, and so on, are not addressed, it will affect the overall progress of the country.

Nineteen per cent of the world's children live in India; 440 million people in the county today are aged below 18 years and constitute 42 per cent of India's total population, i.e. four out of every 10 persons. This is the enormous number of children that the country has to take care of while articulating its vision of progress, development and equity. India has expressed its recognition of the fact that when its children are educated, healthy and happy, and have access to opportunities, they are the country's greatest human resource.

It is rightly stated in the study by Chaudhary (2007) that the subject of child sexual abuse is still a taboo in India. There is a conspiracy of silence around the subject and a very large percentage of people feel that this is a largely western problem and that child sexual abuse does not happen in India. Part of the reason, of course, lies in a traditional conservative family and community structure that does not talk about sex and sexuality at all. Parents do not speak to children about sexuality, as well as physical and emotional changes that take place during their growing years. As a result of this, all forms of sexual abuse that a child faces do not get reported to anyone. The girl, whose mother has not spoken to her even about a basic issue like menstruation, is unable to tell her mother about the uncle or neighbour who has made sexual advances towards her. This silence encourages the abuser so that he is emboldened to continue the abuse and to press his advantage to subject the child to more severe forms of sexual abuse.

Child abuse is shrouded in secrecy and there is a conspiracy of silence around the entire subject. In fact, there is a well entrenched belief that there is no child abuse in India and certainly there is no sexual abuse in the country. Further, certain kinds of traditional practices that are accepted across the country, knowingly or unknowingly amount to child abuse. Existing socio-economic conditions also render some children vulnerable and more at risk to abuse, exploitation and neglect. It is about time that we recognize this and take remedial measures. Lack of empirical evidence and qualitative information on the dimensions of child abuse and neglect makes it difficult to address the issue in a comprehensive manner (Chaudhary, 2007).

Child sexual abuse is an especially complicated form of abuse because of its layers of guilt and shame. It is important to recognize that sexual abuses do not always involve body contact. Exposing a child to sexual situations or material is sexually abusive, whether or not touching is involved. Even though boys and girls are abused, girl children are at more risk. In fact, sexual abuse of girls may be under-reported due to shame and stigma.

Both male and female children are sexually abused. Girls, however, are abused more frequently and for a longer period of time. At least two out of eight girls and one out of six boys are victims of sexual abuse.

Statistics on India reveals that the country has the dubious distinction of having the world's largest number of sexually abused children with a child below 16 years raped every 155th minute and a child below 10 years every 13th hour. Studies undertaken by various NGOs in India reveal that boys and girls are equally vulnerable. In 90 per cent of child abuse cases, someone the child knows and trusts, a neighbour, close relative, family friend and even father is the abuser. This is perhaps due to the fact that in India, children are expected to respect and obey adults.[29]

Scott (1977) reported that between one and 12 children per 1,000 were abused by their parents or guardians. Considering the poverty, illiteracy and large size of families in India, it could be said that five to 15 children per 1,000 children are abused by relatives and employers in our country (see A.K. Singh, 2010).[30]

In India, data from Delhi shows that in the first six months of 1994, nearly two out of three rape victims were children. Rape cases in the city have been on the rise since 1993. Figures indicate that out of a total of 321 victims, 197 girls were minors, of whom 35 were less than seven years and 119 were between 12 and 16 years of age.[31]

Studies conducted by various NGOs and institutions in 1995 and 1997, respectively, in Delhi revealed that more than half the girls surveyed had experienced sexual abuse by family members; 76 per cent women across five cities in India admitted sexual abuse as children.

In India, the only information available annually is the crime data maintained by National Crime Record Bureau. There is a record of only those crimes which can be registered under the IPC or other criminal Acts.

As shown in Table 1.1 cases of crime against children, including kidnapping, sexual assault and rapes in the country increased by about 5 per cent in 2010, as compared to 2009, according to a publication of National Crime Record Bureau.

Table 1.1 *Crime Against Children State-Wise Distribution During 2009 to 2010*

States	*2009*	*2010*
Maharashtra	12.0%	12.2%
Uttar Pradesh (UP)	12.7%	8.7%
Bihar	4.2%	6.9%
Andhra Pradesh (AP)	7.1%	6.8%
Delhi	11.7%	13.6%
Rajasthan	5.8%	4.9%
Gujarat	4.0%	3.8%
Chhattisgarh	5.5%	5.5%
West Bengal	2.0%	3.3%
Madhya Pradesh (MP)	19.2%	18.4%
Other States	15.8%	15.9%

Source: National Crime Record Bureau, 2010.

Table 1.2 shows that there has been an increase in rape cases from 2008 to 2010 and also there has been an increase in the cases of kidnapping and abduction which shows how children are becoming victims of crime.

Table 1.2 *Crime Against Children in India During 2008 to 2010*

Year	*Rape*	*Kidnapping and Abduction*
2008	5,446	7,650
2009	5,368	8,945
2010	5,484	10,670

Source: National Crime Record Bureau, 2010.

The data of National Crime Record Bureau (NCRB) India, 2011–12 reveals that Delhi tops the list of states where highest number of crime against children was committed in 2011. MP and UP recorded the highest number of rape and murder cases of kids, respectively. A total of 33,098 cases of crime against children were reported in the country in 2011 as compared to 26,694 cases in 2010, suggesting an increase of 24 per cent. According to National Crime Record Bureau, the rate of crime against children is biggest in Delhi (25.4%) followed by Andaman & Nicobar Islands (20.3%) Chandigarh and Chhattisgarh (7% each) MP (6%) and Goa (5.1%) as compared to the national average of 2.7. A total of 1,514 cases of murder of children, including infanticide, were reported in the country in 2011 against 1,508 cases in 2010. UP has reported the highest number of such cases (326) accounting for 22.9 per cent of the total murder cases reported in the country.

Prevention of child sexual abuse is the need of the day. Many factors that contribute to the magnitude of the problem of girl child sexual abuse are poverty, illiteracy, lack of economic opportunities, rural to urban migration, population growth, negative attitude towards girl children, political instability and weak implementation of legal provisions.

Hence, this problem needs more efforts through the creation of adequate knowledge on the issue and thereby, to change the mindset of the society.

Girl Child Sexual Abuse in Maharashtra

Girl child sexual abuse is an everyday occurrence in Maharashtra, but few cases get reported. Mumbai Police Commissioner Arup Patnayak said that the issue of girl sexual abuse is serious but unfortunately very few cases get reported. He said that 99 per cent incidences are never brought to us, i.e. only 1 per cent incidences are reported in Mumbai. When the incidences are not at all recorded then how can the Police take any action?[32]

The study by Chaudhary (2007) reveals the fact that majority of the child abusers (sexual abuse) in India are teachers and neighbours, whereas in the state of Maharashtra the abusers are family members. This proves that the persons who are supposed to be responsible for socialization of the children are the ones who are destroying their future.

In the Eleventh Five-Year Plan, the child helpline phone number 1098 will be extended to all districts of the country. According to child line reports in Maharashtra the sexual abuse of children is taking place by family members and owners (workplace).

Table 1.3 *Incidence of Rape, Kidnapping and Abduction of Girls During 2003–08 in Maharashtra*

Year	*Rape*	*Kidnapping and Abduction*
2003	605	337
2004	634	380
2005	634	420
2006	655	552
2007	615	590
2008	690	598

Source: National Crime Record Bureau, 2008.

The incidence of crime committed against the girl children has increased in 2008 by 0.07 per cent when compared to the year 2007. The number of rape cases increased to 690 in 2008 from 615 in 2007 in Maharashtra.

Table 1.4 *Statistics in Maharashtra 2011 (NCRB 2011)*

Crime Heads	*2008*	*2009*	*2010*	*2011*
1. Murder 1-a infanticide 1-b other murder	175	189	211	201
2. Procurement of minor girl	279	292	206	204
3. Rape	690	612	747	818
4. Kidnapping	274	274	216	189
5. Abetment to commit suicide	3	13	05	12
6. Prostitution	13	42	26	20
7. Selling of girls for prostitution	05	02	01	02
8. Buying of girls for prostitution	55	29	27	20
9. Child marriage	05	0	06	02
10. Other crimes	920	1,189	1,277	1,208

Source: National Crime Record Bureau India, 2011.

Note: In the above data there is a record of only those crimes which can be registered under the IPC or other Criminal Acts. Corporeal punishment, use of children for creation of pornography, exposure, fondling are not reflected in NCRB data as they are not an offence under the IPC.

There are no national or state statistics for girl child sexual abuse in India. However, some data is available from the National Crime Record

Bureau. Table 1.4 indicates the reported cases sexual abuse against girl child from 2008 to 2011 in Maharashtra. The table shows there is increase in the leads of crime like murder (infanticide and other murder) rape cases and abetment to commit suicide. Increase in all these crimes indicates lack of protection and security of the girl child in the country. Because the figures show that the girl children are not secured and protected in their own families, these girls need legal protection and rehabilitation to overcome the problem.

Figure 1.1 *Unit-Wise Percentage of Offences Against Children During 2010–11*

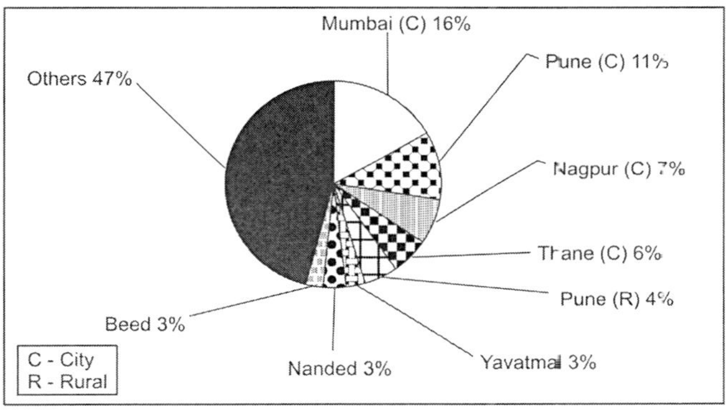

Source: National Crime Record Bureau, 2011.

Figure 1.1 shows unit wise incidence and percentage share of crime reported against children during 2010 to 2011.

The above figure shows the unit-wise percentage of crime against children during 2010 to 2011 in Maharashtra. The highest percentage of crime against children found in Mumbai city, i.e. 16 per cent, followed by Pune 11 per cent; Nagpur 7 per cent, Thane 6 per cent, Pune rural 4 per cent, Beed 3 per cent, and other constitute 47 per cent. Crime against children is increasing day by day which really is a major obstacle in the development of children.

Table 1.5 provides the detail information on child rape victims and their proportion to the total rape victims during the year 2006–2010.

The table indicates the victims of child rape in Maharashtra during 2006 to 2010. The table reveals the fact that the rape cases of minor girls are increasing, i.e. below 10 years and even between 10 to 18 years. The pubescent and adolescent girls are in the higher risk zone. The table also reveals that the share of children rape victims in total rape victims is also increasing which was 42.63 per cent in 2006 but it is 46.99 per cent in the year 2011.

Table 1.5 *Victims of Child Rape (2006–10) in Maharashtra*

S. No.	*Year*	*Age Group (Years)*		*Share of Children Rape Victims in Total Rape Victims*
		Below 10	*Between 10–18*	*%*
1	2006	83	559	42.63
2	2007	99	518	42.35
3	2008	118	576	44.29
4	2009	131	484	41.19
5	2010	108	649	46.99
	% change in 2010 as compared to 2006	30.12	16.10	
	% change in 2010 as compared to 2009	−17.56	34.09	

Source: National Crime Record Bureau, 2011.

The data by child line from 2009 to 2011 in Maharashtra is shown in Table 1.6. The data again proves that the trusted people of the child like parents, family members, caretakers commit the heinous crime of sexual abuse and rape of child in their care. Such incidences have a deep effect on the psyche of the child and the future life of the child becomes a life of shame, guilt, self-pity and fear and the child loses faith in family relationships.

Table 1.6 *Abusers of Girl Children at Home and Outside*

Abusers	*Year 2009 to 2011*
Teachers	25
Neighbours	20
Strangers	32
Family Members	248
Relatives	37
Family Friends	25
Caretakers	11
Owner (workplace)	62

Source: Child Line Report, 2012

Table 1.7 *Type of Sexual Abuse*

Type	*2009*	*2010*	*2011*
Rape	154	93	211
Molestation	59	44	81
Eve-teasing	32	21	96

Source: Child Line Report, 2012

Table 1.7 shows the increase in the crimes against children in Maharashtra which is a serious matter. The table also shows the types of sexual abuse. Cases of rape are 211 in the year 2011, that of molestation are 81 and of eve-teasing are 96. There is an increase in the crime from 2009 to 2011 in all the types. This shows the severity of the problem. Easy availability of minor girls and the tender age of the girls are the causative factors of sexual abuse against girl child. Those girl children find it difficult to break the silence, especially in cases of incest, enforced secrecy and a child's fear of destroying the privacy and security of the family are powerful obstacles in disclosure.

Table 1.8 *Age Group of Victims of Sexual Abuse*

Age Group	*2009*	*2010*	*2011*
Up to 5 years	16	06	08
6 to 10	44	22	122
11 to 15	190	69	188
16 to 18	58	52	54

Source: Child Line Report, 2012.

Table 1.8 reveals that even though children from 5 to 18 years are abused, the age group of 11 to 15, i.e. adolescent girls, is at high risk. The teenage girls are attracted by the gifts and special treatment given by the abusers. Abusers use a number of tactics to gain access to children. Emotional manipulation and verbal coercing were the most common tactics used by the abusers. Most sexual abuse takes place in the context of ongoing relationship between the abuser and the child. This gives the abuser an opportunity to exploit the child's wants and tears.

The subject of girl child sexual abuse is still taboo in our society, so the problem of girl child sexual abuse has not received enough attention. A deep seated fear has always moved in our families to keep our girls and their 'virginity' safe and many kinds of social and cultural practices have been built around ensuring this. This shows that a girl child is unsafe though nobody talks about it.

These girl children need special attention. Apart from girl children requiring special protection and care, there are some children who need to be supported and brought under the purview of effective policies and they are the 'sexually abused girls' – who are regularly denied opportunities for leading healthy, creative and happy life.

Girl Child Sexual Abuse in Beed District

Beed District in Maharashtra is grappling with problems of sex determination tests, female foeticide, girl child sexual abuse, domestic violence, dowry death and harassment. This is due to gender bias in the society and undoubtedly, a male child is preferred over a girl child. The latter is considered a burden and a liability. Due to particular type of social upbringing, abused girls do not seek any help from family and from outside the family setting. The socialization process teaches the girls not to respond, rather to be silent and to bear, adjust and suffer in silence. All this forces the girl child not to break the silence against her sexual abuse.

Girl child sexual abuse is on the rise in Beed District. Beed District is known for its migrant labourers, low sex ratio and for its low socio-economic status (Census 2011) and Beed District is at the bottom of child sex ratio, i.e. 801. In Maharashtra, the highest reduction of about 93 is found in Beed. This is due to negative attitude towards the girl child. Illiteracy of parents leads to increase in dropout rate of girl child in schools. They are engaged in domestic work and most of the time these girls are alone at their house and became easy prey for abusers. Due to all these things, sexual abuse of girl children is increasing day by day.

The rate of girl sexual abuse is higher in the months from January to April, and 11 rape cases of girl children were registered in Beed District in 2011.[33]

Table 1.9 shows the severity of the problem in the District.

Table 1.9 *Registered Cases of Girl Child Sexual Abuse in Beed District from 2006–10*

Type of Abuse	*Year 2006–10*
Rape cases	56 (33.53%)
Molestation	52 (31.13%)
Kidnapping and Abduction	57 (34.13%)
Prostitution	02 (1.19%)
Total	167

Source: Police Station, Beed.

The table shows the type of abuse from the cases of minor girls reported to police station in Beed District during 2006–2010. Kidnapping and abduction cases are the highest, i.e. 34.13 among all other types of abuse, followed by rape cases at 33.53 per cent, molestation at 31.123 per cent and 1.19 per cent of prostitution.

Table 1.10 *Age of Victims of Rape Cases in Beed District*

Age	*3*	*5*	*6*	*7*	*8*	*9*	*10*	*11*	*12*	*13*	*14*	*15*	*16*	*17*	*18*
Number of Victims	1	2	1	3	1	1	1	1	2	3	8	10	10	9	5

Source: Cases Reported to Police Station, Beed, for the Year – 2006–10.

Table 1.10 shows that early age girl children (3 to 10) are also victims of rape. As the age increases the incidence increases. Teenaged girls are the major sufferers of the crimes, the abusers are none other than their parents, family friends, the person known and trusted by them which makes the girl child feel ashamed and guilty and deprives her from her right of carefree and joyfree childhood.

The above discussion proves the statement by Scott (1977) that 'between one and twelve children per thousand (1,000) were abused by their parent and guardians in India'.

Defamation is the primary concern in not getting such cases registered with the police, as the social status of the family and future of the girl child is in danger. So instead of police complaint, the matter is hushed up by the parents. Moreover, illiteracy, poverty, fear of police treatment, unwanted publicity, etc. are contributory factors for treating the matter as closed.

The girl child sexual abuse has now become a global problem irrespective of class, caste, rural-urban region, countries and continents. This problem is a violation of the basic human rights of a girl child and is an outcome of a set of interrelated familial, social, psychological and economic factors. Hence, the problem of girl sexual abuse and human rights violations is one of the most critical matters on the international human rights agenda. In the Indian context, acceptance of child rights as a primary inviolable right is fairly recent, as is the universal understanding of it. There is no understanding of the problem of girl sexual abuse and its extent, magnitude and trends. So awareness and understanding the dimensions/complexities of the problem of girl child sexual abuse is the need of the day.

India is a young nation with about 44 per cent or more of its 440 million people being children. Way back in 1974, the National Policy for Children declared that the nation's children were its most important asset. We need to lobby for the allocation of necessary resources to develop this national asset to its full potential.

Need of the Study

Indian society is facing various problems these days. There is a large child population in India and a large percentage of this population is vulnerable to sexual abuse and exploitation. One of the serious problems is that of girl child sexual abuse. Girl child sexual abuse is not an individual problem. It has become a very important social issue.

Girl child sexual abuse is a grave problem with serious consequences to the society in general and to the concerned child in particular. Though the occurrence is enormous and of wide prevalence, not much is said about it due to low priority accorded to girl children by parents and care givers.

In Beed District of Maharashtra, it was found that due to backwardness and poverty, many people do not have settled families. They are engaged in seasonal work of sugarcane cutting and move from place to place in search of work along with their family. The children from such families have to suffer a lot. They do not get proper schooling and have to live in a disorganized family. The girl children in this particular area are an easy prey to the potential abusers who exploit the situation and sexually abuse the girls.

A girl child is vulnerable to sexual abuse and is abused frequently and for a longer time. In a patriarchal structure of Indian family, meagre or no attention is paid to her well-being. Her nutrition, her health, her education, secondary status and deprivation of girl child, her security, her small physical needs, her socialization and her emotional needs of love and affection are the last priority in the family. The girl child is the first victim of poverty, ignorance and social taboos. The situation of a girl child in our country is the result of deep-rooted biases that can only improve with a change in attitude that treats a female only as an object of sex.

Unfortunately, the phenomenon of girl child sexual abuse in our country has not yet been brought to the forefront for various reasons. Wrong notions of dignity and status of women in society, puritanical attitude of parents, their punitive and authoritative child rearing practices have been purposeful socio-economic norms and are justified on the grounds that they are persisting for centuries and are thought to be good for the proper upbringing of the child and necessary for the sustenance of society.

Awareness about the subject among people in the society and punishing the guilty is urgently needed. Girl child sexual abuse is not only dangerous to the child psychology but is also dangerous for our society in future as it may lead to several social crimes because an abused child never understands the value of humanity. Thus, it is very essential to look at this problem seriously.

The study of the subject is also needed to take the responsibility to focus on the issue and to make the society aware of it to prevent the incidence by not tolerating the incidence but to safeguard the rights of children and let them enjoy their childhood and help them to become healthy citizens of India.

There is a gross under-reporting of crimes against children, which in itself is an indication of the low priority accorded to children by parents, caregivers and the police.

Taking into consideration the seriousness of the problem the researcher studied 'Girl Child Sexual Abuse' in Beed District in Maharashtra.

There is limited previous research on child abuse, especially on girl child sexual abuse. As Rodney Hammond (2009) says that 'while it is generally known that sexual violence against girls is a global problem, very limited data exist on the extent of this problem in the developing world. Obtaining valid data is a key step towards mobilizing policy and other positive intervention'. Taking into consideration the need explained in the above statement the researcher studied the subject in selected areas about girl sexual abuse, to find out its extent, nature, causes and consequences. The researcher also considers suggestions given by Asha J. Rane in the book, *Research on Families with Problems in India (1991)*. Emphasizing on the limited literature on girl sexual abuse, she says that whatever available data is there, it is focused on physical abuse and other studies focus on both boys and girls abuse. Some studies are on women childhood experience or on all the forms of child abuse, but special studies on girl child sexual abuse are very limited. So the study is contributing on the extent, nature causes, consequence and coping strategies of girl child sexual abuse in the family and outside, in different social and economic settings. The findings of this research contributing to step forward to mobilizing policy and other positive interventions, by suggesting intervention strategies required to work with abused girl and her family. This study also helps to work on the valuable suggestions given by the key informants who are working in the particular field.

This is a specially focused study on sexually abused girl children but the researcher does not presume to claim these finding to be representation of the entire country but there are patterns in these accounts that other survivors can relate to and there is much to learn from these experiences for those trying to help the most vulnerable and voiceless group, i.e. sexually abused girl children.

The study tried to create awareness among all the important sections of the society, the social workers, researchers, doctors, advocates, police personnel, parents, policy-makers, to take immediate actions to prevent the evil of girl sexual abuse and bring confidence to the girl child so that she may feel proud of herself, of being a 'girl child'.

Theoretical Framework

'Integrated model' and 'systems theory' has been adopted for the present research as theoretical framework.

Integrated Model of Child Abuse

Kewalramani's study (1991) of child abuse focused on the major premise of this model and the interdependence between parent, child and situation. This model focuses on four factors in child abuse: (1) Family environment, (2) Structural stresses, (3) Individual characteristics of parents and (4) Sub-cultural learning.

The model requires knowledge in five different areas: (1) Child development, (2) Socialization processes, (3) Family interactions, (4) Learning principles and (5) Sources of arousing anger, aggression, hatred, etc.

These areas point out that: Child abuse can be viewed in terms of the degree to which a parent uses negative or inappropriate control strategies with her/his child. Employing 'normal' methods (meeting the child's needs, adequate control, positive disciplining and clear communication) contributes to a child's social, emotional and intellectual development, whereas taking recourse to 'abnormal' methods (neglecting child's needs, inadequate control, negative disciplining, conflict between parents, addiction of father, unclear communication, negligent parenting, being indifferent and unresponsive and not paying due attention and over-reliance on coercion) in child rearing inhibits a child's development and causes child abuse. Factors like unemployment and dissatisfaction with job affects an individual's behaviour which leads to child abuse.

Systems Theory (Fouche and Oliphant, 1977)

According to Fouche and Oliphant, there is a link between basic principles of system theory and sexual abuse. The focus is not only on the victim as a child who has been sexually abused but also on the context of abuse.

The abuse forms a part of the larger pattern of dysfunction such as marriage problems, financial problems or other dysfunctional behaviour.

The family system forms a pattern of behaviour, which acts as the basis of family functioning. When these patterns of behaviour are operating to maintain the abusive relationship, they can be seen as dysfunctional and not to the benefit of the child.

Behaviour in the system (including the behaviour regarding the sexual abuse), the sexual abuses are circular in nature. The system is constantly in a state of stability and change, indicating that the family tries to cope with the abuse by means of certain patterns of behaviour, for instance, family may decide to cope with the sexual abuse by means of secrecy.

Draucker indicates that it is essential to acknowledge that sexual abuse occurs within a larger context, often important factors of sexual abuse according to him are family composition, for example, the loss of a parent through divorce, death, separation, and the role of the other significant caretakers, the survivors birth order and the number of siblings in the family.

Draucker explains the social factors in the eco system includes the socio-economic class. Other significant family pathology or stresses, parental alcoholism, emotional or physical abuse, mental illness, criminal behaviour and extra family resources. He identifies the characteristics of abusing families. These elements are denial, inconsistency and unpredictability, lack of empathy, lack of clear boundaries, role reversal, closed family system, incongruent communication, conflict, deterioration of relationships and strained marriage relationships.

Research Methodology

A researcher's primary goal, distant as well as immediate, is to explore and gain a greater understanding of the subject matter of her/his research. Stated in other words, social research is a systematic method of exploring, analysing, and conceptualizing social life in order to extend, correct or verify knowledge, whether the knowledge aids in construction of a theory or in the practice of an art.[34] Therefore, research has become an essential activity of our social life.

A scientific study is a means to an end, that is, it aims to solve a problem, practical or theoretical or methodological. It aims at discovery, verification, validation and finding relationships among the accumulated data. These feats can be accomplished only by means of two scientific methods that is, logical and systematized application of the fundamentals of science to the general and overall questions of a study, and scientific techniques which provide precise tools, specific procedures and technical, rather than philosophical, means for getting and ordering the data prior to their logical and statistical manipulation.[35] This kind of research or scientific work is of vital importance when we want to understand and to study the nature, extent and causes of the problem. All these factors are focused in the present study of girl child sexual abuse in Beed District.

Child abuse is a state of emotional, physical, economic and sexual maltreatment meted out to a person below the age of 18 and is a globally prevalent phenomenon. However, in India, as in many other countries, there has been no understanding of the extent, magnitude and trends of the problem. The growing complexities of life and the dramatic changes brought about by socio-economic transitions in India have played a major role in increasing the vulnerability of children to various and newer forms of abuse.

Child sexual abuse has serious physical and psycho-social consequences which adversely affect the health and overall well-being of a child. There is a large child population in India and a large percentage of this population is vulnerable to abuse, exploitation and neglect.

The researcher focuses on the need of the study as there is a record of only those crimes which can be registered under the IPC or other Criminal

Acts. Corporal punishment, use of children for creation of pornography, exposure, etc. are not reflected in National Crime Record Bureau data as they are not offences under the IPC.

The discussion of sex or sex-related topics are still taboo in Indian society. The sexually abused girl children are often afraid and ashamed to being abused and report of being sexually abused is very less due to the stigma attached to this crime. There is a gross under-reporting of crimes against girl children, there is a conspiracy of silence around the subject as it is a hidden fact. It is much higher than generally perceived and taken cognizance of, which in itself is an indication of the low priority accorded to children by parents, caregivers and the police. The data available on this issue is very limited. Hence, the researcher believes that the study of this subject is the need of the day.

So the researcher studied 'Girl Child Sexual Abuse' within limited scope, i.e. restricted to Beed district. The aim of the study is to understand the extent, nature, causes and consequences of sexual abuse and to suggest coping strategies. The present study intended to address a set of following objectives.

Objectives

1. To study the extent of girl child sexual abuse.
2. To study the socio-economic background of the victims of sexual abuse.
3. To find out the nature and causes of girl child sexual abuse.
4. To study the consequences of sexual abuse on victims.
5. To assess the attitude of family members towards the victims.
6. To suggest the strategies and rehabilitative programmes for victims.

Hypotheses

A hypothesis is a conjectural statement of the relation between two or more variables. Hypotheses are always in declarative sentence form, to variables. Hypotheses carry clear implications for testing the stated relations.[36]

Hypotheses framed in the light of objectives:

1. Lower economic condition makes girl child vulnerable to sexual abuse.
2. Girl child sexual abuse occurs mainly within kinship.
3. Deterioration of morality and values leads to higher incidence of girl child sexual abuse.
4. Urban and rural divide exists in girl child sexual abuse.
5. Sexual abuse leads to mental and physical disorder in victims.
6. Attitude of family members is negative towards the victims of sexual abuse.

Operational Definition

Operational Definition of Girl Child

For the purpose of this study, girl child is defined as a girl not having completed 18 years of age.

Operational Definition of Girl Child Sexual Abuse

Girl child sexual abuse is inappropriate sexual behaviour with a girl child. It includes fondling a child's genitals, making the child fondle an adult's genitals, molestation, intercourse, incest, rape, sodomy, forcible kissing, exhibitionism, abduction, pornography and prostitution. To be considered as girl child sexual abuse, these acts have to be committed by a person responsible for the care of a child or related to the child (parent, relatives, extended family members, peer, older child, friend, neighbour, baby sitter, caretaker or stranger). Following indicators were decided for the study:

Indicators of Girl Child Sexual Abuse

1. Sexual assault.
2. Making the child fondle private parts.
3. Touching private body parts of the child.
4. Making the child exhibit private parts.
5. Exhibiting private body parts to child.
6. Exposure – children forced to view private body parts.
7. Exposure – children forced to view pornographic material.
8. Forcible kissing.
9. Sexual advances during marriage situations.
10. Sexual advances during travel situations.
11. Whistling.
12. Singing vulgar songs.
13. Passing sexual comments.
14. Threatening to touch.
15. Torture by using vulgar language on mobile.
16. Looking in a wrong way.

Universe

For this study, Beed District in Marathwada region of Maharashtra, a state in India has been selected. It is essential for the researcher to understand the universe thoroughly for the proper study of the problem undertaken. Socio-economic and political background and cultural heritage are the important factors in the development of any region. Healthy social status, sound economic conditions and favourable geographical features contribute to the all-round development of any area.

Beed District is located in the Deccan black basalt stone ranges of Balaghat. The most significant river in Maharashtra is Godavari which flows on the border line of Georai and Majalgaon taluk. Geographical area of Beed District is 10,693 sq. km. For the administrative purpose, the district comprises two subdivisions. One section consists of five talukas (1) Beed (2) Georai (3) Patoda (4) Ashti (5) Shirur kasar. Other section consists of (1) Ambajogai (2) Kaij (3) Majalgaon (4) Dharur (5) Parli (6) Wadwani taluk. There are eleven Tehasils and excluding urban area there are eleven Panchayat samitees.

In Maharashtra, there has been a decline in child sex ratio from 913 to 833 during the decade 2001–11. This shows that there is increase in the shortage of girls per thousand boys from 87 in 2001 to 117 in 2011. The highest reduction of about 93 is found in Beed District. This shows the negative attitude towards girl child. The population of 0–6 age group is 34,44,122. The male child population is 1,91,115 and the female child population 1,53,007. Beed District is at the bottom of child sex ratio which is 801 per thousand.

Lack of educational and technical facilities and specialized vocational training leads to unemployment and poverty. The marginal farmer and landless labourers, large scale migration of sugarcane harvesters on account of unemployment is a peculiarity of the district and women and adolescent girls also migrate to work for their livelihood. Health and medical facilities in the district are also insufficient. Illiteracy, poverty, ignorance, superstition, large scale migration of people and negative attitude towards girl children, results in girl dropout rate, female foeticide and sexual abuse. So these girls are engaged in work (domestic or outside). Girls from this district are worst sufferers of sexual exploitation. The National Highway (211) from Ahmedabad to Hyderabad passes through Beed. This has given rise to dhabas, making minor girls from nearby villages vulnerable to trafficking and sexual exploitation. Moreover, raids conducted in Mumbai brothels have revealed that a number of minor girls are from this district. There are instances of young girls being sexually exploited in *Tamasha* centres under the pretext of dance and entertainment. These minor girls are ignorant about HIV/AIDS. Number of police recorded cases also reveals the fact that minor girls are sexually abused by their parents, family members and close relatives. Another disturbing fact of the district is addiction to tobacco, alcohol, drug among adults and youth. Connection between substance abuse and sexual abuse is a harsh fact. Hence, the negative attitude towards girl child and addiction, illiteracy, poverty, lack of parenting, interactions lead to sexual abuse of girl children. The researcher felt the need to disseminate information about children's rights among children and parents and in the community, economic and social empowerment of women and girl children and awareness about the importance of girl child in the society as an asset and not a burden. For this purpose, the researcher selected Beed District and studied the extent, nature and causative factors of girl child sexual abuse and to suggest coping strategies and measures to prevent or control the problem.

Sampling

For the purpose of this study, Beed District in Marathwada region of Maharashtra was selected as universe. Universe was divided into rural and urban area. Among 11 taluks of Beed District, two taluks Kaij and Ambajogai, were selected purposively for the purpose of study on the basis of police recorded cases of sexual abuse against girl children.

Only school-going girl children were selected for the purpose of study. Twenty schools were selected randomly (only 20 schools were given response). An interactive orientation was conducted with the girl children discussing child sexual abuse and giving them intimation on the UN convention of the child, especially on articles regarding abuse. Critical topics, such as how sexual abuse is never a child's fault, were also emphasized. Girl children appeared in Focused Group Discussion, i.e. 500 girl children were selected as a respondent which was followed by one-to-one interaction. There is no equal number of girls from each class and school because researcher selected only those girls as respondents who came forward in group discussion as a victim of sexual abuse.

The sample included sexually abused school-going girl children in the age group of 11–18 years. These girls were divided into two groups 11–14 and 15–18; girls of Middle and High school were selected. The girls of 11–18 year age group were selected purposively since this age group girls could interact properly on the sensitive issue like sexual abuse and they can share their abusive experiences with the researcher.

Case Study Method

Case study method was also used in this research. Case study is a type of research method that investigates one or a few cases in depth, using appropriate methods. As one of the methods in qualitative research, it favours intensive analysis of one or a few cases using in-depth unstructured interviews, observation and narrative rather than depending on numerical reporting. The method shares with other qualitative research the quality of developing rich insights that have direct relevance to real world behaviours.[37]

Stake (1988) viewed case study as the 'Study of a bounded system emphasizing the unity and wholeness of that system, but confining the attention to those aspects that are relevant to the research problem at the time'.[38]

In Beed District, 167 total cases of girl child sexual abuse were recorded during the year 2006–2011 in 11 Tehasils of Beed District.

According to the availability of the cases 10 cases, were analysed and studied with the help of case study method. Unreported 10 cases and 10 cases from key informants were also analysed and studied with the help of case study method.

Hence, for a fuller understanding of the phenomenon and process and to study in depth by integrating different perspectives, case study method was used in the present study to study the reported and unreported cases selected according to their availability.

Key Informants

Key informants are another important source of data collection in the present study. The 40 experts working on the issue concerned were from different fields – 10 advocates, 10 doctors, 10 social workers and 10 police personnel. These were selected purposively from two selected Tehasils as key informants and they were interviewed with the help of interview–guide to understand their opinions, experiences and suggestions regarding the issue of girl sexual abuse.

Research Design

As this study attempts to find out the characteristics and nature of girl child sexual abuse, the 'Descriptive Research Design' was found suitable. To portray accurately the characteristics of a particular situation or group or individual, the Descriptive Research Design is to be useful and hence it was employed.

Tools and Techniques of Data Collection

Taking into consideration that the child is sensitive to such issue, friendly attitude was used to share the girl's experience of sexual abuse. Primary and secondary sources were used for collecting data.

Primary Data

Focus group discussions, one-to-one interaction, interview schedule, interview technique, and case study method were used.

Focus Group Discussions (FGDs)

FGDs were conducted by the researcher starting with story-telling and showing some charts related to sexual abuse. The purpose of this discussion was to establish rapport with the girl children.

The orientation programme makes the respondents to know the background and purpose of the study. After attending orientation programme the girl children were given a choice as to whether they wanted to participate in the research or not, their participation was strictly a decision they had to make. The girl children who were approached in focus group discussions were selected as a sample.

One-on-One Interaction with Girl Children

The girls who were approached with the help of FGDs were then called for one-to-one interaction. This was conducted to elicit specific information from them and was conducted on the basis of guidelines developed by a report on child abuse by Chaudhary (2007). Interview schedule was prepared to conduct one-to-one interaction.

Interview Schedule

Interview schedule was prepared for one-on-one interaction which includes open and close ended questions in which each question was judged in the context of its relatedness to the objectives of the study.

Before commencement of the data collection, the pre-testing of the interview schedule was carried out on ten victims of sexual abuse with the view of detecting their shortcomings. The questions were modified in content, language, and sequence and then finalized.

Case Study Method

Thirty cases of girl child sexual abuse were studied by the case study method.

Interview with Key Informants

Forty experts working on the issue of girl child sexual abuse were selected as key informants. They were interviewed with the help of interview guide.

Secondary Sources

In secondary sources, reported cases in police station, a report on child abuse by Ministery of Women and Child Development, Government of India (2007), studies of NGOs like Tulir, Rahi, Sakshi, etc. along with books, journals, research articles, reports, websites were used.

All measures were undertaken to protect the confidentiality of the respondents. All efforts to ensure privacy and comfort, within the available setting, were provided to the respondents.

Data Analysis and Interpretation

Data collected through observation, group discussion, interview schedule, key informants were analysed in the light of objectives and parameters developed by the researcher.

Chapter Scheme

The present study is divided in the following chapters:

1. Introduction
2. Socio-Economic Status of Sexually Abused Girls
3. Stories of Voiceless Girls

4. Nature and Causes of Girl Child Sexual Abuse
5. Consequences of Sexual Abuse on Girl Child
6. Rehabilitation of Victims of Sexual Abuse
7. Conclusions and Recommendations

Basic Concepts

The meanings of some basic concepts used in this research are as follows:

Victim

The word victim is usually used to denote the person who has been abused by the activity of others. It is someone who is badly treated or taken advantage of, injured or destroyed while attaining an object or in gratification of a passion. This is, therefore, an appropriate term, especially as one of the key elements of child sexual abuse is that of being used for an adult's sexual pleasure or of being taken advantage of. It must be emphasized that a victim in relation to child sexual abuse is in no way responsible for or in any way contributing to the exploitative activity of the perpetrator.[39]

Abuser

An abuser is one who acts specifically in relation to the following meaning of abuse to violate, to misuse anyone's confidence. The term is generally used interchangeably with perpetrator and offender.[40]

Perpetrator

The word perpetrator is used in relation to the person or people who are directly abusing a child or children. Although it can be applied to the person responsible for any other form of mistreatment, it tends to relate to those committing child sexual abuses. It is not used to refer to other adults who may have played a role but were not directly involved, such as a non-abusing parent who might have been aware of the abuse but unable to intervene (Source: RAHI, New Delhi).

Exhibitionism

This term is used to describe the exposure of the genitals as a deliberate act to gain satisfaction. Closely related to exhibitionism is a form of reverse voyeurism where the child is made to watch the sexual activities of adults or pornographic material.

Pornography

Pornography is both a contact and non-contact abuse. Porn material is publicly available in a variety of form such as audio, video, written and still photographs depicting sexual act or body parts. The viewers cannot establish bodily contact and can yet use the porn material to excite and satisfy themselves. Children can be exploited for the use of pornography without having to be touched. They could be required to dress in erotic clothes or pose in sexual positions or they could be engaged in sexual acts, violated or even killed.

Contact Abuse

Fondling

This refers to touching the child's body for sexual gratification.

Masturbation

Children can be forced or enticed to rub the perpetrator's genitals (Doyle, c. 1994); it is important to note in the case at Child Sexual Abuse (CSA) that mutuality of needs/desires is assumed by the perpetrator (adult) to justify his behaviour and reduce guilt.

Penetration

The term intercourse, either vaginal or anal, is usually referred to for penetration by the penis. However, children can have all manners of objects inserted into the vagina or anus.

Oral Sex

Kissing– kissing might sound relatively innocent and a affectionate act towards children but it can be highly sexualized and frightening for children.[41]

Incest

Incest is sexual intercourse between two people who by blood relationship are either parent and child, brother and sister, grandparent and grandchild. Incest between a child and a related adult has been identified as the most widespread form of child sexual abuse with a huge capacity for damage to a child.[42]

The legal definition of incest applies to acts of sexual intercourse between a man and a woman within the prohibited relationships. These are a man with a woman who is his daughter, sister, mother, or granddaughter and to a woman with a man who is her father, brother, son or grandfather.[43]

Modus Operandi

'Modus operandi' (Latin) means 'method of operation'. A method of procedure, especially a distinct pattern or method of operation that indicates or suggests the work of a single criminal in more than one crime.[44]

The abusers have some specific tactics which were used by them to sexually abuse the girl children. When sexually abusing a child, the abuser must make a series of decisions or plans prior to committing the deviant act.

This planning causes the offender to experience a sense of excitement that further motivates him until he is at the point of committing the offense. The tactics used by the abuser include verbal and/or physical intimidation, seduction or the use of enticements such as candy, money or other gifts. Emotional blackmail of victim, emotional manipulation and verbal coercion were the most common tactics used by the offenders. The abuser gradually extends the affectionate touching to include sexual behaviour, all the while 'testing' the child's response. If no overt resistance is observed, the sexual abuse continues.

Experiences and Observation

As it was stated earlier that the subject of the study 'Girl Child Sexual Abuse' itself is a limitation and the respondents, i.e. girl children who are voiceless part of the society is a challenge to the researcher. It became very difficult for the researcher to make them vocal on the issue, because the issue of girl child sexual abuse is an unspoken subject in our country even though it is prevalent. Hence, the researcher planned for the orientation of the girl children on the subject. The initial experiences and observations of the researcher were not positive as there was no response from the schools; most of the schools denied the permission for study by saying that this is the western concept and this will not happen in our country and we do not want to make our children know such bad things. Request was being made to the Head Masters/Mistress by explaining the seriousness of the subject. Hence, a few teachers gave permission for the study and only those limited schools were selected for the present study.

Another experience was about the girl children who were not ready to even listen to the discussion. When the researcher started the orientation, a number of girls went outside the classrooms one by one. But when the researcher talked about some true cases and showed the charts related to the subject and the girls were asked only to listen and watch the charts, they began to participate.

Gradually, many of the girls started to cry, they became emotional and they asked the researcher if they could discuss alone with researcher. Focus group discussions (FGDs) made the girl children understand and become open about the subject which they later discussed in one-to-one interaction. Interview schedule made it easier for them to share their experiences about sexual abuse.

During home visits for case studies, parents were not ready to give information, some parents asked whether any scheme is there for the victims, they need some financial support from the government for the treatment of child after the incident. Even though their daughters were suffering from the problems, some parents told that this is not a subject of discussion but it is a secret matter. They told that defamation would never allow girl children's marriage and society will keep aside such girls as 'damaged goods'. Due to conspiracy about the subject, the girls were ashamed and afraid to discuss freely about their experiences of sexual abuse.

It was observed during the home visits that the parents were ignorant about the legal procedure, medical procedure and also how they were exploited in society due to poverty, illiteracy and ignorance.

Some girls told about their helplessness to oppose the persons who sexually abuse them and these girls asked the researcher what can be done to solve their problem. Some girls were so silent that it took a lot of time to make them speak. In schools, girls were hesitating to discuss and they asked the researcher a number of times not to tell anybody about their secret incident. They said that for the first time somebody had enquired about their problems so affectionately.

The girl children and parents share their experiences with the researcher after heart-to-heart dialogue and emotional sympathies shown by the researcher.

Many of the key informants, especially doctors, were not given permission for interview but some advocates, doctors, social workers and police persons, who are really committed to the work, were given permission for interview and they expressed their opinions and gave suggestions about the subject.

Limitations of the Study

- One of the major limitations of the study is the subject itself, i.e. sexual abuse and also the respondents like girl children. It is extremely difficult to get responses from girl children on such a sensitive subject, because of their inability to fully understand the different dimensions of sexual abuse and to talk about their experiences. It is difficult to collect data on the subject due to the conspiracy and silence around the subject.
- It is a hidden issue in the area under study so the schools were not responding well during the initial stage. Many schools rejected our consent letters as they said such things are not happening in our area.
- Younger children were not able to understand the concept properly and they participated in less number.
- It was very difficult to select reported cases from 11 tehsils. Because most of the victims had migrated/shifted/married. There were no proper addresses of some victims so they were not available on those addresses.
- Very often children do not even realize that they are being abused. Some of the respondents have stated that till the interview was conducted with

them, they did not realize that they had been abused. The incident is a painful and shameful one not to be ever told to anyone.

The study was challenging in itself due to its sensitivity. Despite all the limitations mentioned above and the operational difficulties, the study has been able to throw light on many important findings that will help the policy-makers to formulate policies and schemes for girl child protection.

Review of Literature

Child sexual abuse is the biggest kept secret in India due to societal denial, ignorance and silence owing to the discomfort generated out of acknowledgement. It is a universal problem that occurs across gender, caste, religions, ethnic communities, occupational and socio-economic groups.

Abuse of girls is usually kept hidden under the guise of family honour and issues of 'purity'. Overlooking of child sexual abuse has happened not only in the sphere of society and community, but in the professional area as well. Therefore, there is a scarcity of empirical information on child sexual abuse within the Indian context and consequently the indigenous body of knowledge on the subject is very limited.

The researcher has taken the review of literature in this concerned area to understand the magnitude of sexual abuse in India, the nature of child sexual abuse in the family and outside, the causes and consequences of child sexual abuse and the available intervention strategies for its prevention and management.

The present review has pointed out the prevailing dearth of research on child sexual abuse in the family and outside in India and abroad.

The first published work dedicated specifically to child sexual abuse appeared in France in 1857, *Medico-legal Studies of Sexual Assault* by Auguste Ambroise Tardieu, the noted French pathologist and pioneer of forensic medicine.

Research work on child sexual abuse could be said to have started even before Freud, in 1860, when French forensic physician Ambroise Tardieu published several papers on battered children, rape and child sexual abuse. He was immediately shouted down by society and his contemporaries. Later, Freud's student, Ferneczi, confirmed child sexual abuse and pointed out that it leads to severe psychological distress. However, he added, being listened to comforted child sexual abuse victims. He died in 1933 and nobody ever accepted his insights in child sexual abuse. Incidentally, in 1946, when the American pediatrician and radiologist, John Caffey, discovered the physical evidence of child battering by means of X-rays, he was shouted down as people preferred to believe that children had problems. No one wanted to see the obvious that parents could be physically battering in children just as they did emotionally. It was only in 1962, when Henry

Kemp's book, *The Battered Child Syndrome* was published that the family evil came to be accepted.

In 1953, Alfred Kinsey and his research sampled over one thousand women. One in four reported child sexual abuse and 90 per cent said they were petrified by the encounters.

By the late 1970s and early 1980s lot of work was being done on the subject and in the early 1990s it became part of the women's movement.

Castelino (1985) studied the incidence and prevalence of childhood sexual victimization and its long-term influence on social and sexual behaviour, on the basis of a survey by 133 postgraduate students from varied disciplines. An adapted version of David Finekelhor's questionnaire and the Bell's adjustment inventory were administered to groups of not more than 20 students.

The major findings of the study indicate that a majority of the respondents belonged to middle or high economic strata of society. It was revealed that almost 26 per cent of the respondents had been sexually abused in childhood between the ages of 3 and 12 by persons who were below the age of 35 years. The mean age at which the respondents were sexually victimized was 9 years.

Only 16 per cent of the females were victimized by strangers and the study confirmed the well-established fact that sexual abuse largely occurs within the child's intimate social network. Castelino (1985) found that sexual abuse occurred primarily in homes, their own, the older partner's or a friend's. In brief, Castelino's study provides evidence that one out of every three girls and one out of every 10 boys has been sexually abused in childhood among the highly educated and middle class population in Bombay city.[45]

Another study, conducted by Mehta et al. (1979), studied 130 cases of suspected rape in girls between the age of six months and 18 years who were admitted to the remand home, Bombay (New Mumbai), over a period of 15 months. These cases were examined medically to confirm the suspicion of rape.

The researchers found that over 77.68 per cent of the cases were more than 14 years of age and 6.15 per cent were between the age of six months and six years. Most of the girls belonged to poor socio-economic strata and came from various slums in Bombay. A majority of them had poor educational background and more than one-third of the girls were illiterate. A majority of the girls had some knowledge about sex. Of the 130 victims, 23 had conceived, and of them six delivered after full term.

Surprisingly, 36.16 per cent of the victims were willing copartners in the sexual activity. Among the accused of the crime of rape, neighbours were responsible in 57.53 per cent of the cases. The remaining were friends, relatives and known hooligans from the same area. Shockingly, two fathers and eight uncles were responsible for committing the heinous crime on the child in the family.[46]

A 1992 survey studying father-daughter incest in Finland reported that of the 9,000 15-year-old High school girls who filled out the questionnaires, of the girls living with their biological fathers, 0.2 per cent reported father-daughter incest experiences; of the girls living with a stepfather, 3.7 per cent reported sexual experiences with him. The reported counts included only father-daughter incest and did not include prevalence of other forms of child sexual abuse. The survey summary stated 'The feelings of the girls about their sexual experiences are overwhelmingly negative'.[47]

In 1994, a paper was presented by sociologist David Finklhor, an internationally recognized expert on research on the incidence and prevalence of child sexual abuse, and director of the Crimes Against Children Research Centre; the countries covered in the paper, were Australia, Austria, Belgium, Canada, Costa Rica, Denmark, Dominican Republic, Finland, France, Germany, Greece, Great Britain, Ireland, Netherlands, New Zealand, South Africa, Spain, Sweden, Switzerland and the United States.

As per the paper's abstract: 'Surveys of child sexual abuse in large-non clinical populations of adults have been conducted in at least 19 countries in addition to the United States and Canada, including 10 national probability samples. All studies have found rates in line with comparable worth American Research, ranging from 7 per cent to 36 per cent of women and 3 per cent to 29 per cent for men. Most studies found females to be abused at 1.5 to 3 times the rate for males. Few comparisons among countries are possible because of methodological and definitional differences; however, they clearly confirm sexual abuse to be an international problem.'[48]

SAMVADA's 1996 study on students in Bangalore (New Bengaluru) states that 47 per cent of the respondents had been sexually abused; 62 per cent of whom had been raped once and 38 per cent of whom had suffered repeated violations.

A study on girl child sexual abuse was conducted by Trupti Panchal in 1997. A total of 1,176 of child sexual abuse were registered between 1990–95 in Mumbai and there were only 57 reported cases on girls under 10 years who were sexually abused. All the 57 cases were selected for the study.

Conclusions of the study were that the child sexual abuse is clearly a violation of trust of the child and the family by the abuser. The child was threatened not to disclose the abuse. He has control over the child because of the child being less powerful.

According to a survey with 350 school girls in New Delhi by SAKSHI in 1997, 63 per cent had experienced child sexual abuse at the hands of family members; and 25 per cent of the girls had either been raped, made to masturbate the perpetrator or engage in oral sex.

Another 1997 study on middle and upper class women from Chennai, Mumbai, Delhi, Kolkata and Goa by RAHI (Recovering and Healing from Incest) Foundation revealed that 76 per cent of respondents had been sexually abused as children, with 71 per cent been abused either by relatives or by someone they knew and trusted.

First comprehensive, global study UNICEF's study on Violence on Children conducted by the United Nations on all form of violence and first global study to engage directly and consistently with children. Children have participation in all regional consultations, help in connection with the study eloquently describing both violence they experience and their proposals for ending it.

- The report includes the following overview statistics (Section II, B pp. a–10) with references to specific studies provided for each, almost 53,000 children died worldwide in 2002 as a result of homicide.
- Up to 80 to 98 per cent of children suffer physical punishment in their homes with a third or more experiencing severe physical punishment resulting from the use of implements.
- 150 million girls and 73 million boys under 18 experienced forced sexual intercourse or other forms of sexual violence during 2002.
- Between 100 and 140 million girls and women in the world have undergone some form of female genital mutilation/cutting. In Sub-Saharan Africa, Egypt and Sudan, 3 million girls and women are subjected to genital mutilation/cutting every year.
- In 2004, 218 million children were involved in child labour, of whom 126 million were in hazardous work.
- Estimates from 2000 suggest that 1.8 million children were forced into prostitution and pornography and 1.2 million were victims of trafficking.[49]

Survey conducted in 2001 by Save the Children, Sweden, found that 68 per cent had faced physical abuse, 46.6 per cent faced severe abuse leading to injuries, 32.2 per cent had their private parts touched by the abuser, 20 per cent were forced to have sexual intercourse.

An empirical study in 2009 in Delhi was carried out by Abhishek K. Singh to assess the nature, extent pattern and causes of abuse and to analyse the effect abuse has on a child's role performance and his development. The study was focused on 170 children in the age group of 10–16 years of the 170 case studies, 120 were cases of physical abuse, 23 of sexual abuse and 27 of and 38.4 per cent were girls. The age groups of the interviewed children were 10–16 years.

1. Results are physical abuse.
2. Boys are more battered than girls.
3. Non-working children are beaten more than working children.

4. Maximum number of abused children are from poor families.

Sexual Abuse

1. Girls are more often prime victims of sexual abuse than boys.
2. A high proportion of children become victims of sexual abuse when they are 14 years or above in age.
3. Male victims are abused by one person but female victims are generally assaulted by more than one person.

Emotional Abuse

Boys are more emotionally maltreated than girls. Aggressive imitable and domineering nature of parents results in emotional abuse.[50]

Tulir CPHCSA's study in 2006, conducted among 2,211 school going children in Chennai, indicates child sexual abuse prevalence rate of 42 per cent, children of all socio-economic groups were found to be equally vulnerable. While 48 per cent of boys reported having been abused, the prevalence rate among girls was 39 per cent; 15 per cent of both boys and girls had been severely abused.[51]

The first ever 'National Study on Child Abuse' in April 2007, covering 13 states in India and a sample size of 12,446 children was released by the Ministry for Women and Child Development showing these stark reality figures:

- More than 53 per cent children report facing one or more forms of sexual abuse.
- Almost 22 per cent faced severe sexual abuse, 6 per cent sexually assaulted.
- Fifty per cent of sexual offenders were known to the victim or were in positions of trust (family member, close relative, friend or neighbour).
- Onset of abuse is from 5 years of age.
- Boys were equally at risk as girls.
- Severest sexual abuse is in age group of 11–16 years.
- 73 per cent of sexual abuse victims were in age groups of 11–18 years.

The World Health Organization (WHO) estimates that 150 million girls and 73 million boys under 18 years have experienced forced sexual intercourse or other forms of sexual violence involving physical contact. Much of this sexual violence is inflicted by family members of other people residing in or visiting a child's family home – people normally trusted by children and often responsible for their care. A review of epidemiological surveys from 21 countries, mainly high and middle-income countries, found that at least 7 per cent of females (ranging up to 36%) and 3 per cent of males (ranging up to 29%) reported sexual victimization during their childhood.

According to these studies, between 14 per cent and 56 per cent of the sexual abuse of girl, and up to 25 per cent of the sexual abuse of boys, was perpetrated by relatives or step-parents. In many places, adults were outspoken about the risk of sexual violence their children faced at school or at play in the community, but rarely did adults speak of children's risk of sexual abuse within the home and family context. The shame, secrecy and denial associated with familial sexual violence against children foster a pervasive culture of silence, where children cannot speak about sexual violence in the home, and where adults do not know what to do or say if they suspect someone they know is sexually abusing a child.[52]

As per a survey carried out by SAMVAD, Bangalore, of 348 girls up to 18 years, among the students from schools and colleges around Bangalore (Now Bengaluru), approximately 24 per cent were found to have experienced sexual abuse at least once in their lives. Another study in Tamil Nadu has shown about 23 per cent of rape victims as girls, under 16. Around 60 per cent of victims were reluctant to name the offender. This was a clear indication that the abuse had happened within the home and the offender was too close for a complaint. These incidences clearly confirm that the high incidence of sexual abuse of girl children is by someone known or trusted by them.[53]

A survey conducted in Swaziland by UNICEF, the Centres to Disease Control and Prevention (CDC), and local partners in 2007 illustrated the scope of the problem, with approximately one in three girls a victim of sexual abuse prior to the age of 18, and three-quarters of the perpetrators being men and boys (including boyfriends, husbands, and male relatives) from the neighbourhood the victims resided in.[54]

Bitter Chocolate (2000) is the first book in India on the issue of child sexual abuse. The author is Pinky Virani. This book has been translated in several Indian languages. Based on real cases of child sexual abuse, the book opens the hidden fact of child sexual abuse in India.

A study of sexual abuse of girls and women was conducted by Maharshi Karve Institutes women study and research centre in 2007 Pune, and Siddhivinayak Kala Vanijya Mahavidyalaya. A study of sexual abuse of girl children with 180 girls was conducted. The finding of the study was that victims or her parents were not ready to complain against the abuser. Parents suggested to their children to ignore the incidence. Faith and trust on police has declined and most of the girls wanted awareness camps about sexual abuse.

Invisible Tears is a first book written by Abigail Lawrence in the year 2010. This is the story of Abbie's struggle to survive, the grim details of child sexual abuse of the worst kind, from the perspective of a little girl.

This book has been written to bring to public attention the horrors that some girl children go through and live with sexual abuse. After raising her own children, Abigail Lawrence's book is based on a true story.

More work is needed to know the nature, extent and prevalence of incident of child sexual abuse so that measures can be suggested that measures to tackle the problem.

To conclude, it may be emphasized that an increase in research in the field of girl child sexual abuse will help in creating greater awareness about the phenomenon of girl child sexual abuse in our country and facilitate the formulation of suitable intervention strategies for its prevention.

Notes

1. Quoted statement taken from Anand Sirohi's *Modern Perspectives on Social Work*, Vol. III, Dominant Publishers, New Delhi, p. 11.
2. Quoted statement taken from the 'Report on Child Abuse' by Ministry of Women and Child Development, Government of India, 2007.
3. Thukral, G.E. and Abbasi, I.R. (2007), 'Ensuring Child Protection', *Seminar*, Magazine, New Delhi, p. 19.
4. Ibid., p 19.
5. Bajpai, Asha (2007), 'Who is a Child?', *Info Change News and Features*, Magazine, p. 5.
6. Ibid., p. 23.
7. Sinha, P.K. (2011), 'Higher Education in India', *Human Touch*, Vol. VIII, New Delhi, p. 28.
8. Shivkumar, A.K. (2007), 'Why Children are Neglected?', *Seminar*, New Delhi, p. 14.
9. Human Touch Bureau (2011), *The Children of India: Victims of Malnutrition*, Vol. VIII, New Delhi, p. 31.
10. WHO (2005), *World Report on Violence and Health*, World Health Organization, Geneva.
11. NIPCCD (2010), *Statistics on Women in India*, New Delhi, p. 2.
12. Ibid., p. 4.
13. www.indianchild.com.
14. Shrivastava, Nidhi (2010), 'Children at Risk of Developing Unstable Personality in Modern Society', in Nidhi Shrivastava (ed.), *Family in Modern Society*, Ritu Publications, Jaipur, p. 98.
15. Singh, K. (1991), *Criminology and Social Disorganization*, Prakash Kendra, Lucknow, pp. 130–131.
16. Srivastava, S.S. (1996), *Criminology and Criminal Administration*, Central Law Agency, Allahabad, p. 4.

17. Human Touch Bureau (2004), *Child Abuse: A Priority Issue for Immediate Action*, New Delhi, p. 5.
18. Rane, J. Asha (1994), 'Dynamics of Child Abuse and Interventions', in Murli Desai (ed.), *Family and Intervention*, Tata Institute of Social Sciences, Bombay, pp. 165–166.
19. WHO (2012), *World Report on Violence and Health*, World Health Organization, Geneva, p. 59.
20. www.wikipedia.org, accessed on 18 August 2012.
21. Buchanan, M.F. (1986), *Sexual Abuse of Children*, DVD Video. The University of Leeds, Audio and Visual Service, Leeds, p. 9.
22. Ibid., p. 6.
23. Singh, A.K. (2010), 'Child Abuse', *Human Touch*, Vol. VII, New Delhi.
24. Hini, Robert (2012), 'Sexual Abuse: A Big Problem for All of Us', *The Record*, Perth, Australia.
25. UNICEF (2011), *Together for Girls*, Swaziland, p. 4.
26. Hayward, Ruth Finney (2000), *Breaking the Earthenware Jar: Lessons from South Asia to End Violence Against Women and Girls*, UNICEF, New York, p. 83.
27. Ibid., p. 84.
28. SAATHI (1997), *A Situational Analysis of Violence Against Women and Girls in Nepal*, Kathmandu, p. 8.
29. Human Touch Bureau (2004), 'Child Abuse: A Priority for Immediate Action', *Human Touch*, New Delhi, p. 5.
30. Singh, A.K. (2010), 'Child Abuse', *Human Touch*, Magazine, Vol. VII, New Delhi, p. 11.
31. NCRB (1993), Crime in India Report, Delhi.
32. Sirsat, J. (2012), 'Nati Pisatlali', *Lokmat*, Daily Newspaper, 20 May, p. 7.
33. Munde, V. (2011), 'Beed Zhilyat Chaar Mahinayat 11 Balatkar', *Loksatta*, 29 April, p. 1.
34. Young, P.V. (1956), *Scientific Social Surveys and Research: An Introduction to the Background, Content Methods and Analysis of Social Studies*. Prentice Hall, Englewood Cliff, N.J.
35. Ibid., p. 32.
36. Kerlinger, F.N. (1964), *Foundations of Behavioural Research: Educational and Psychological Inquiry*, Holt, Rinehart and Winston, Inc., New York.
37. Vijayalakshmi, B. (2008), 'Case Study Method in Social Work', in D.K. Lal Das and Vanila Bhaskaran (eds), *Research Methods for Social Work*, Rawat, Jaipur, p. 286.
38. Ibid., p. 286.
39. RAHI Foundation (1998), *Voices from the Silent Zone: Women's Experiences of Incest and Childhood Sexual Abuse*, RAHI, New Delhi, p. 7.
40. Ibid.

41. Panchal, Trupti (1997), Documentation of Police Cases of Sexually Abused Girls in Mumbai City between 1994–95, The Special Cell for Women and Children.
42. Ibid., p. 8.
43. Porter, Ruth (ed) (1990), CIBA Foundation, *Child Sexual Abuse Within the Family*, Tavistock, London, p. 1.
44. Webster's II (1984), *New Riverside University Dictionary*, Houghton Mifflin, New York, p. 762.
45. Rane, J. Asha (1991), 'Research on Child Abuse in Families', in J. Asha Rane (ed.), *Research on Families with Problems in India*, Vol. II, Tata Institute of Social Sciences, Bombay, p. 456.
46. Ibid., p. 457.
47. Porter, Ruth (ed) (1990), CIBA Foundation, *Child Sexual Abuse within the Family*, Tavistock, London, p. 4.
48. Hopper, J. (2010), 'Child Abuse: Statistics, Research, and Resources', www.jimhopper.com.
49. UNICEF (2003), 'Child Protection: Child Trafficking Statistics', New York, p. 14.
50. Singh, A.K. (2010), 'Child Abuse', *Human Touch*, Vol. VII, New Delhi, p. 12.
51. TULIR-CHCSA (2006), Doesn't Every Child Count? Research on Prevalence and Dynamics of Child Sexual Abuse Among School Going Children in Chennai, TULIR-CHCSA, Chennai, pp. 4–5.
52. Buchanan, M.F. (1986), Sexual Abuse of Children, DVD Video, The University of Leeds, Audio and Visual Service, Leeds, p. 9.
53. SAKSHI Foundation (2007), Child Sexual Abuse, Draft Manual, New Delhi, p. 3.
54. Reza, A., et al., (2009), 'Sexual Violence and its Health Consequences for Female Children in Swaziland: A Cluster Survey Study', *Lancet*, 373 (9679), p. 4.

2

Socio-Economic Status of Sexually Abused Girls

Socio-economic conditions play a major role in increasing the vulnerability of children to various and newer abuses. To find out the relationship between sexual abuse of girl children and their socio-economic background, the factors such as education, occupation and income of parents of the victim are analysed in this chapter.

Child abuse is a violation of the basic human rights of a child and is an outcome of a set of interrelated familial, social, psychological and economic factors. The growing complexities of life and the dramatic changes brought about by socio-economic transaction in India have played a major role in increasing the vulnerability of children to various and newer forms of abuse. Existing socio-economic conditions also render some children vulnerable and more at risk to sexual abuse.

The girl child is the first victim of poverty, ignorance and social taboos. The situation of a girl child in Indian families is the result of deep-rooted biases which treat the female child only as an object of sex. The girl children from the families which are below poverty line and whose caretakers are illiterate are the worst sufferers.

Thus, the utter vulnerability and defenseless façade of children make them an easy target of adult treachery and lust. Faced by restrictions, ignorance and an indifferent environment in the family, teenage girls are easily attracted by scheming adults who lure them with affection and freedom from the confines of a drab existence.

Therefore, the teenage girls seek to escape to better socio-economic conditions, which the accused seem to offer. Parental inadequacies, poverty, illiteracy are the factors discussed and analysed in this chapter with the help of following tables and graphs.

Table 2.1 shows the age-wise classification of victims. In this study, 500 school going girl children are selected. According to the data, the school going girl children were divided into two groups, i.e. 11–14 years and

15–18 years of age. The percentage of girls of age group 15–18 years is higher, i.e. 73.80 per cent and the percentage of girls of age group 11–14 years is lower, i.e. 26.20 per cent.

Graph 2.1 *Age-Wise Classification of Victims*

Year 2011

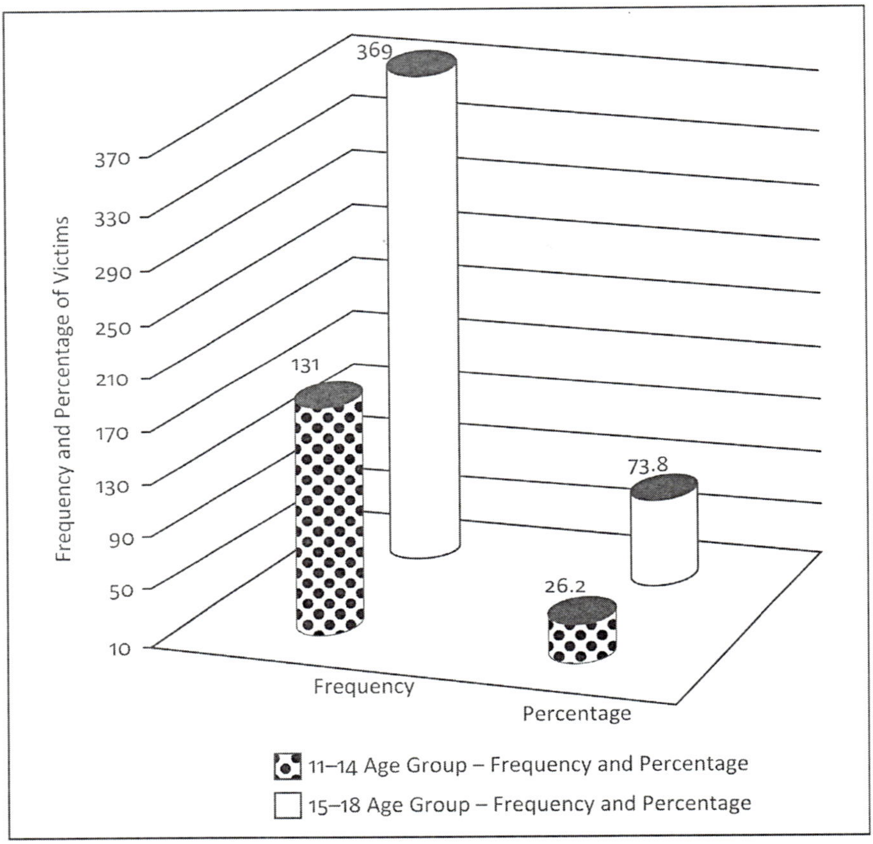

Table 2.1 *Age-Wise Classification of Victims*

Year 2011

S. No.	*Age Group*	*Frequency*	*Percentage*
1	11–14	131	26.20
2	15–18	369	73.80
	Total	500	100.00

Source: Primary Data

Among the age group of 11–14 years, highest number is 62 girls belonging to 14 years of age, and lowest number is 19 girls belonging to 11 years of age. Among the group of 15–18 years, highest number is 255 girls belonging to 15 years of age and lowest number is 24 girls belonging to 18 years of age. There is no equal number of girls from each class and age because the researcher selected those girls as respondents who came forward to share their experiences during group discussion. The age group of 11–18 years is selected specifically with the intention that they can answer well during the group discussion and they can break their silence by sharing their abusive experiences.

This data shows that sexual abuse is prevalent among girls of all ages. Girls belonging to 11–14 years of age participated in the group discussion in less number due to their hesitation to break the silence about the abuse. In fact due to their lower age, they were not aware or did not even realize that they were being abused. On the other hand, girls belonging to 15–18 years of age participated in large number in the group discussion as these girls were rather eager to share their experiences and told that they did not know how to tell and whom to tell about their experiences because their parents did not believe them when told about their abuse. Instead of support, these girls were blamed by their parents saying that it was her own fault and the girl should keep quiet.

Hence, the pubertal and adolescent period girls seem to be most at risk and they need psychological support and proper way to come out of this situation so that they can enjoy child rights by getting proper schooling at proper age and happy childhood in a happy and healthy family environment which is the need of all girl children.

Table 2.2 *Marital Status of the Victims*

Year 2011

S. No.	*Marital Status*	*Reported*	*Unreported*	*From key informants*	*School going girl children*
1	Married	03	05	04	–
2	Unmarried	07	05	06	500
	Total	10	10	10	500

Source: Primary Data

Table 2.2 shows the marital status of the victims. In the present study, 30 cases were studied with the help of case study method and interview of 500 school-going girl children was conducted with the help of interview schedule. Among the 500 school-going girl children, all the girls were unmarried. Among 30 cases (10 unreported, 10 reported and 10 from key informants), 12 girls were married (i.e. three from reported, five from unreported and four cases from key informants) and remaining 18 girls were unmarried.

The study revealed the fact that even though the girls were below 18 years they were married. Instead of giving them psychological support or medical treatment, parents arrange marriage of their daughters without thinking about their daughters' emotional and psychological situation or even about the adjustment problems they are likely to suffer after marriage. Disreputation and stigma attached with the incident of sexual abuse make the parents to do so.

Graph 2.3 *Caste-Wise Distribution of the Victims*

Year 2011

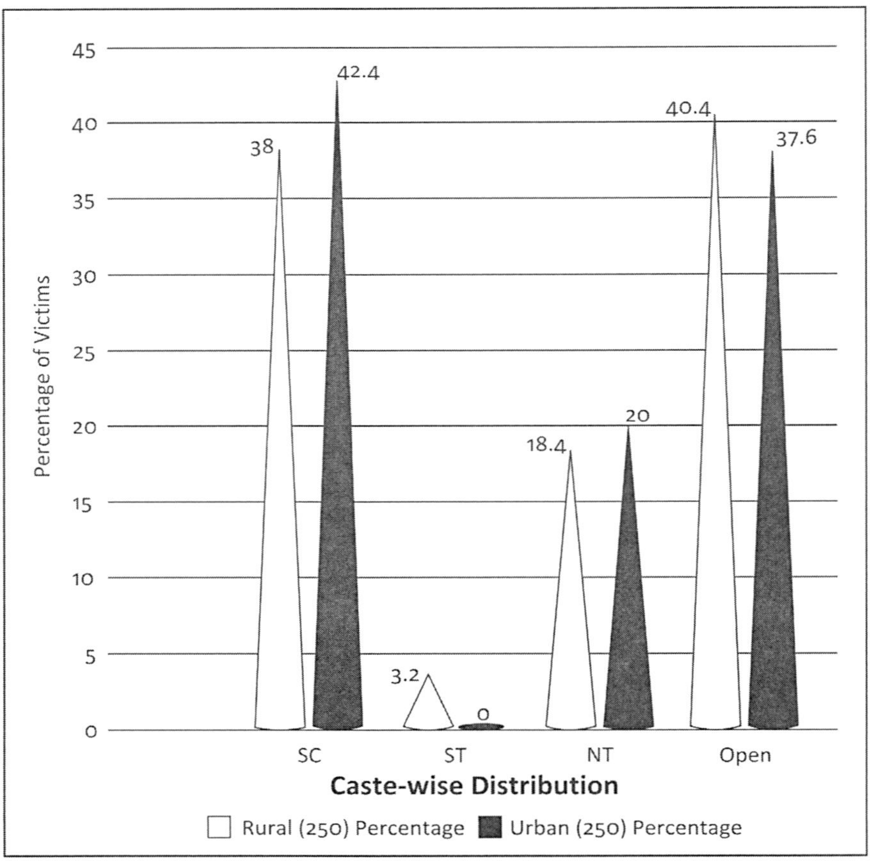

It was found that the married girls suffer from a feeling of guilt and shame and the incident of sexual abuse never allows them to trust their new close relationships, because they have been sexually abused by trusted and known persons. Consequences of the incident are that they have to face adjustment problems in their married life.

It was also found that reported girls were facing marriage problem due to the stigma. So the victim has to suffer various problems due to the incident of sexual abuse in her life.

Table 2.3 *Caste-Wise Distribution of the Victims*

Year 2011

S.No.	*Caste Group*	*Rural 250*		*Urban 250*	
		Frequency	*Percentage*	*Frequency*	*Percentage*
1	Scheduled Cast (SC)	95	38.00	106	42.40
2	Scheduled Tribe (ST)	8	3.20	0	0.00
3	Nomadic Tribe (NT)	46	18.40	50	20.00
4	Open	101	40.40	94	37.60
	Total	250	100.00	250	100.00

Source: Primary Data

Graph 2.3 and Table 2.3 show the caste-wise distribution of the victims. The percentage of open category respondents is the highest, i.e. 40.40 per cent in rural area. Followed by SC category respondents at 38 per cent, NT category respondents were 18.40 per cent and lowest percentage is of the respondents of ST category, i.e. 3.20 per cent. Whereas, in urban area, the percentage of SC category respondents is higher, i.e. 42.40 per cent, followed by open category respondents at 37.60 per cent, NT respondents 20 per cent and ST respondents were not available in schools during group discussion.

Open category students participated in more number in rural areas during group discussion; on the other hand, even though SC students were present in the classroom, they participated in less number in the group discussion. It indicates that caste is still dominant in rural areas and this caste discrimination stops them from participating in the discussion. It was found in the urban areas that SC students came forward to participate in the group discussion to share their experiences. This shows the changing scenario in the urban areas which allows them to participate in discussion and it proves that the caste is losing its impact in urban areas compared to rural areas. The non-availability of ST girls shows that the STs have not come in the mainstream of the society yet.

Graph 2.4 *Educational Background of the Victims*

Year 2011

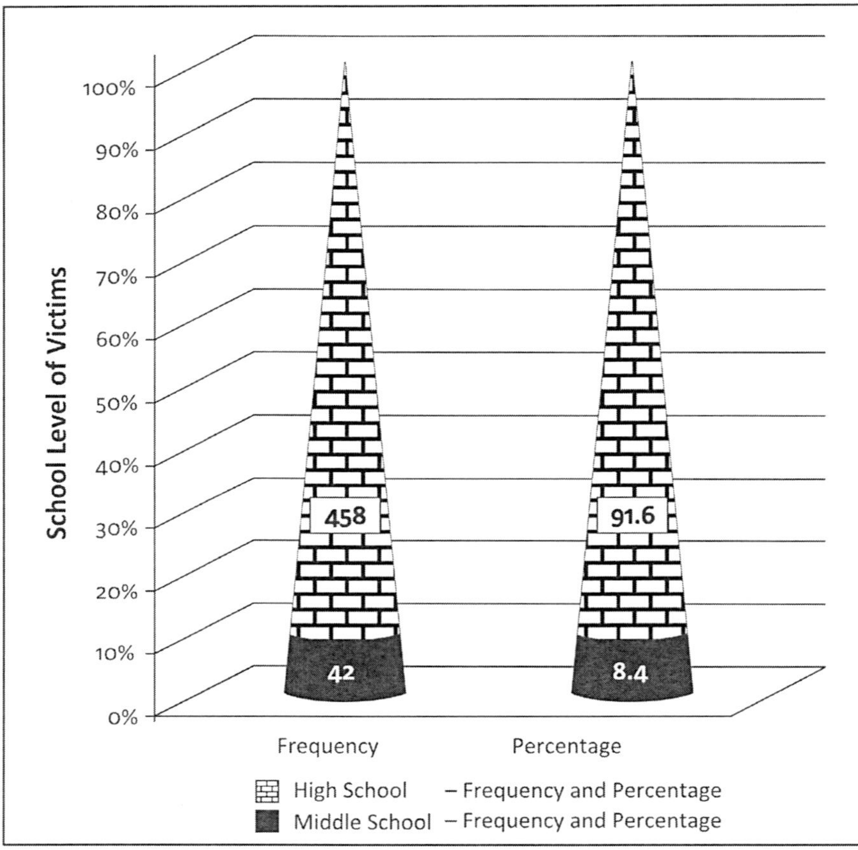

Table 2.4 *Educational Background of the Victims*

S. No.	*Education*	*Frequency*	*Percentage*
1	Middle School	42	8.4
2	High School	458	91.6
	Total	500	100.00

Source: Primary Data

Table 2.4 reveals that middle school girls are very less, i.e. 8.4 per cent in comparison to high school girls, i.e. 91.6 per cent. While VI to VII standard girls belong to Middle school, VIII to X standard girls belong to High school.

The girls belonging to Middle school participated in the group discussion in less number. Even though sexual abuse is prevalent among the girls of all classes, the girls from Middle school are confused and also feel guilty to share their experiences of sexual abuse. They are not aware or do not even realize that they are being abused due to their young age On the other hand, the girls from High school participated in group discussion in large number and told that they do not know to whom and how to tell their experiences of sexual abuse because the family atmosphere does not permit them to share such feelings. This shows that there is lack of interaction between parents and children and disbelief of parents force the girls to keep quiet. Hence, they need timely counselling to come out of this problem.

Table 2.5 *Co-Relation between Girl Child Sexual Abuse and Type of Family*

Year – 2011

Type of Family	*Rural 250*		*Urban 250*		*Total 500*	
	Abused Girls Frequency	*Not Abused Girls Frequency*	*Abused Girls Frequency*	*Not Abused Girls Frequency*	*Abused Girls Frequency*	*Not Abused Frequency*
Joint Family	151 (71.23)	16 (42.11)	46 (31.51)	07 (6.73)	197 (55.03)	23 (16.20)
Nuclear Family	61 (28.77)	22 (37.89)	100 (68.49)	97 (93.27)	161 (44.97)	119 (83.80)
Total	212	38	146	104	358	142

Source: Primary Data

Table 2.5 shows the prevalence of sexual abuse of girl children in joint and nuclear families in rural as well as in urban areas. The percentage of abused girls in joint families is higher, i.e. 71.23 in rural areas, whereas the percentage of sexually abused girls in joint family is lower in urban area, i.e. 31.51 per cent. The percentage of sexually abused girls in nuclear family is highest, i.e. 68.49 in urban area whereas the percentage of sexually abused girls in nuclear family is lowest, i.e. 28.77 in rural area.

The available data shows that total joint families are 220 and total nuclear families are 280. The prevalence of sexual abuse in joint families from both the areas is higher, i.e. 55.03 per cent and the percentage of sexual abuse in nuclear family from both the areas is lower, i.e. 44.97 per cent.

Thus, the figures in the above table show the hidden facts in the Indian families. Home is considered as a secured place for all family members and it is believed that the family gives protection to its family members and kinship. It is unfortunate that family members are abusing their own children which puts a question mark in such relationship and in such type of families. Girl child is not safe in her own house. It shows that these families are losing their morality and the girls have lost faith in the family members that they cannot live comfortably and happily in these families.

The above figures are alarming and asking us to be aware of the extent of the problem of girl child sexual abuse in families. Though sexual abuse of girl child is higher in joint families, the figures of sexual abuse in nuclear families are not negligible. So, it can be said that the extent of sexual abuse is more in joint families, but it also exists in a large number in nuclear families and it clearly indicates that sexual abuse is spread over all types of families. Family which is a primary unit of the society is gradually losing its function of building morality and faith in the relations and to protect its family members. This is really a serious problem as children from such families will not create a good society.

This study proves the prevalence of sexual abuse of girl child within the families, which is a hidden reality. The result of study contradicts the popular myth that sexual abuse does not take place within joint families, and that it happens within nuclear families only. This is often mistakenly attributed to the element of greater degree of supervision, especially by elders in the joint families. This study proves that the prevalence of sexual abuse within joint families is in large number than in nuclear families. The percentage of sexual abuse of girl child is higher in joint families as number of people having greater access to children is higher and they win the trust and make the children feel special in order to abuse them sexually. Due to trust in the elders or other family members, lack of awareness about abuse and general silence on the subject in the family, the girls are disbelieved or blamed for their abuse. So, even though sexual abuse is prevalent in the family, due to above causes the girl children keep quiet and do not disclose their abuse.

Table 2.6 *Occupational Status of Father of the Victims*

Year 2011

S. No.	*Occupation*	*Rural (250)*		*Urban (250)*	
		Frequency	*Percentage*	*Frequency*	*Percentage*
1	Daily wage earner	70	28.00	61	24.40
2	Agricultural worker	66	26.40	35	14.00
3	Rickshaw driver	8	3.20	19	7.60
4	Gavandi	17	6.80	21	8.40
5	Private job	10	4.00	15	6.00
6	Government servant	13	5.20	44	17.60
7	Self-employment	13	5.20	15	6.00
8	Unemployed	53	21.20	40	16.00
	Total	250	100.00	250	100.00

Source: Primary Data

Father's occupation plays a vital role in the family, as occupation decides the income and income helps to fulfil the needs of the family members. Table 2.6 shows that 28 per cent respondents' fathers are daily wage earners in rural area which is higher than all other occupations followed by agricultural worker at 26.40 per cent, Gavandi (masons) at 6.80 per cent, 3.20 per cent are rickshaw drivers which is the lowest of all occupations. Government servant and self-employment are same percentage, i.e. 5.20 per cent, 4 per cent respondents' fathers are doing private jobs like working in private companies and sugar factories as servant or teacher in private schools where there is no guarantee of regular payment. The government servants are Zila Parishad (ZP) teachers; servants in civil hospital, health workers, etc. and self-employment includes running STD booths, panshops, kirana shops and hair cutting saloons, etc.

In urban area also 24.40 per cent respondents' fathers are wage earners followed by government servants at 17.60 per cent, 14 per cent agricultural workers, 8.40 per cent gavandi, 7.60 per cent rickshaw drivers, the percentage of private job and self-employment is same, i.e. 6 per cent. Self-employment includes auto-rickshaw driving for school-going children, running STD booths, tailoring, having panshop, 'kirana' shops, saloon, milk selling, etc. Private jobs include work in press, tutors in computer institute, etc.

The number of respondents whose fathers are government servants earning fixed salary are very less in both the areas. All other occupations of fathers of the respondents have no certainty of job and no fixed income as unemployment exists in both the areas. The data shows that the percentage of respondents whose fathers are unemployed is higher in rural area, i.e. 21.20 per cent, whereas it is 16 per cent in urban area. Hence, most of the respondents are from lower income group families.

This percentage of unemployment is alarming due to uncertainty of job. So, the fathers of the respondents get leisure time and this leisure time makes them addict and addiction leads to tension and quarrel in the family and such tensed families are not having healthy environment and interactions with their children. In this situation, the teenaged girls are easily available to the abusers by giving some valuable gifts which are not given by their parents as their income does not permit them to fulfil the needs of their teenaged girl children. However low income, tension in the family and no guarantee of job are all the important factors of sexual abuse of girl child.

Table 2.7 shows the different occupations of victim's mother. The percentage of daily wage earner in rural area is 50 per cent which is higher than all other occupations. Followed by 34 per cent agricultural worker, 5.20 per cent private job, 4 per cent self-employment, the percentage of housewife and domestic worker is same, i.e. 2.80 per cent; 1.20 per cent government servant which is the lowest among all.

Table 2.7 *Occupation of Victim's Mother*

S. No.	*Occupation*	*Rural (250)*		*Urban (250)*	
		Frequency	*Percentage*	*Frequency*	*Percentage*
1	Housewife	07	2.80	53	21.20
2	Agricultural worker	85	34.00	48	19.20
3	Domestic worker	07	2.80	55	22.00
4	Daily wage earner	125	50.00	50	20.00
5	Private job	13	5.20	16	6.40
6	Government servant	3	1.20	11	4.40
7	Self-employment	10	4.00	17	6.80
	Total	250	100.00	250	100.00

Source: Primary Data

In urban area, the percentage of domestic worker is 22 per cent, which is higher than all other occupations, followed by that of housewife at 21.20 per cent, daily wage earner 20 per cent, agriculture work 19.20 per cent, and self-employment 6.80 per cent, which is the lowest among all other occupations.

This shows that a large number of women in urban and rural areas remain outdoors for earning money. It was stated earlier in Table 2.6 that most of the respondents' fathers are unemployed in both the areas. So mothers of this victim bear the responsibility of working to earn for the family and this working keeps them away from home and they have no time to interact with their child. Girl children are having no regular schooling due to their work at home and responsibility of siblings and thus these girls are most of the time alone in the home as the parents are always at work. The male family members or others take advantage of this situation and sexually abuse the girl children. Even though women in the family are sometimes aware of this fact, but they are unable to protect the girl children from abuse as they cannot afford to abandon their work outside and are forced to keep silent because of fear of social stigma and male dominance in the family.

Table 2.8 shows different income groups of respondents. These income groups were divided into five different income groups. In rural area 40.40 per cent respondents belong to the income group of ₹ 10,001–₹ 15,000 which is the highest of all other income groups. Whereas, in urban area 32.80 per cent respondents belong to the income group of ₹ 15,001–₹ 20,000 which is the highest of all other income groups; more than ₹ 25,000 income group is the lowest in both the areas which are 1.60 in rural area and it is 13.60 in urban area; 30.40 per cent families are earning less than ₹ 10,000 in rural areas and 16.40 per cent in urban areas.

Table 2.8 *Annual Income of Families of Victims*

Year 2011

S. No.	*Income Group*	*Rural 250*		*Urban 250*	
		Frequency	*Percentage*	*Frequency*	*Percentage*
1	5,000–10,000	76	30.4	41	16.4
2	10,001–15,000	101	40.4	42	16.8
3	15,001–20,000	59	23.6	82	32.8
4	20,001–25,000	10	4	51	20.4
5	25,000 and More than	4	1.6	34	13.6
	Total	250	100.00	250	100.00

Source: Primary Data

Graph 2.8 *Annual Income of Families of Victims*

Year 2011

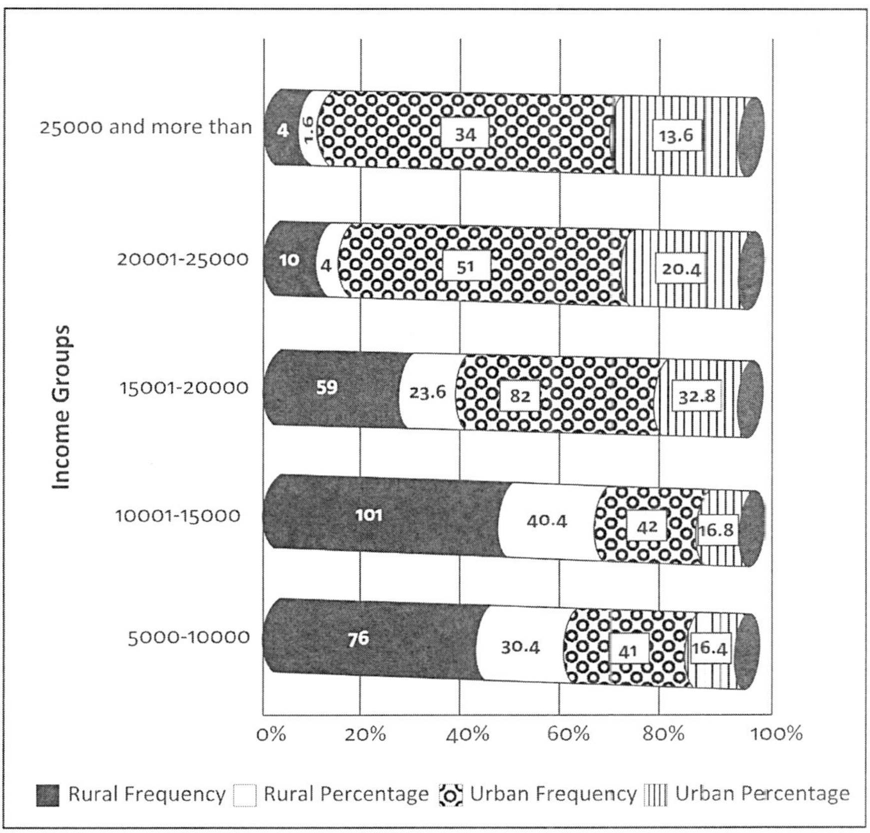

Thus, overall in rural areas 94.40 per cent families belong to lower income group, 4 per cent to middle income group and 1.60 per cent to higher income group, whereas in urban area 66 per cent families belong to lower income group, 20.40 per cent to middle income group and 13.60 per cent to higher income group.

The study reveals the harsh fact that 'poverty' is at the root of sexual abuse of girl children in both rural and urban areas. Beed District is known for its migration, poverty, female foeticide and low literacy level of girls. Poverty makes the girl to minimize her wants but her teenage desires lures her to fulfil her wants. The abusers, i.e. relatives, family friends, neighbours, etc. know very well of this vulnerability of the girl and try to lure her by giving things which are not normally available to her in her family. The parents of lower income group are unable to fulfil even the basic needs of the members of the family. The income is not guaranteed and, therefore, the earning members are always under stress and tension. This leads to addiction and quarrels in the family. There is no sharing, love and interaction between the parents and children and among children in the family. Children are deprived of proper upbringing and are unable to decide what is right and what is wrong. This situation helps the potential abusers to emotionally exploit the child, misuse her trust and abuse the girl child sexually.

As it was discussed earlier in Tables 2.7 and 2.8 that low income and unfulfilled needs and demands of teenage girl children go together. The unfulfilled demands of her age tempt her to receive valuable gifts from the abuser, makes her an easy prey of the abuse without knowing the result of their abuse due to their lower age, ignorance and trust on the abusers. This study reveals the fact that even though the sexual abuse is prevalent in all income group families, girls belonging to lower income group are at high risk. Most of the respondents in the present study are from lower income group families.

Table 2.9 *Time Given to Household Work by Victims*

Year 2011

S. No.	*Working Hours*	*Rural*		*Urban*	
		Frequency	*Percentage*	*Frequency*	*Percentage*
1	One hour	59	24.28	53	24.09
2	Two hours	60	24.69	50	22.72
3	Three hours	52	21.40	43	19.54
4	Four hours	30	12.35	25	11.36
5	Five hours	19	7.82	15	6.81
6	More than five hours	23	9.47	14	6.36
	Total	243		220	

Source: Primary Data

Table 2.9 shows the time given by victims to household work in rural and urban areas. The percentage of time of one hour devoted for household work in rural area is 24.28 per cent and it is 24.09 per cent in urban areas. The percentage for two hours in rural area is higher, 24.69 per cent, and it is 22.72 per cent in urban area and the percentage for three hours in rural area is 21.40 per cent and it is 19.54 per cent in urban area. The time of four hours in rural area is 12.35 per cent and it is 11.36 per cent in urban area. Time of five hours devoted for household work in rural area is 7.82 per cent and it is 6.81 per cent in urban area and in case of more than five hours it is 9.47 per cent in rural area and it is 6.36 per cent in urban area.

The study reveals that the girl children from both the areas are giving time for household work. There is not much difference in the devoted time in cases from both the areas, because the girls from both the areas are belonging to lower income group. These girls are made to shoulder the responsibility of their siblings and to do the household chores as their parents are mostly away from home for earning. Girls at home have to prepare food, wash utensils and clothes and look after their younger brothers and sisters. Besides doing some or the other work at home, sometimes they have to go for outside work with their mother to earn for the family. This results in their irregular schooling and school dropout. In such a situation, the elderly who supervise them and the relatives who visit the home, misuse the situation by gaining her trust through their power, or authority or even by love and sympathy and they succeed in sexually abusing the girl child.

As discussed in the previous tables, the minor age of girl child, lack of awareness of consequences, temptation of age and trust in family members and relatives make them easy prey of abusers and, sometimes, these girls are also abused by the owners at work place. The percentage of girls who are not giving time for household work is higher in urban areas, which is 12 per cent (30 girls) where as it is 2.8 per cent (7 girls) in rural area. In urban area some girls are going for tuitions, some families are allowing them to get their education. However, a large number of girls from both the areas are belonging to lower income group families and their parents have to keep themselves away from home for earning and these girls are made to give much time for household work and shoulder the responsibility of their siblings, which deprives them from their right of recreation and education.

Table 2.10 reveals the medium of entertainment of victims. Among all medium of entertainments, the percentage of television as a medium of entertainment is higher than any other medium of entertainment. Chitchatting with friends is 10.6 per cent and play is just 2.6 per cent. Some respondents have given multiple modes of entertainment but television is common among all multiple groups.

Table 2.10 *Medium of Entertainment of Victims*

Year 2011

S. No.	*Medium of Entertainment*	*Frequency*	*Percentage*
1	Television	314	62.8
2	Mobile	08	1.6
3	To play	13	2.6
4	To go to cinema	15	3
5	Internet	04	0.8
6	Chitchatting with friends	53	10.6
7	Television, mobile, cinema	20	4
8	Television, internet, cinema	13	2.6
9	Mobile, television, chitchatting	25	5
10	Chitchatting, playing and television	35	7
	Total	500	100.00

Source: Primary Data

The study reveals that mobile and internet, the new technology, is not used by the girls. They are far away from these new modes of communication and entertainment. Going to cinema is not allowed, but 62.8 per cent girls are watching TV at home; 10 per cent girls from 11 to 14 years resort to chitchat with their friends and 15 to 18 years girls are not allowed to go outside for chitchatting. So the television is the only medium of entertainment for girl children in both the areas. We can see the impact of TV on their dressing pattern, their use of cosmetics, their behaviour. At their impressionable age, they are overtly made aware of sexual behaviour and relationships. This mindset of these girls, supported by their ignorance, poverty, lack of parental supervision, curiosity about sex, makes them an easy prey for potential abusers. In teenage years, these girls are unaware of hard facts of life which are quite different from the life shown in movies and TV serials. This age is an age of attraction for opposite sex, this is an age of curiosity and they always want to look like beauty queens or heroines in serials and movies and they are attracted by the gifts offered by the abusers and become victims of sexual abuse. These girls are denied healthy means of recreation such as reading, playing games and mixing with peer groups. It is the responsibility of their parents to give these girls proper education, proper entertainment, recreation and, thus, help them become healthy citizens. Parents should guide their children at this age and contribute to create a healthy nation.

Hence, socio-economic factors play a major role in increasing vulnerability of girl children. Even in the 21st century, attitude towards girl children is negative in the home and society. A study of girl children who are victims of sexual abuse reveals the well known but sad fact that a girl is an unwanted child and she is treated as a financial burden, an economic liability. The upbringing of a girl child is not paid attention to. Her nutrition, her health, her education, her security, her small physical needs, her socialization and her emotional needs of love and affection are the last priority in the family. The girl child is the first victim of poverty, ignorance and social taboos. There is a tendency to spend less, as far as possible, on her basic needs of food, clothing, games and entertainment, etc. To pay for her education is considered as waste. Instead of sending her to school, the girl child is made to help her mother in domestic work of sweeping, washing utensils and clothes and looking after younger siblings. Sometimes the girl child is also sent to work outside along with her mother or even alone to work in fields or to work as domestic help.

In the present study, majority of the cases are from lower economic group of the society and all girls are unmarried. Fathers were generally occupied in semi-skilled or unskilled and manual work. Most of the girl children are having mothers working as daily wage earners and domestic workers. Only few parents are government employees

Sexually abused girl's family environment and atmosphere is not cordial and friendly. The elders in the family suffer from lack of education, moral values and culture. Men are given to addiction and the women are living under an emotional stress and tension. There were frequent quarrels, bitterness and unhappiness in the family because of lack of adequate amenities. The children are deprived of emotional bonds between children and parents that is necessary for the proper upbringing of the children. The atmosphere in the family is devastatingly damaging to the psychology of the children. The family which is known as a place of security, love and affection and protection of family members is losing faith and trust of the girl children as they are not secure in their own families. Mother is always away from home for earning money due to addiction and unemployment of her male partner and the role of housekeeper is entrusted to the girl child. The mother in the family has no time to take care of her children, to educate and monitor them and to interact with them. The left-alone girl child is an easy prey for potential abusers and a victim of sexual abuse.

Thus, the institution of family is under stress and strain for various reasons and child, specially the girl child, is the victim of such situations. A girl child in the family or in outside world, has to face double jeopardy, these children are always living a life of ill-treatment, torture at the hands of parents and society.

This present study reveals that sexual abuse of girl children is more prevalent in lower income group families. The poverty of the family renders it unable to fulfil the needs of their girl children and the teenage girls are tempted by the gifts, money and items of luxury and false promises offered by the abuser, and these girls become victims of sexual abuse. Due to their lower age, they are unaware of the consequences of sexual abuse. Due to the abuse these girls suffer from inferiority complex, become devoid of self-confidence and self-respect and lose the capacity to communicate with outside world. They cannot differentiate between right and wrong. The media, TV with its serials, film songs, reality shows and movies have a negative effect on their mind. The 'make-believe world' of this mode of entertainment accompanied by lack of proper education and neglect by parents, make these innocent girls vulnerable to deceit and exploitation.

Thus, the main factors that contribute to the magnitude of the problem of girl child sexual abuse are poverty, gender discrimination, illiteracy and caste system, family environment and weak implementation of legal provisions. Hence, a girl child who is a future mother, with such unhappy childhood and in such socio-economic background, runs a greater risk of being victimized.

3

Stories of Voiceless Girls

The girl child sexual abuse is emerging as one of the most horrific offences in Beed District. The aim of the present study is, therefore, to understand the nature, causes and consequences of girl child sexual abuse and also to suggest remedial measures and coping strategies.

An extensive number of cases of girl child sexual abuse are selected by the researcher because after a study in depth, using appropriate methods, they can provide more valid portrayals of the person under study, better bases of personal understanding of what is going on and solid grounds for considering action. The case studies are highly appropriate when the goal is individualized outcome. It helps for fuller understanding of the phenomenon and processes. It provides great details that help the researcher to understand the complexity of human behaviour. Case studies are particularly useful where one needs to understand a particular problem, a unique situation or a special person in great depth. It is useful in capturing the emotive aspect of human behaviour. A case study can be defined as 'a type of research method. The general objective of the case study is to develop as full an understanding of the subject of the research as possible'. According to Goode and Hatt, the case study is not a specific technique. It is a way of organizing social data so as to present the unitary character of social object being studied.[1]

Thus, case study method is flexible and can deal with a wide spectrum of evidence. Documents, systematic interviews, direct observations and even traditional surveys can be incorporated in case study.

Thirty cases are selected in the present study. Among them school-going girl children were identified through group discussion in schools, 10 cases reported to police station and 10 cases from information available from key informants were selected for the case studies.

These cases under study include the cases of incest, rape, sodomy, intercourse, molestation, prostitution, pornography and exhibitionism. These are the different forms of sexual abuse which are included in the definition of sexual abuse of girl children. Thus, the selected case studies in the present study are representing the above-mentioned different forms of sexual abuse.

The family is the first building block of the society. The size and structure of the family and its capacity to sustain itself has played an important role in how children are raised. Institution of family is under stress and strain for various reasons and child, specially a girl child, is the victim of this breakdown of family structure. A girl child is exploited and abused within and outside the family. The following case studies prove this statement.

Case Studies (Names of all girls are changed)

Sexual Abuse by Grandfather

The status of a grandfather in an Indian family is that of a grand old man. The girl child holds the old man in high esteem as she has seen her parents and other people in the family almost worshipping him. The child looks at the patriarch with awe and respect. The child does not feel anything wrong when the loving old man caresses her. But the girl child is shocked and bewildered when the same old man makes the girl an object of his lust.

'My grandfather tells me to sit in his laps and asks me to touch his "parrot". He always loves me more and tells me not to tell this to others. I feel uncomfortable, but he forces me to do so', says Ashwini. Ashwini, a 12-year-old girl, living in a joint family with her father, mother, brother, grandfather, uncle and aunt. There was always a quarrel between Ashwini's grandfather and grandmother, as her grandfather was having a sexual relationship with another woman, a poor widow from the village. Finally, Ashwini's grandmother left her home and went to her father's house, leaving her two grown-up sons in the care of the old man.

Ashwini's father is a driver and mother is an agricultural labourer. Both of them often have arguments. Ashwini's father is an alcoholic. Even her grandfather is addicted to alcohol. Ashwini's mother does not like this. After the quarrel, every now and then, she goes to her father's house. There is no one to look after Ashwini as everyone is busy in their work. Her grandfather used to ask her not to go with her mother and promised to look after Ashwini. Her grandfather usually took her to the farm. There, he exposed his private parts and asked the child to fondle them. This had started from the age of four for Ashwini. This continued until she reached the age of 12 years. She kept mum as he loves her very much and looks after her in the absence of her parents, as her father visits the village two or three times in a month due to his work as a driver.

One day, as usual Ashwini's grandfather took her to farm and raped her. By chance some people saw this act and beat him, as he and his family are known for their misconduct.

The mother of Ashwini came to know of this and she reported the case in police station. The abuser, her grandfather, was tried and on being found guilty was imprisoned for seven months only.

The act of Ashwini's grandfather is not only a gross violation of the child's body but also of the trust that a dependent child has on her caretaker and that too being her own grandfather. Now, Ashwini's mother went to her father's house with Ashwini and she asks to show her a place which is secure for her child.

Joint family system is the backbone of Indian culture, and is known for its values like trust in relationships, love and affection for family members and emotional bonds between one another in the family. The above case reveals that the Indian family is fast losing its value identity. The elders in the family, who are most trustworthy caretakers of the children, are violating the trust of the children. Instead of giving support to the children in difficult situation, they themselves, by their conduct, are putting a question mark on their relationship with children (Source: direct interview with the victim).

Sexual Abuse by Cousin

Some children are more vulnerable than others because they belong to divorced or reconstituted families. Such families not only affect parent-child relationship but also relations between siblings. Children in such families are neglected and they are at risk of sexual abuse by family members.

Eight-year-old Anjali sat aloof, silently and there was a fear on her face. She sat on her two legs because she had injury in her vagina. The stitches were not properly done and she felt uncomfortable to sit. She always complained about pain in the stomach. Her treatment was not done properly. After the stitches, they went only two or three times for check-up. Her mother has no time and nobody else is there to take care of her. Mother says that the child has no relief from the pain in stomach, because the treatment given was of no use and they have no money to take her to a well-equipped hospital for treatment and the mother said that Anjali was not the only child. They have six children in their family and poverty never allows them to give the daughter proper treatment. The first priority is to fulfil the basic needs of the family from the earnings.

Anjali is the second daughter to her mother from her first marriage. Her step-father's is also a second marriage. His children from first marriage and second marriage are all living together. It is a reconstituted family. Anjali's father is a drunkard and always beats his wife. They would quarrel very often. Anjali's mother works at a brick kiln and her husband does not work regularly. She is the sole bread winner in the family.

They are living in their ancestral house in which Anjali's uncle also lives with his family separately, Anjali's 20-year-old cousin brother always came to play with her, he spent lot of time with her when he was alone, and he loved her very much. She liked him very much because her step-siblings quarrelled with her. In Indian family, the status of a cousin is almost that of a real brother. Anjali's cousin used to take her outside, in the farm and used to abuse her. He did different acts like touching her genitals, masturbating in front of her and forced her to watch. From the age of five years, he abused her by forcing her for oral sex and other sexual acts. He always asked her to keep silent because it was a secret between them.

One day Anjali's cousin brother took her outside the village as usual and raped her by tying her hand to the tree trunk. Some villagers saw her in unconscious condition, bleeding from her vagina. They brought her home. Villagers stopped her parents from reporting to the police saying that it may defame their family. It will create difficulties for her marriage. But one social worker helped them in reporting the case and the boy is in jail now.

The case proves that children under reconstituted families are at a high risk as they are neglected, denied affection and deprived of emotional needs. It is generally found that people discourage the parents of the victim from reporting the matter to the police for fear of defamation.

This story shows that the children have adjustment problems in reconstituted families. The girl from first marriage of the woman feels lonely in the new family. Ill-treatment at the hands of step-father and cousins is a common complaint. The girl is forced to do domestic work and also made to work outside to earn. Lack of communication between parents, no or little interaction with mother deprives the girl of her teenage needs of love and affection and small needs. Forgetting the values of relationship of brother and sister, the cousins sometimes abuse the trust of the girl and sexually abuse her. She loses faith in the relationship. Love for family life is lost forever (Source: direct interview with the victim).

Sexual Abuse by Father

Sexual abuse is itself a trauma to the child, but when it is caused by a trusted close person like father, how can the child believe in such relationship. This is discussed in case study No. 3.

Nagina an eleven-year-old girl studying in VI standard. She has three elder sisters. Her parents are doing the work of scrap dealer. They have no other source of income.

Nagina's mother is the second wife of Nagina's father. Nagina is going to school and also doing domestic work and helping in their bhangar selling work. Nagina says, 'sometimes the sisters go out in the night and come back dressing nicely and bring lot of things and money in the morning'. Her father says that 'these three daughters are for others and you are only for myself'. He always takes her to market gives her the things she likes. When her mother and sisters go out, he holds her in his arms and kisses her. He always does some other sexual acts with her. He tells her not to tell to anybody. She too loved her father but somehow did not like him touching her thighs and breast and genitals. She never told her mother as she felt her mother loved the three sisters more and there is always a quarrel between her parents as her father is alcoholic, he is not doing work properly and mother earns for the family. Her mother never liked her father.

One day when her mother and sisters were away to the market, her father came in saying that nobody is caring for him, they are enjoying the life and why he shouldn't. He went near Nagina. She was sleeping. He asked her for intercourse. From that day, it became routine for Nagina. She was helpless and more confused as what to do. One day her mother came to know this and she reported the case of rape against her husband and now the father is in jail.

The story speaks of how the sexual abuse made the girl child feel as spoilt, violated and now a bewildering complex of guilt, anger and shame prevails. Father and daughter relationship is considered very sacred, lovely and trustworthy as father is a protector and caretaker of the child. The story shows how this sacred relationship of father and daughter became unhealthy, fearful and how a protector became a destructor (Source: direct interview with the victim).

Sexual Abuse by Grandfather

Yellama, a 14-year-girl goes to her grandfather's house in the holidays. Grandmother died when Yellama's mother and aunty were kids. Her grandfather lives in the village and looks after his farm. Yellama's parents were employed and they sent their child to her grandfather whenever he called her in the holidays so that she should not be alone and bored in her house. Her grandfather loves her very much and gave her whatever she wished. Yellama's grandfather took her to the farm. He used to sleep with her and made 'fun' with her. At night he used to call her in his room and show her a different type of film in the dark. Then he used to do all those things shown in the film with a 14-year-old girl. This continued for five years.

The girl thought of telling her mother about what her grandfather was doing to her, but fearing that her mother might not believe her as the man is her mother's father, so she kept mum and she disliked her holidays which are generally very much liked by children. She thinks she lost her childhood.

After some days, the girl said that she was not feeling well so her mother took her to hospital and they came to know that Yellama is pregnant. Her parents were shocked and started beating the girl and asked her about the person responsible for this. She told about her grandfather's behaviour towards her. It was unbelievable for them. They never reported the case as it was a family matter and feared disrepute.

The story is an example of how the 'child sexual abuse' within the family violates the dependent child's expectations of parental care, leading to confusion of roles. The child loses faith in the family and family members. The girl is depressed and confused. She lost the sense of self-worth and dignity and developed an attitude of self-sacrifice. She even thought of committing suicide.

The child kept mum as she might have felt that other family members would not believe her if she accused the old man of untoward behaviour. As grandfather, he is supposed to be her caretaker and protector. Moreover, the Indian culture taught her to respect and trust the elders in the family. This teaching did not allow her to speak about the abuse. Lack of interaction in the family forced her to stay silent. This story makes it clear that secrecy, i.e. keeping mum increases the abuse of girl child within the family (Source: interaction with the victim).

Sexual Abuse by Cousin

Incest, i.e. sexual relationship between a child and a related adult, has been identified as the most widespread form of child sexual abuse with a huge capacity for damage to a child. Children who received supportive response following disclosure had less traumatic symptoms and were abused for a shorter period of time. But the children who did not receive support from family members and others, had more traumatic symptoms and they were abused for long period of time.

Kamala's mother died when she was seven years old. Her father was working in a sugar factory nearby. He came home once in a week and he was alcoholic. It was a joint family in which Kamala, her two aunts, two uncles, a grandmother and her five cousins were living together. She was the only child of her parents. She had to do household work and also attend school. Her cousins were all brothers and she was the only female child. She liked to sing and wanted to become a singer.

When she was nine years old, her elder cousin brother who was 22 years old, told her that he knows one Guruji and he would take her to him. The cousin was a powerful person in the family as a job holder because except her father other male members were working in the farm. Her cousin brother brought a harmonium and some new clothes for her and some CDs of songs. She got impressed by him, as her teenage desires were being fulfilled by him. She believed him to be a good brother. He took her to Guruji's school twice in a week, while returning he took her to a temple outside the village and abused her. He forced her to expose her private parts and he exposed his private parts and forced her to fondle them. He said that it was a new game between both of them and it was their secret and she should not tell it to anybody. He promised her that he would give protection to her in her life and he would fulfil her wish to become a singer. It continued for three years and when she was 13 years old, he asked her for intercourse. Every night he used to call her in his room upstairs and had an intercourse with her. He told her that whenever he called her she should follow him.

She never spoke about her abuse in the family as her father had no proper interaction with her due to his addiction. She thought family members would not believe her if she spoke the truth.

The cousin brother, a powerful person in the family, sexually abused this helpless teenage sister who trusted him as a protector and caretaker. Now she is depressed and anxious about her future.

This story speaks about the truth that sexual abuse that occurs in a context of granting of special privileges, may be as traumatic and bewildering to the child as violent molestation. If the home and surroundings are not congenial enough and basic needs of food, clothing, education and hobby are not met, the child is likely to fall a prey to sexual abuse.

Absence of normal family life adversely affects the physical and emotional well-being of the child. The girl suffers with loss of appetite, lack of trust in family adults, fear of men, severe sleep disturbance and wants to be alone. Dreamy age of the girl is converted into an age of fear and depression.

This case also reveals that addiction of the father, tensed atmosphere in the family, presence of an authoritative cousin in the family, absence of congenial environment makes the girl suffer her abuse by the cousin. Family is a secure place, but abuse of girl child also occurs in the family and the abuse is by none other than the nearest and trusted member of the family. No wonder Indian family is fast losing its relevance and sanctity (Source: interview with a social worker).

Sexual Abuse by Paternal Uncle

It is important to realize that child sexual abuse not only occurs in rural areas but it also occurs in urban areas and slums. Poverty, lack of education, absence of congenial atmosphere and overcrowding have been found as prominent factors in the occurrence of child sexual abuse in slum areas of towns and cities.

This story of sexual abuse of a poor girl reveals this fact. He said, 'I cannot live without you. If it is not possible for you to marry me, do not marry anybody else. I can give you money to live happily'. Vidya said, 'I am helpless and I am in confusion about what to do. I cannot ask my family members because they will not believe me'. These were the feelings of Vidya, a girl of 14 years. Her paternal uncle of 34 years sexually abused her since the age of 8 years. He used to give her chocolates and took her to a garden. He used to visit their house daily as he was living in the same slum area. He showed her some dirty pictures when she was alone in the house. He said that he loved her very much. He gave her dresses, ear-rings, bangles and also a mobile as gifts. She liked him very much as her parents were not capable of bringing such things for her. Her father was a daily wage earner. Mother was ill. She had two brothers and three sisters. It was a large family with low income. The paternal uncle gave money whenever needed. Because he helped everyone in difficulty, he was loved and trusted by all in the family. His wife had left him as she had an affair with a man in her father's village. The possibility that the man could be an abuser is not considered by her parents and nobody objected to her going out with him and did not doubt when she came late from outside. He was satisfying his sexual urge by abusing Vidya in and outside the home or in lodges some times.

Her mother was ill and Vidya had to attend to her. It was difficult for Vidya to go outside so the uncle gave some sleeping pills to Vidya asking her to give the pills to her mother and then leave the house to meet him. He also gave her oral pills to avoid pregnancy and asked her to be relaxed.

The girl knew that the man was her paternal uncle and the marriage in this relation is prohibited. But the uncle said that he would keep her happy without marriage. She became irregular to school. She was in stress; she thought that if she told her mother it would affect her health. Disclosure of the matter might lead to defamation of the family as she was the eldest daughter in the home. But her uncle assured her and asked her not to worry as everything would be fine.

This went on for about six years and the girl was in a dilemma, she felt guilty and even thought of committing suicide as she felt it to be an end of the road. She developed an inferiority complex and had sleeping problems.

The story indicates the truth that a child is at high risk when children are neglected; parents are experiencing financial problems, no communication between children and parents, and between husband and wife. In this situation, the abuser lays the trap taking advantage of the situation, attracts the child towards him by giving things and by giving emotional support and wins the trust and misuses the trust of the child for sexual abuse of the trapped child.

The story also speaks about how the poverty, tensed atmosphere in the family and teenage years of the girl, tempted her to believe the person who abused her sexually. A girl child, especially if she is poor, is considered as a commodity devoid of any personal choice and desire (Source: direct interview with victim).

Sexual Abuse by Perverted Father

Personality disorder is responsible for child sexual abuse, abuser often had a propensity for impulsive and/or antisocial act that extended beyond the parenting role. A parent, according to this explanation, may abuse his child due to unmet emotional needs. Emotional scars from his own abusive family background affects his ability to care for his own offspring. Such a father abused his own girl child.

Gauri was eight years old when her Baba started playing with her some different, odd games. He used to touch her vagina, inserting objects like pencil, pen, etc. He touched different parts of her body. One day when she was 11 years, her mother saw what her Baba was doing. The mother was shocked and quarrelled with her husband, saying why he became so shameless and inhuman with his own child. He promised her that he would not do it again.

He was a teacher. His wife said that he was not talking much, not laughing, always sat silently, did not mix with others. He was always interested in playing with children especially the girl children. He loved Gauri very much and he was doing all her work from the day of her birth. But all the time, he abused the child by making different sexual acts with the girl.

That was a Sunday when Gauri's mother went to the market at 4.00 pm. Gouri and her father were watching TV. When she returned from market, she saw her child lying unconscious and bleeding from her vagina. Her father was sitting in the corner. She rushed to him and started beating him. In return he pushed her and beat her on the back. He was not having any feeling of guilt also.

The 13-year-old girl had injured her vagina and also had psychological problem. She took her child to the hospital immediately and then reported the case to the police. The man was sentenced to life imprisonment. Mother's dream of happy home came to an end.

The story indicates the truth that the closer the relationship between the offender and the child, the greater the resultant trauma. When an outsider abuses a child, she turns to the family for support. But if the abuser is a family member, i.e. father, the child learns that the person, who is supposed to protect and love her, is the person who hurts to such an extent that she loses faith in parental relationship. This results in greater trauma. This may produce in the child an anxiety and fear and may potentially worsen the impact of trauma.

This case again proves that the relationship which is most trusted in the Indian family, the relationship of father and daughter, is losing its value and strength bringing down the man to the level of beast (Source: interview with police inspector).

Sexual Abuse by Paternal Uncle

Many a times, the mother knows that the brother of her husband is sexually abusing her girl child, but she dares not to tell this to her husband as she feels that her husband would not listen to her or accept his brother as the culprit. Silence of the mother and the girl child increases the strength of abuser to abuse the girl.

'My "chacha" masturbates and shows me different naked photographs and asks me to do all that is shown in the photographs. I do not like all this but I am afraid to say "no"', says 15-year-old Julie, who is being abused by her paternal uncle since last four years.

John, her paternal uncle visits her home every weekend. He lives in a place 20 km away from her town. He is working as a manager of her father's hotel. Julie, a student of X standard, used to study at night in her room and her uncle, over the weekends, comes to help her in her studies. At that time he touches her private parts, masturbates her, shows her naked photographs and forces her for intercourse. She is afraid of weekends as she is unable to tell about her problem to anybody. Her uncle is very close to her parents and they believe him to be a very sincere responsible person and loyal to their family.

Once she told her mother that her uncle was a bad person, her mother had beaten her and told her to keep quiet and not use bad words against her uncle. Her mother was shocked but was not in a position to avoid it because of her own powerlessness. He was a trusted and close person, but he was sexually abusing the girl. Julie became silent, helpless and lost her trust in family relationship.

Sexual abuse by close relatives is a fact of life for many children in India as it happens in all kinds of families and in all areas. It disturbs the child and makes the child self-blaming, guilty, causes mistrust in herself and in others (Source: direct interview with victim).

Sexual Abuse by Uncle

Rukmini's father lived elsewhere with his second wife. Rukmini's mother lived in the house with three children and made a living by selling liquor. The mother had no time for domestic work as she was always busy with her business. Rukmini could not go to school regularly as she had to do the domestic chores, like cooking, washing and in addition she had to take care of her younger siblings. The father of the children would visit them once in a month. Sister of Rukmini's father and her husband lived in the adjacent house. The 34-year-old uncle of Rukmini was jobless and a drunkard. One day Rukmini's mother went to another town for some work and during the night when Rukmini was sleeping alone with her younger brother and sister, the man next door, her uncle, entered her room, took her to the other room and raped her. Rukmini told her mother next day about the incident and the mother lodged a complaint with the police, but the man is absconding and the police have not yet traced him.

The abuser in this case used the girl child to satisfy his own sexual gratification due to lack of moral values in the man. Unsettled families lead to child neglect and such situation tempts the potential abuser to exploit the children in their own home. The days of playful enjoyment in the life of the child are now full of horror, sorrow, guilt and shame. Inadequate control of the family, neglect of the child's needs by the family and helplessness of the child all taken together has resulted in the sad incident (Source: direct interview with victim).

Sexual Abuse by Brother-in-Law

Sheela's mother works as a farm labourer. Her father died one year back. Sheela goes to school but also works on the farm during vacations. Sheela has no brother. Two of her sisters are married. One of her sister's husband asked her mother to allow her to accompany them when he and his wife were going for sugarcane cutting as Sheela's sister was pregnant and needed help. So, 14-year-old Sheela accompanied her sister to do household work and also to do work of sugarcane cutting.

One night when she was sleeping outside the hut she felt someone's hands on her breasts. She looked up and saw that it was her brother-in-law. He threatened her not to shout and abused her. This went on for about four months of the sugarcane cutting season. She was frightened and was under pressure. She was in utter confusion about what to do and whom to tell. She dared not complain to her sister against her brother-in-law. Sheela's story is an example of how sexual abuse by a close relative is all the more damaging as the girl cannot protest against the abuser and the abuse continues. Life becomes bewildering as the child tries to cope with the feeling of hurt and fear when the near relative betrays the trust of the child. The child loses faith in relationships and it becomes very difficult for the child to trust any other person and the relationship (Source: interaction with doctor).

Sexual Abuse by a Brother-in-Law

Beed District is known for its migrant labourers. People migrate for sugarcane cutting for six to eight months every year. These people are mostly landless labourers and people with small or uneconomical holdings.

There is no other source of income for them at their place of residence and poverty compels them to go to distant places in search of job.

During this season, the girl child in the family has either to accompany her parents or stay at home in the care of grandparents looking after younger brothers and sisters. Away from the watchful eyes of their parents, the girl children are an easy prey for the scheming adults around them. The abusers tempt the girls by giving gifts or by indulging in sweet talk and the innocent teenaged girls are victims of sexual abuse.

Asha was just three years old when her father died. Her mother was a mental case. She had one married brother and one married sister. Both the families were engaged in sugarcane cutting in the other state. Asha also accompanied them leaving her school. At the sugarcane farm, they lived in huts. Her brother-in-law used to sing songs and make comments on Asha. He took opportunity to misbehave with her whenever she was alone and went to the extent of even raping her on occasions. She became pregnant and the brother-in-law ran away leaving her to the mercy of her sister and brother. They blamed her for the incident and tortured her mentally and physically. They asked her not to let this incidence be known to anybody as that would make it difficult for them to get her married. The girl at her tender age does not know what to do with a child to be born of her. She is just passing her days uncertain of her future. This case is also an example of a poor teenaged girl being sexually abused by a near relative. The stigma attached to her character and the negative attitude of the family members weigh heavy on the mind of this girl and she has to live a life of loneliness, feeling guilty and resigned to her fate.

It is sad to find that the caretakers, family members, even parents, commit the heinous crime of sexual abuse and rape of the child in their care. Such incidences have a deep effect on the psyche of the child and the future life of the child becomes a life of shame, guilt, self-pity and fear losing faith in family relationships. Rarely can the child grow into a healthy and happy adult. The unfortunate girl child needs ventilation of emotions and help to cope with psychological problem (Source: direct interview with victim).

Sexual Abuse by Paternal Uncle

Jyoti was 13 years old when her father died. Her mother was a daily wage earner and she had four children, three younger to Jyoit. Jyoti at this tender age was burdened with the responsibility of her siblings and also of domestic work. She was staying at home and did not go to school. She had an uncle who was alcoholic and criminal minded. This man had established physical relations with her mother and used to stay for the night in their small house. After a year or two, he started visiting Jyoti during day time in the absence of her mother and other children. He started abusing the grown-up girl. She could not dare to tell her mother as she thought that mother would only blame her and would not say anything to the man as they were intimate with each other.

By finding no other option, she fled from the home and was sitting all alone at the bus stand. A lady befriended her and took her to her house. The lady enquired about her, showed sympathy, gave her food and shelter, and assured protection from the man. After a few days, the lady pushed the girl into prostitution. One day this child prostitute was rescued by the police in a raid and was sent to remand home. Her bitter experience of life at home and also in the outside world made her depressed and withdrawn. She needed a long-term psychological treatment which was not available at the remand home.

The way of life of the mother in this case had resulted in spoiling the life of the girl and landed her in more trouble in an eagerness to escape from the abuser (Source: reported – direct interview with victim).

Sexual Abuse by Male Cousin

Sexual abuse of girl child does not always take place in poor and uneducated families. It also occurs in the well-to-do, happy homes of middle-class people. Fourteen-year-old Anita's parents are government employees and are having a house of their own. Her parents want her to become a doctor. They send her to coaching classes. They have provided her a separate room for her studies. In their anxiety to see their daughter get good marks in her entrance exam, they asked her cousin, her aunt's son, a student of final year engineering, to guide and help her in her studies. The young boy is tempted to touch her checks, thighs, and even breasts when they were alone in her room. She is restless, mentally disturbed and cannot concentrate on her studies. He also shows her some dirty pictures and speaks in a very vulgar language on phone. He tells her that it would create difficulties for her marriage, and nothing would happen to him if she tells others about him. She is very upset and is not being able to sleep properly in the night.

In their naivety, the parents do not suspect that the young boys are also likely to be tempted to do untoward things when the situation is favourable. In this case, the parents of the girl are also responsible for the plight of the girl. They should have been more cautious and should not have allowed the girl and the boy the privacy to indulge in sexual encounter (Source: unreported – direct interview with victim).

Sexual Abuse by Brother-in-Law of Sister

Ameena, a 15-year-old girl from a small village came to the town for her higher education. As there was no hostel for girls, she had to stay with her elder sister's family. Her sister worked as domestic help in some houses in the locality and the sister's husband worked in a factory. Ameena went to school up to 12.30 pm. After returning from school, she would do some domestic work and keep herself engaged in her studies. A young man, brother-in-law of her sister, was having a kirana shop in a nearby village and would often come to town for purchases, etc. Having come to know that Ameena is usually alone in the house in the afternoon, his visits to the town and to the house of his brother increased. He was not discouraged from doing so by her sister. He would bring costly gifts for Ameena, would take her out to market, to hotels and even to cinema houses. Knowing full well that he was a married man, the girl and her sister allowed him to develop physical contacts with Ameena. It was only when Ameena was pregnant that she and her sister realized their mistake.

This case reveals that the grown-up girls, though child by definition, allowed herself to be exploited and abused and her sister did nothing to protect the girl. No wonder that the girl felt shame and guilt as it was her fault and is depressed. It cannot be denied that due to ignorance about sex and the age of the girl, she was carried away by her own temptation and did not pay attention to consequences of her behaviour. The conduct of her sister also was quite opposite to what was expected of her as the guardian of the girl. Though there was clearly a violation of the trust of the child and her family, an easy access to child and no discouragement from her guardian sister, for reasons best known to her, helped the young married man to abuse the girl (Source: unreported – direct interview with victim).

Sexual Abuse by Neighbour

Geeta, a 13-year-old girl is studying in VIII class. Her 25-year-old neighbour is a photographer by profession. He started visiting her house and succeeded in gaining the affection and trust of her family members. This is the typical 'modus operandi' of the persons intending to sexually abuse girls. He photographed her and gave her gifts on her birthday. He also called her to his photo studio and photographed her in different poses. He told her that she was a beautiful girl and with photogenic features, had good prospects in modelling profession. He persuaded her in giving some revealing and half naked photos. These photographs were used by him to force her to succumb to physical intimacy.

Geeta's father is an addict and the mother is a wage earner in the family. Brother is also a spoilt boy. The atmosphere in the family is not congenial and friendly. No help was available to her to get rid of the nasty man. In a disorganized family there is no interaction between the children and parents. This prevents the girl from discloser of the abuse and the helplessness of the girl only increases the abuse.

The teenage years of the girl, the temptation and absence of normal family life are the causes for the plight the girl finds herself in. The scheming neighbour took advantage of the situation and abused the girl. Normally, children look upon their neighbours as their well-wishers. They expect parental care and love from them, but such incidences show that the girl children do so to their own peril (source: unreported – direct interview with victim).

Sexual Abuse by Neighbour

Fifteen-year-old Pinky is worried, confused, disturbed and generally quiet. She is afraid of her middle-aged neighbour. Her father is in another place for his job. He comes once or twice a month to see his family. Her mother is a working woman and goes to bed early as she is tired from her work and has to get up early the next day. It is the matriculation year for Pinky and she studies till late in the night. This night time is used by the elderly man next door to disturb her. He would come to her window and show obscene pictures on his mobile phone to her. Sometimes he would also show his private parts to her. He is known as a good person in the area and she is afraid nobody would believe her even if she told about his untoward behaviour to others. She is in utter confusion as whom to tell and how to tell. She is unable to concentrate on her studies and the important year of her studies is being spoiled and wasted.

Child sexual abuse is a grave form of abuse because of its layers of guilt and shame. It is important to recognize that sexual abuse does not always involve body contact. Pornography is a serious form of sexual abuse which results in serious emotional harm. Exposing a child to sexual situations or materials which are sexually abusive is equally damaging to the psyche of the child. Effect of such situations on the mind of the child is far-reaching as the child is tormented by shame and guilt. The symptoms like depression, anxiety, fear and eating disorders are seen in a child who is exposed to such abuse. The child loses interest in studies and in playing with other children and thus the very childhood of the child is spoiled. Sometimes the effect of this abuse remains for a long time on the psyche of the child. The behaviour of the neighbour in this case is most disgusting and reprehensible (Source: unreported – direct interview with victim).

Sexual Abuse by Neighbour

Incident of sexual abuse makes the child develop negative sense of self as the child feels ashamed. Sushma, a 15-year-old girl, was living in a village with her parents, grandparents, two brothers and two sisters. Father was a farmer and her mother also worked on the farm. Sushma's grandfather was the head of the family and being a retired government servant commanded an unquestioned authority in the family matters. All decision-making power was centred on him and nobody dared to oppose him. Sushma's parents were asked to live on the farm along with their other children. Only Sushma was allowed to reside with her grandparents and was said to be the most loved one of her grandfather. Raju, a 25-year-old boy from the neighbourhood developed intimacy with her by promising her to marry. Her resistance to his advances was dismissed by him by saying that they were lovers and nothing was bad when the boy and a girl were in love with each other. Moreover, they were to marry soon. After abusing her sexually he disclosed that he had no intention to marry her and that it was his hobby to have affairs with girls like Sushma. She was shocked and attempted suicide by drinking pesticide which was easily available in her house.

As it was a case of attempted suicide, the village elders tried to hush up the matter by arranging the marriage of the two lovers. Though both of them belonged to the same caste and Sushma was from a well-to-do family, the parents of boy refused to have her as their daughter-in-law saying that the girl was an illegitimate child of her grandfather. Village people suspected that Sushma's mother had illicit relationship with her father-in-law. The patriarchal atmosphere in the family and the dominating nature of her father-in-law had not allowed her to avoid the advances of the old man. The stigma of illegitimate birth attached to the child became an obstacle in the way to her happiness.

The head of the family had not only spoiled the life of his daughter-in-law but also the life of his granddaughter. Breakdown of the value system of the family and lack of morality has made the life of the family members pitiable (Source: reported – direct interview with victim).

Sexual Abuse by Neighbour

Chaya was just four years old when she became a victim of sexual abuse by an elderly neighbour. Her parents were wage earners. Whenever they were away for work, leaving her alone at home, she would go to the neighbour's house to play with their child. 'Balu Mama', the neighbour, would call her to sit in his lap. He would touch her private parts. The girl child, in her innocence, did not understand his motive behind the 'touch'. The man was alcoholic and usually quarrelled with his wife. After one such incident the woman left her husband and went to live with her parents. One day this man, perverted as he was, made the girl sit in his lap, removed her clothes, forced himself on her and tried to penetrate her. There was partial penetration and the poor child suffered vaginal injuries. After a day or two, the girl complained of pain and difficulty in passing urine. The mother was alarmed and on inspection it was found that the girl's vagina was swollen and reddened. On enquiry, the girl told her mother what had happened.

The mother reported the matter to the police. The girl was sent for medical examination, but rape was not reported as there was no penetration. The sole statement of the child was not believed and the charge of attempted rape was not proved against the accused. The poor mother was shocked and lost faith in criminal justice system. The unfortunate girl had to live with the memory of the ugly incident throughout her life.

This case points out the lacuna in justice system dealing with cases of child sexual abuse. The offence was of an attempted rape. The victim/complainant was just a four-year-old child. The court ought to have believed her statement to give the verdict 'guilty' even though there was no corroborative or medical evidence. There was no reason for the girl to speak lie, or to make a statement that was not true (Source: reported – direct interview with victim).

Sexual Abuse by Neighbour

'I loved Pintya as he looked like a hero from cinema', says 14-year-old girl, Varsha, about her 25-year-old boyfriend. He gave gifts to her on her birthday, on Valentine's Day, and also on some festivals. Both her parents were wage earners and the mother was in a relationship with a farmhand. There were always quarrels between Varsha's mother and father on this issue but the father of Varsha, somehow, could not dissuade her mother from her wrong-doing as she was also earning and maintaining the family. One day, Varsha eloped with Pintya to Pune and they lived there for about six months. Varsha found that her lover was a pickpocket and had been jailed several times. They returned to their village and stayed at the farm of one of his friends outside the village. This friend also abused her as he gave them shelter. Varsha repented and returned to her parents and was fortunate that they received her and now she stays with them. But her future is dark.

Due to her age and temptation, she eloped with her friend not knowing the consequences of her imprudence. She had to return to her parents with a feeling of bitterness and hopelessness. Her father reported the case to police. Tender age, poverty and innocence about the consequences made the girl meet the boy at cinema halls and in public park. Before long, the girl developed complete trust and faith in the boy, sufficient for her to decide to leave her parental home and elope with him to an unknown destination, without realizing the consequences (Source: reported – direct interview with victim).

Sexual Abuse by Known Person (School Peon)

After her special class was over in the evening, Seema had to stay in her classroom. The teacher and other students had left. Seema was copying some notes given by her teacher and the teacher had asked her to give the original notes to the peon of the institute, an old man. After completion of her writing when she went to the peon to hand him over the notes, she was bewildered by the behaviour of the old man. He snatched her dupatta, pulled her in his arms, tore her churidar and tried to rape her. She shouted very loudly and some boys who were playing in the ground outside came running, and helped to free her from the clutches of the old man.

The boys also gave a beating to the peon, thought till then to be a gentleman. Even though the head of the institution came to know of the incident, he was not ready to report to the police saying that the institution would be defamed. There is no information whether the culprit was removed from the job or not. Seema told her parents about the incidence and did not go to school the next day. She thought other students from her school were talking about the incidence, and a feeling of shame and self-blame filled her mind. Her parents were also of the opinion of withdrawing her from the school. However, some other members of her family persuaded her parents to send her to some other school as it was her X class. Though she went to school again, she was not the innocent, joyful girl any more.

Such incidents make children depressed and they adopt on attitude of self-sacrifice, either positively withdrawing from the surroundings or acting out in a self-destructive way like thinking of committing suicide.

In the Indian culture, the elders – due to their age and experience – are respected and trusted persons. This case of Seema shows how the trust of the girl and his own age was misused by the elderly peon in an attempt to abuse the girl. This shows the deterioration of value system and morality in the society. Even senior citizens forget their age and behave in an uncivilized manner (Source: direct interview with victim).

Sexual Abuse by Known Person

Ayesha, 17-year-old girl, and her mother lived in a village. Ayesha's father had died of cancer. Both, the mother and the daughter, worked as labourers at a brick kiln. The owner of the kiln used to bring his tiffin and shared his lunch with them. They believed that he was a good person and was helping them. Though married, he became close to Ayesha and visited their house at night also. He even talked of leaving his wife for the sake of Ayesha. One evening he gave some tablets to her saying that she would feel better as she was tired. She slept and when she woke up in the morning, she found herself naked in the room and no one else was there. The owner of the brick kiln met Ayesha the next day and behaved as if nothing had happened. He would give tablets to her every night and rape her. He gave her money and mobile phone and said that he wanted to make her happy anyway. The 35-year-old man abused Ayesha for about two years. Mother of the girl, a poor lady kept quiet and did not raise her voice in protest as she thought that nobody would help or support her.

Ayesha has now become a psycho; she does not go to work, speaks to nobody and sits silently at home. There was an attempt to suicide also. Perhaps, she expected the man to marry her. Poverty made Ayesha a victim of sexual abuse. The mother and daughter felt helpless as there was nobody to help them in the situation.

This story reveals that poverty, ignorance and illiteracy made Ayesha an easy prey of the abuser who exploited the poor adolescent girl due to her poverty and helplessness (Source: interview with doctor).

Sexual Abuse by Known Person

Fifteen-year-old Kalawati was living on their farm with her grandmother. Her parents had gone to Karnataka for sugar cane cutting. A young man of 35 was working on the farm during day time and an old worker gave them company during the night time. The young man gained the trust of the girl and of the old woman by helping them in various ways. They believed him and thought that he would protect them from any ill. Gradually, the girl became close to him. Taking advantage of the situation, the young man started regularly abusing her by giving gifts like clothes, chappals, bangles, cosmetics which were never given to her by her parents. She was impressed and was tempted to do anything that the young man wished her to do. The young man assured her of marriage but when she became pregnant he refused to do so. The old lady was bewildered and was unable to decide what to do as the parents of the girl were far away. The young man suggested abortion and also volunteered to give money required. The poor girl was shocked and suffered a trauma from which it was difficult for her to recover.

Migration of parents, helplessness of grandmother, poverty, ignorance as to the consequences of sexual intercourse due to the teenage years of the girl, and not having healthy family environment made it easy for the abuser to exploit the girl. This again shows the violation of her trust and deterioration of morality and value system in society which made the girl suffer (Source: interaction with doctor).

Sexual Abuse by Known Elderly Person

Kalpana, a fifteen-year-old girl, and her friend came from village to a town for their high school education. They attended tuition classes for X standard. There was a 50-year-old man, a bank employee, in the neighbourhood. He used to come and sit in their room till late in the night and help them in their study of mathematics. He spoke so nicely that the girls in their innocence believed him to be their well-wisher. One day, Kalpana's friend went to her village as her mother was sick. The old man volunteered to give Kalpana company for the night and abused her in the night. This went on for about a week as Kalpana's friend was away to her village. The tender girl was abused by the so-called gentleman. The parents of the girl were shocked but did not report the incident to the police for fear of stigma and defamation. After the old man was transferred to other town, it was found that he had abused many other girls before, in this fashion. The poor girl suffered physically, had headache, disturbed sleep, anxiety and eating disorders. She lost weight and looked pale and sick. She did not do well in her exam and had to discontinue her education.

Sexual abuse hurts the child and it may lead to low academic achievement, poor concentration and it also affects the ability of the child to develop trustworthy and intimate relationship with adults. Due to the age of the abuser, the girl did not expect him to behave in this manner and he misused her trust.

Indeed, because of social stigma and shame attached to the victims, sexual offences remain one of the most misunderstood and under-reported crimes which gives strength to the abusers to abuse the innocent, tender girls. The girls should be taught to respect the behaviour instead of age of a person (Source: unreported – direct interview with victim).

Sexual Abuse by Known Person

Shilpa was a 13-year-old and was studying in VII standard. She lived with her mother in a rented house in the town. Her father was a teacher and lived in some other town with his second wife. Shilpa's mother had to work for their living. Deepak, brother of the house owner, was a young man of 30 years and worked as a truck driver in Mumbai. This young man visited his brother very often and developed friendship and intimacy with Shilpa. He gave her costly gifts and asked her to accompany him to Mumbai tempting her to the attractive way of life in Mumbai and also by giving her false promise of marriage. He also took her to his native place, introduced her to his relatives as his would-be wife. Both stayed there for a week with his disabled parents. He gained her confidence and repeatedly abused her.

One fine morning, he just dropped her at the bus stand of her town and went away with a promise to return soon. She waited and waited for him; neither did he return nor talked to her on the phone. The heartbroken girl now stays with her grandmother who only blames the poor girl for the incident. Shilpa's other relatives also blame her for the unfortunate incident in her life.

Separation of parents, neglect of the girl by the family were the situations taken advantage of by the man who lured the poor girl to the life of her dreams. The harsh realities of life are revealed to the girl at a great cost (Source: unreported – direct interview with victim).

Sexual Abuse by Known Person

Rohini, a 13-year-old girl, was a victim of sexual abuse. Father was a marginal farmer living in a joint family of his parents, his step-mother, wife, three daughters and a son. Two elder daughters were married and Rohini, the youngest daughter, was a mentally challenged girl. Her brother attended school. As she was not going to any school, she helped her parents in household work and on the farm also. Once two young boys, knowing that there was no one else in the house except Rohini, entered the house and molested her. She started crying and could not understand what they were doing to her. She was an easy prey. Two elderly women heard her cries and came to her help but it was too late and the boys ran away after having molested the girl. Body of a girl was an object of enjoyment for the boys and the poor girl only felt that some horrible thing had happened to her! This case was registered in the police station and the family is still waiting for judgment.

The unfortunate girl is victim of both, her pitiable situation and the mischief of the boys. The girl ought not to have been left unattended. The boys were cruel and deserve harsh punishment for the crime committed by them, but the case also highlights the necessity of some special care to be given to such children (Source: reported – direct interview with victim).

Sexual Abuse by Known Person

The two boys were vagabonds and rowdy ones from the locality. They were out of the control of their parents also. They would tease the girls of the area. One day, when Sangeeta, a 14-year-old girl, was about to leave for her school, they pushed her inside her house. Her parents had already gone for work and her younger siblings had also left for school. As she was all alone in the house, the boys started misbehaving with her. She got horrified and started shouting but nobody came to her help. After the boys left, she went to the farm to her mother crying and told her mother about the incident. Her father in the evening told the police and the Sarpanch of the village but they refused to entertain the complaint. Even the police did not take cognizance of the case as there was no rape and just warned the young boys and let them free. The boys were not brought to book and were not punished. When the police, which must give protection to people, refuse to do their duty, no wonder the antisocial elements in the society are emboldened and are a constant threat to the society (Source: reported – direct interview with victim).

Sexual Abuse by Known Person

After Sujata's birth, her mother died and her father left home leaving Sujata to her aunt's care. Aunty had four children of her own and the uncle was always ill and did not work for living. When Sujata was just five or six years old, the aunty would ask her to do all household work. She was not sent to school and was treated as a burden on the family. When she was a little grown-up, say at the age of 13, she was sent to work as house maid in other houses. A young man took advantage of the situation, gave her money and gifts and developed physical contact with her. He also made her believe that someday he would marry her. One day, the young man sent her to one of his friends and the girl, lured by money and gifts, was made to live the life of prostitute. The 'aunty' was only interested in the money brought by her and gradually the girl started believing that money was everything in life and love and morality were all meaningless. Her experiences of harsh reality of life made this 13-year-old girl become insensitive to the goodness of life.

The young girl, now, has an infection of STD and is HIV positive. Sexual abuse at an early age spoiled the childhood and damaged her mental and physical wellness.

An orphan is generally forced to work for earning, exposing the child to the vagaries of the society. The girl in this case had no home and the relative exploited her by pushing her into a life of prostitute. The people around, instead of helping her to free herself from the life of drudgery, only took advantage of her situation. This harsh reality of life only told the unfortunate girl that money was everything in life and love, morality and character are all meaningless things without any worth (Source: unreported – direct interview with victim).

Sexual Abuse by Known Person

Vimala's father lost his leg in an accident and was unable to do physical labour. Vimala's mother had to shoulder the responsibility of earning for her husband, three children and also her in-laws. Vimala, a girl of 15 and a student of IX standard had to leave school and accompany her mother for sugar cane cutting on a farm. They were staying in a camp near a sugar factory. Vimala sang well and used to sing songs while doing her work. This youthful good-looking girl soon drew the attention of an officer of the sugar factory staying nearby and he persuaded her to give up hard labour and to work as house maid in his house instead. He would give good dresses and gifts to her and much more money than she expected. He also promised a job for her disabled father at the factory. Gradually, he developed intimacy with her and established physical relations. This went on for nearly six months, the period of sugar cane cutting season. He did not arrange for any job for her father at the factory and Vimala and her parents had to return to their village. Vimala could not adjust with her life at the village and went into depression. She also attempted suicide.

This case of Vimala is an example of a girl child who had to suffer the ignominy of sexual abuse and its consequences of stress and strain. The family had to move from place to place in search of job, forcing children to leave their school and live the life of nomads. Persons like the factory officer take advantage of plight of such girl children; abuse them with an attitude of 'use and throw'. The life of the girl was spoiled (Source: unreported – direct interview with victim).

Sexual Abuse by Teacher

The teacher-student relationship is considered sacred in India. A teacher is an idol for the student and they respect him. Fatima, a school girl of VII standard, was abused by her teacher. Salma, mother of Fatima, had lost her husband in an accident leaving behind his parents and three daughters and two sons. Salma was burdened to earn for the family. Fatima was sent to her maternal uncle for schooling. After few days, one male teacher of her school made himself dear to her by helping her and gaining her faith. Fatima in her innocence trusted him. He gave her costly gifts and took her to his farm. He had a two-wheeler and a four-wheeler as well. The girl was also attracted towards the man as he had a good personality. Many a times, he took her to his house and she stayed there with him for the night. The wife of the 40-year-old man was helpless as she had two daughters and a son from her husband and was afraid that the future of her children would be jeopardized. Fatima's uncle knew about the affair but was silenced by the teacher by offering money. He even blackmailed her by taking her photographs. False promise of marriage was also given to continue the illicit relationship. When the teacher refused to pay any more, the maternal uncle of Fatima reported the matter to the police; a case was filed and the culprit is on bail. The girl returned to her mother. She suffers from physical and mental illness, happy days of childhood are lost forever and the future of the girl is hopeless.

This story of Fatima is an example of an immoral behaviour of a teacher with his student, unworthy of his profession (Source: direct interaction with victim).

Sexual Abuse by Stranger

Kasturi's parents died in an accident when she was just 11 years old. Her maternal uncle brought her to his home. One day, when her uncle and aunt had gone to their farm for work, a lady who was their neighbour, asked Kasturi to accompany her to the city to make some purchases. The girl initially refused but somehow was persuaded by the lady to go with her. Once outside the village the lady handed over the girl to two young boys who were already waiting by the road side. The boys forcibly took the girl to the bushes and raped her. They threatened her not to tell about the incident to anybody. However, there was physical injury and the blood stained under garments of the girl were noticed by her aunt. On being questioned, the girl had to tell her aunt about the incident. Instead of reporting the case to the police, her guardian scolded and beat the girl calling her a girl of bad character. Instead of giving her any support they insisted on her to leave their house. The girl had nowhere to go, and therefore, was depressed. For no fault of her, the girl was blamed. In fact, the girl was the victim of deceit. She was dependent on her uncle and aunt and they were denying her any support. This shows the negative attitude of the society towards the girls who are victims of sexual abuse. The boys went scot-free when they could have been easily identified and punished (Source: unreported – direct interview with victim).

These case studies prove that sexual abuse of girl children is disturbing, abhorrent and very often unimaginable. Unfortunately, it exists in our society. Girl children are sexually abused within and outside the family by the family members and other relatives or by known persons or by the persons in authority. These are the persons who wield moral and physical authority over the child and are responsible for socialization of the child. Many a times these very persons are damaging the child's future by sexually abusing the child. These persons by virtue of their power over the child due to age, relationship or position of strength in the family use children to meet their own sexual urges.

In the present case studies, the abusers are grandfather, father, male cousin and brother-in-law, paternal uncle, relatives, neighbour, teacher, the persons at work place, other known and trusted persons.

In a joint family, the status of cousin is almost that of a real brother but sexual abuse by male cousin makes the girl lose faith in the relationship. Father and daughter relationship is considered very sacred, lovely and trust-worthy as father is a protector and caretaker of child in Indian families. But some of the above cases prove that such sacred relationship of father and daughter has become unhealthy, fearful and they also prove that how a protector has become a destructor. The relationship of paternal uncle is also sacred in the Indian families but such relationship is also losing its value and some cases prove that how these persons fall to the level of a beast. The teacher-student relationship is also considered sacred in India. A teacher is an idol for the student and they respect him but again in some case studies, it was found that there was immoral behaviour on the part of the teacher with his student which is unworthy of his profession.

Girl children are among the most vulnerable members of our society because of their age and dependency on adults. For many of the victims, the continuing sexual assaults of childhood are a guilty secret which they have never been able to share. They regard themselves as spoilt, debased and violated, and experience a bewildering complex of guilt, anger and shame. Some victims never acquire a positive self-image. The models, their parents presented, are confusing. Hence, it is sad to find that caretakers, family members, even parents, close relatives commit the heinous crime of sexual abuse and rape of the girl child in their care. Such incidences happen in all kinds of families and in all areas. It disturbs the mental equilibrium of the child and makes the child self-blaming, guilty and forces her to mistrust herself and others.

Sexual abuse of girl children is caused in a number of situations like lack of communication between parents and children, little or no interaction with mother, no respect for relationship, tensed atmosphere in the family, addiction of father, poverty and deterioration of value system and morality in the family and society. Absence of congenial environment in the family, ignorance and illiteracy of the parents, inadequate control of the family over children, presence of an authoritative person in the family who thinks it to be his privilege to exploit the girl children in the family, the lust of the elders, an easy access to the child and helplessness of the girl child are some other factors responsible for girl child abuse. Neglect of girl child by parents because of separation of parents or a reconstituted family could be another situation that is taken advantage of by neighbours and other people to sexually abuse the lonely children. Lacunae in the criminal justice system and negative attitude of society towards abused girl children compel such children not to disclose their abuse and suffer in silence. Temptation, immaturity of age and not knowing the consequences of sexual behaviour on the part of the girl are some of the important factors that are found responsible for this phenomenon of sexual abuse of girl children in the Indian society.

These girl children, suffering with the stigma and shame surrounding the abuse, often struggle with a feeling of being the 'damaged one'. In such situations the response of the victim's family has a tremendous effect on the outcome. Supportive responses from the victim's family and friends can go far to lessen the impact of the abuse while negative responses compound the damage done. All these girl child victims can be helped to overcome the situation, by asking them to become confident and self-dependent. They should be told that it was not their fault and they have every right to live with respect and dignity of a human being.

Interviews with Key Informants

Researcher also conducted interviews of 40 key informants who are working in the concerned field. These are the persons who, because of their position in the society, are aware of the phenomenon of girl child sexual abuse. These people were willing to share their knowledge with the researcher, and their experiences, observations, opinions, suggestions were very valuable. They were 10 social workers, 10 doctors, 10 advocates and 10 police personnel who helped the sexually abused girls to face the situation, to cope with the trauma and sufferings.

These various informants were the key to the researcher's understanding of the subject. They provided much information through formal conversations and specific interviews. These key informants were persons with special skills, were knowledgeable and because of their status and the capacity of responsibility dealing with cases of sexual abuse, were in a position to throw light on different aspects of the problem in sexual abuse.

Their observations and perspective were immensely helpful to the researcher in the study of this complex evil of sexual abuse of girl child in society. Even the difficulties encountered by these people in discharging their duties and the problems faced by them in handling cases of sexual abuse acted as a valuable guide for the researcher in understanding this social problem.

An interview guide was prepared and key informants or the persons who know the problems were made to speak their mind on the matter. These key informants helped this researcher a lot, to gather information efficiently and to gain a special understanding of the subject.

Doctors

This researcher interviewed about 10 persons from the medical profession. The case is referred to a doctor only when the injury is not simple and cannot be treated at home. When the case is referred to the police, as in case of rape, sodomy, etc. then, because of legal procedure, the police have to get the medical examination done as early as possible. The medical examination of the accused also goes, to a large extent, to prove the offence if the accused is immediately caught and apprehended and this medical examination of the culprit is done before it is too late. The time factor in the examination of such cases is very important in order to get the accused convicted by a court of law. Conviction of an accused for the offence and the award of the deterrent punishment generally desists the prospective offender from committing such offence in future. Very often a girl child, who is a victim of sexual abuse by an adult, suffers physical injury, the case is referred to doctor only when the injury is not simple and cannot be treated at home. Secondly, the parents approach the doctor when the girl is pregnant. They insist on abortion to avoid disrepute. Doctors are persuaded to terminate the pregnancy even if there are no medical grounds for it. The possibility of the girl committing suicide or being killed in such situations is not rare. Therefore, the doctors agree to do so for money or on humanitarian grounds.

The girl who is a victim of sexual abuse, particularly when the girl is a child, suffers from a severe psychological wound. This injury to the mind of the child is more damaging than the physical injury. The child goes into depression, feeling shame and guilt and owing to the attitude of the family members and the society at large to blame the child itself for what has happened to her, makes the child lose her hope for a happy life in future and many a times the child is driven to commit suicide. If not, the girl child suffers from maladjustment with world around her. She is lucky if she could come out of this successfully with the help of sympathy of the near and dear ones and proper psychological counselling and treatment. This aspect of medical assistance to the girl is also called 'save the girl' programme. Female foeticide, child sexual abuse, neglect of health and education, child marriage, early and multiple pregnancies, domestic violence and dowry deaths are the many social evils the women suffer in society and doctors are the people who can do much to eradicate this evil.

Police Personnel

About 10 police officers working on different posts were interviewed on the subject of girl child sexual abuse. An analysis of their experiences, measures taken by them in handling the persons involved, difficulties faced by them in securing the punishment of the accused by court of law and most important of all is what they think that the parents, family members, relatives, friends and other people of the locality should do to prevent the occurrence of such cases has been carried out. According to the police officers, such incidents take place in the four walls of the home of the child.

It is the grievance of the police that hardly 5 per cent of the number of actual cases are reported to the police. The parents or other family members waste lot of time in their decision-making; 'to do or not to do' is the question. When the case is referred to the police, as in case of rape, sodomy, etc. then, because of legal procedure, the police have to get the medical examination done as early as possible. The medical examination of the accused also goes to a large extent to prove the offence if the accused is immediately caught and apprehended and this medical examination of the culprit are done before it is too late. The time factor in the examination of such cases is very important in order to get the accused convicted by a court of law. Conviction of an accused for the offence and the award of the deterrent punishment generally desists the prospective offender from committing such offence in future.

Whenever there is delay in reporting the offence, it becomes difficult to apprehend the accused. Immediate medical examination of both the victim and the accused, which is very necessary from the point of view of evidence of the offence, cannot be done and this results into acquittal of the accused in most of the cases. If the girl is from economically poor and socially or politically uninfluential strata of the society and the offender is an influential person, the people of the girl are afraid of or unwilling to report the case at all. Even if the case is reported, the complainant is very reluctant to disclose her identity, the parents or other relatives make an absurd demand that the abusers be severely punished but the incident should not get any publicity as the reputation of the family is at stake.

The stigma that is generally attached to the victim and her family by the society dissuades them from pursuing the matter to its logical end. No witness comes forward to testify before the court about the identity of the accused or about the incident itself. The accused often gets acquitted for want of sufficient evidence to prove the offence. The general tendency is to push the matter under the carpet as the child's parents feel that the court case in the matter would result into character assassination of the girl and her future would be in jeopardy. Compensation in terms of money induces them to settle the matter rather than seeing that the offender is punished. Witnesses turn hostile and the prosecutor is helpless. Some police personnel even admit that there is political pressure making the investigation of the case difficult.

Social Workers

Social workers, specifically those working in the field of child welfare or orphanage, or child homes and observation homes, come across cases of sexual abuse of girl children. Their experience throws some light on the plight and suffering of the girl children who are victims of sexual abuse. The role of social worker in dealing with such cases is very important as they are the persons who give psychological support to these victims and try to understand their problems allowing the victim to express their feelings and, thus, help them in rehabilitation.

If any of the girl child in the family can be noticed by the social worker, he gives some warning sign of the impending danger and parents or guardians could be made aware of the possibilities of sexual abuse of the girl child.

The conclusion that can be drawn from the interviews of social workers is that the incidences of sexual abuse of minor girls are increasing in Beed District. Among the cases of sexual abuse of minor girls reported in the institutions and in the police station, most of the victims are from low and lower middle social-economic groups. Even though sexual abuse is prevalent in other socio-economic group, they remained under-reported and undisclosed due to disreputation and stigma attached to such abuse.

The causative factors for sexual abuse of girl children found by the social workers are:

(a) No cordial atmosphere in the family
(b) Quarrels between parents
(c) Bitterness and unhappiness in the family due to lack of adequate amenities
(d) Temptation of teenage girls
(e) Poverty
(f) Ignorance
(g) Illiteracy
(h) Large families
(i) Migration

People expect the social worker to represent their case to the police and also before the court of law. They also expect the social worker to console and give moral support to the child which is their own primary duty in such cases. The family members also expect a social worker to help them to settle the matter by making available some monetary compensation to the victim from the abuser. The social worker by way of counselling can help the child to get some relief from stress and strain of the ugly incident. It is possible that the children are made aware of the lurking danger by speaking to them in suggestive manner telling them about hygiene and sex education. A social worker can have exchange of ideas with parents and other family members in the form of social education that the family atmosphere should be congenial and friendly. There should be interaction between the children and the elders in the family so that the children feel free to discuss such things with their caretakers. This, too to some extent keeps the probable abuser away from the child.

Hence, the social workers are working as agents of change, they help the parents to change, to adopt different coping skills and alternative values about child rearing, they facilitate an interaction between children and parents and, thus, help them to release their stress.

Advocates

In medico-legal cases of sexual abuse that go to the court of law, the institutions of police, medical experts and advocates play a very important role. On receipt of a complaint, it is the duty of the police to investigate the case and file a charge sheet against the accused. Medical examination and evidence provided by doctor dealing with the case goes to a large extent to prove the guilt of the accused. It is the duty of the advocate, as police prosecutor, to prove the offence beyond reasonable doubt and secure appropriate punishment for the accused found guilty. However, advocates who are private practitioners appear in the court of law to represent the accused and, therefore, are more interested in getting the 'not guilty' verdict from the court. Though they appear generally as defense lawyers, advocates are well aware of the phenomenon of sexual abuse in the society. They know the mental state of the complainant and members of her family, they know the loopholes in the investigation by the police. As members of the society they are familiar with the attitude of the people towards the unfortunate victim and her family members. They can see the integrity of their brother professional – the police prosecutor and even the presiding judge. All these factors make an advocate a knowledgeable person to be interviewed by a researcher of the study of girl child sexual abuse in society. In the opinion of these advocates and prosecutors, the matter should be reported to the police as early as possible and medical examination of the victim and also that of the accused done without delay.

The advocates are of the opinion that efficient investigation of the case is very necessary, some amendments in law such as in-camera hearing of the case, presence of women judges and lawyers, and burden to prove his innocence to be placed on the accused as the victim is a child, are some of things that can be thought of. According to them, the cases in which the family members of the victim refuse to cooperate with the prosecution are not rare as they are tempted to compromise and settle the matter outside the court. Many a times, they do so under pressure or just to avoid bad publicity. Measures are to be taken to deal with the curse of child sexual abuse in the society.

The conclusions that can be drawn from interviews of various advocates are that the crime is on increase because the offender rarely is punished for the offence. There are many factors responsible for this state of affair. Primarily, it is the reluctance of the family of the victim to report the matter to the police. In such cases, very often, stigma is attached to the victim and her family and it is the victim who is made to feel guilty, rather than the accused. Hardly 5 per cent cases are reported and then also the police are reluctant to take cognizance of the offence, and to bring the accused to book. The so-called well-wishers of the family and the police discourage the victim and her family from filing the case. Many a times the poverty of the victim's family tempts the family to compromise and settle the matter outside the court for money. Witness, even if there is any, is unwilling to testify before the court. Prosecutors are not very keen to secure punishment in the trial. Conviction rate in Maharashtra is 3 to 4 per cent, which shows the pathetic state of criminal justice system. Victims are mostly from low income group and are minors. Parents do not listen to their children and most of the times the children are asked to keep quiet. Very often there is inordinate delay in reporting the matter affecting the availability of medical and other evidence. The date, time and place of offence are not properly recorded and the plea of alibi is easily available to the accused. The burden is always on the prosecution to prove the offence committed by the accused and the accused is acquitted for want of conclusive evidence. The various forms of sexual abuse, other than rape and sodomy are not well defined in the criminal law though they are equally damaging to the psyche of the victim.

According to the key informant's interview in the present study, the causative factors for girl child sexual abuse are neglect of girl child, absence of love and affection for the girl child in the family, lack of dialogue and communication between the members of the family, which make the girl vulnerable. The neglect of the child is the consequence of the lack of awareness of the caretakers. Parents should always have a watchful eye for their children. They should promptly take note of any unusual and abnormal behaviour of the child and channels of communication and interaction between the elders and children should always be kept open. The child should feel free to talk about anything that has happened to it which is not to its liking and instead of blaming the child; the caretaker should see that the child is not an easy prey for the sexual abusers.

Note

1. Goode, W.J. and Hatt, P.K. (1952), *Methods in Social Research,* McGraw-Hill Book, New York.

4

Nature and Causes of Girl Child Sexual Abuse

In this chapter, the nature and causes of girl child sexual abuse are discussed. For the proper understanding of this problem it is important to know the causative factors and the nature of the problem. In-depth study helps to prevent or to suggest coping strategies of the problem.

Child abuse, in one form or another, has existed in almost all the societies throughout history. However, the recognition of child abuse as a social problem is of recent origin. The research on child abuse in India has, therefore, not received much attention, especially girl child sexual abuse. This, perhaps, could be attributed to a lack of conceptual clarity and low reporting of cases of girl children. This situation has reinforced the prevalent myth that child sexual abuse is rare in Indian society.[1]

The subject of girl child sexual abuse is still a taboo in India. There is a conspiracy of silence around the subject and a very large percentage of people feel that this is largely a western problem and that child sexual abuse does not happen in India. Part of the reason of course lies in a traditional conservative family and community structure that does not talk about sex and sexuality at all.

Thus, the problem of girl child sexual abuse is neglected in Indian society, though a large percentage of child population is vulnerable to sexual abuse, exploitation and neglect; there is also inadequate information about the extent of girl child sexual abuse in the country.

In our country, awareness of the sexual abuse of girl children have yet to grow. The girl children who talk about or disclose their sexual abuse are most frequently met with denial, minimization, or blame. We have yet to proceed from silence about the abuse, to awareness.

The girl child is never able to talk about sexual abuse because our society has never allowed them to voice their fears, has attached stigma and tended to hush and bury the abuse. In our country, families experiencing child sexual abuse often go on as if nothing has happened. In that case, children learn that there is no one they can trust and none to share with. The children feel that sharing leads not to help but to harm or neglect that it is not safe to tell the truth. As a result they feel shame and keep secrecy and silence.

There is a need to have empirical data on various forms of girl child sexual abuse in the family and outside. Large scale research studies with multidisciplinary approach are necessary to study the extent, nature and causes of girl child sexual abuse and to suggest suitable intervention strategies.

Hence, while there is a need to break the silence of these girl children and help them to come out from their prison of secrecy and pain, at the same time, it is also important to punish the guilty. An attempt is being made to suggest measures for policy-making, suggest preventive, primitive and rehabilitative services for sexually abused girl children. Hence, the researcher in the present study focused on extent, nature, cause and consequences of girl child sexual abuse.

The various forms of girl child sexual abuse found in the study are rape, sodomy, prostitution, molestation, abduction, incest, sexual intercourse, touching private parts of child, fondling of child's genitals, making the child fondle an adult's genitals, exhibitionism and pornography. The problem of girl child sexual abuse is prevalent in the secure place like home and neighbour's house, and even in public places like market and while travelling. More surprisingly the abusers are the persons known and trusted by the children. Hence, the extent, nature and causes of girl child sexual abuse are analysed with the help of following tables.

Table 4.1 *Family Atmosphere of the Victim*

Year 2011

S. No.	*Nature of Atmosphere*	*Rural*		*Urban*	
		Frequency	*Percentage*	*Frequency*	*Percentage*
1	Friendly	25	10.00	40	16.00
2	Tensed	131	52.40	121	48.40
3	Mixed	94	37.60	89	35.60
	Total	250	100.00	250	100.00

Source: Primary Data

Table 4.1 reveals that the percentage of families with tensed atmosphere in the family is higher in rural area, i.e. 52.40 per cent, whereas 48.40 per cent families in the urban area are having tensed atmosphere in their homes. This is followed by 37.60 per cent in rural areas and 35.60 per cent families in urban area that have mixed atmosphere. Only 10 per cent families have friendly atmosphere in the rural area. It is lower than the percentage of (16%) families with friendly atmosphere in urban areas.

There is little difference between rural and urban areas in the percentage of tensed families and mixed atmosphere in the families.

The above figures show the severity of the problem and divide between urban and rural families. Still rural families are deprived from education and other exposures. In modern times, the family is fast losing the family values of love, affection, morality and emotional bonds among the family members. Tensed atmosphere in the family is high in rural area, i.e. 52.40 per cent, and it is also quite high in urban area, i.e. 48.40 per cent. This compels the children to keep quiet as they are afraid of even speaking to their parents about their problems. There is no interaction between parents and children and lack of friendly relations in the family results into fear psychosis in children which is a hindrance to their healthy development. Such families restrict their children from enjoying their liberties like outdoor games and mixing with friends from the same age group. Tensed atmosphere at home makes the child feel inferior, lose self-confidence, keep quiet and, therefore, vulnerable to abuse. Most of the time, children are indoors and exposed to negative impact of TV at home. Due to silence of girl children, they are easily carried away by allurements and become an easy prey of the abusers who exploit them for their personal sexual gratification.

Table 4.2 *Frequency of Quarrel Between Parents of Victims*

Year 2011

S. No.	*Frequency of Quarrel*	*Frequency*	*Percentage*
1	Frequently	148	31.89
2	Always	316	68.10
	Total	464	

Source: Primary Data

Table 4.2 reveals the frequency of quarrel between the parents of victims. The highest number respondents, i.e. 68.10 per cent, reported that their parents quarrel always and 31.89 per cent reported that their parents quarrel frequently.

It is known that parents are models for their children. What will be the future of children if there are frequent quarrels in the family? The fact that 68.10 per cent parents quarrelled 'always' makes us think of the scene in the family. What the children learn from their parents and how such parents can give psychological, emotional support to their children and how can they protect their children from any abuse? There is no surprise if children feel insecure in their own families in such conditions. That 7.2 per cent children did not answer properly shows the severity of problem of quarrels between parents and tensed atmosphere in the family. It was observed that the girl children were afraid to talk about the quarrel between their parents. Such situation makes the girl children keep mum while answering the questions about their abuse. They have no interactions in their families and there is no affection and emotional bond between the parents and children. When these girl children are not feeling safe in their own families, they are being deprived of their child rights.

Graph 4.1 *Nature of Punishment for Mistakes Committed by Victims*

Year 2011

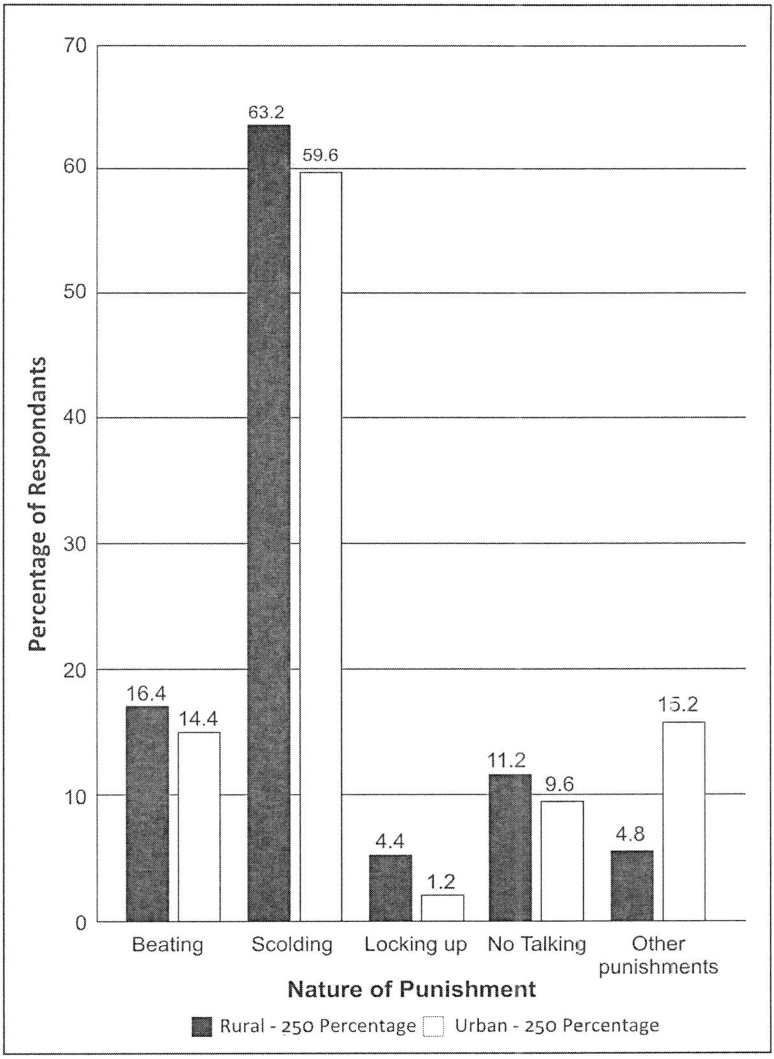

The above discussion makes it clear that the quarrel between parents leads to tension in the family. The girl child in such families is living in tensed mind and would not share her feelings with others. These demands of teenage years are not fulfilled by the parents. In such an environment, the child keeps quiet even when she is sexually abused in the family itself. This silence works actively because it is the main perpetrator as it puts a curtain before the eyes of the parents and they do not see the reality. Tensed atmosphere and quarrel between the parents in the family silences the child. Hence, recurrence of the abuse of a girl child in the family is possible because of this silence on the part of the girl.

Table 4.3 *Nature of Punishment for Mistakes Committed by Victims*

Year 2011

S. No.	*Nature of Punishment*	*Rural 250*		*Urban 250*	
		Frequency	*Percentage*	*Frequency*	*Percentage*
1	Beating	41	16.40	36	14.40
2	Scolding	158	63.20	149	59.60
3	Locking	11	4.40	3	1.20
4	No talking	28	11.20	24	9.60
5	Other punishments	12	4.80	38	15.20
	Total	250	100.00	250	100.00

Source: Primary Data

Graph 4.1 and Table 4.3 shows the nature of punishment for mistakes committed by victims. 'Scolding' as the type of punishment is higher in both the areas, i.e. 63.20 per cent in rural area and 59.60 per cent in urban area. The percentage of beating is in second place, i.e. 16.40 per cent in rural area but 'other form of punishment' is in second place in urban area which is 15.20 per cent. The percentage for 'no talking' is in third position in rural area, i.e. 11.20 per cent, but 'Beating' holds third place in urban area which is 14.40 per cent. The punishment of 'locking' is higher in rural areas, i.e. 4.40 per cent, whereas it is comparatively less in urban areas, i.e. 1.20 per cent. The 'other' option in rural area includes punishments for girl children such as giving food late, giving more work (agriculture work and household work), and not purchasing new clothes during festivals, etc. In urban areas, the other punishments include not sending them outside, insulting in front of the friends, etc.

The above table shows that scolding is higher in both the areas. 'Beating' type of punishment is higher in rural areas. 'Locking' also is inhuman. The nature of punishments used by the parents makes the girl child upset and it leads to mental strain. 'No talking' of parents, especially mother, makes the girl child feel very sad. Neglecting her emotions and disturbing her by using bad words is an emotional abuse and this shows the negative attitude towards girl children by their parents. Even though there is little difference about nature of punishment between the areas, 'the girl child' gets punishment in both the areas for her mistakes only because she is a 'girl child'.

As discussed in Table 4.3, family atmosphere is very important for healthy development of child. Tensed atmosphere makes the girl stay quiet without sharing her emotions; she does not tell about her exploitation. In the same way, nature of punishment also makes the girl child feel inferior, of low dignity and helpless. It creates distance and lack of rapport between the parents and child and makes her feel insecure in her own home. There is no emotional support offered to her by her parents. In such a situation, the potential abusers get a chance to step in pretending as well-wishers and using the opportunity to win the trust of the girl. He then not only abuses the girl once or twice but frequently because her silence emboldens him.

Table 4.4 *Addicted Persons in the Family of Victims*

Year 2011

S. No.	*Addicted Person*	*Frequency*	*Percentage*
1	Father	385	82.61
2	Brother	55	11.80
3	Uncle	11	2.36
4	Grandfather	15	3.21
	Total	466	

Source: Primary Data

Table 4.4 shows that a large number (385) of girl children who were victims of sexual abuse disclosed that the father was alcohol addict. With 82.61 per cent families having the head of the family addicted is quite a distressful situation as this results into disharmony, frequent quarrels between parents and tension affecting the childhood of the girl in the family. Some 11.80 per cent of girls reported that the brother was given to addiction. Only 6.80 per cent (34 girls) girl children did not have this problem in their families.

Addiction of the parents leads to quarrel between husband and wife. Husband beats his wife and children, making the atmosphere in the family full of tension, there is no proper communication among parents and children, this again leads to more quarrels. Families having one or more member addicted are found to have high level of stress and conflict, ill treatment of children, lack of parental care and addiction of a family member also causes breakdown of family relationships. The girl child loses faith in the parents. This unhappy and unhealthy environment in the family is one of the leading causes of girl child being a victim of sexual abuse.

In this situation, this girl child does not feel that she would be properly understood if she tells about the sexual abuse by the close family member or acquaintance. She does not feel secure in her home, so she prefers to keep quiet and suffer in silence, aggravating the evil. To her horror she discovers that there is a degradation of moral values in the family members. This forces her to avoid disclosure which leads to recurrence of the incident and the abusers are found to take advantage of the situation that the girl is in, and continue to sexually exploit her.

Table 4.5 *Opinion of the Victims About Gender Discrimination*

Year 2011

S. No.	*Particulars*	*Rural*	*Urban*
1	Familial Discrimination	75	70
2	Economic Discrimination	75	65
3	Cultural Discrimination	40	30
4	Educational Discrimination	60	55
	Total	250	230

Source: Primary Data

Gender discrimination among children prevails in the families from both urban and rural areas. Indicators of the discrimination decided for the study were: (i) Familial discrimination (ii) Economic discrimination (iii) Cultural discrimination (iv) Educational discrimination.

(i) Familial discrimination includes: Food, housework, going outside, punishment for mistake, punishment for not returning home in time, and ill-treatment.
(ii) Economic discrimination includes: Sending to trip/excursion, to buy new clothes, to bring medicines, buying of books, buying of vehicles and the given pocket money.
(iii) Cultural discrimination includes: Playing, going to cinema, watching TV, and visiting friends.
(iv) Educational discrimination includes: Sending to school, to participate in school programmes and to participate in sports competition.

In rural area, familial and economic discriminations are found more often followed by cultural discrimination and educational discrimination. In urban area, familial discrimination is found in more cases followed by cultural discrimination, economic discrimination and educational discrimination.

Even though gender inequality is clear in both the areas, the discrimination is doubly profound for girls from the rural area. Indicators of discrimination in the present study show that girls from rural area are more discriminated at the familial level, economic, educational and cultural levels. Girls' involvement in school declines, their participation in sports and other programme is less with diminished household earnings and social position.

Gender discrimination among children prevails in the families from both urban and rural areas. In rural area, girls are made to do housework in 97 per cent cases, whereas boys are not at all asked to help their mothers in her domestic work; 80 per cent girls are not allowed to participate in playing games and 99 per cent of girls are prevented from going to cinema houses. Boys enjoy the freedom of visiting friends, whereas 60 per cent girls are discouraged from doing the same. About 70 per cent girls are denied new clothes and other things. Outdoor sports and excursion is a taboo. Also, 80 per cent girls receive punishment for not coming home within time limits; 95 per cent will not be spared for even small mistakes. Overall, ill-treatment is meted out to 99 per cent girls as compared to boys.

In urban areas, there is a little difference in comparison to rural area in this aspect. In urban area, about 40 per cent girls are not allowed to visit friends; 70 per cent girls are not allowed to play games; 94 per cent girls are prevented from visiting cinema houses. Nearly 85 per cent girls are not spared for mistakes; 90 per cent girls are victims of general ill-treatment. Almost all boys are free to enjoy these privileges in urban as well as rural areas.

The above figures clearly indicate gender discrimination and that the girls get ill-treatment in their homes. They are forced to do house work, are not sent to school regularly. They are not allowed to participate in outdoor games and play with children of their own age group. They are also discriminated in health care. Their small mistakes are also not forgiven and a harsh punishment like not giving food, not purchasing new clothes, etc. is given. Punishments like scolding, public insult, physical torture and beating is a common thing. All this goes to make the girls feel inferior and lose their status in the family; it discourages them from voicing their grievance, forcing them to tolerate ill treatment and sexual abuse.

Girl children from rural area are discriminated against in almost all activities such as not sending the girl children to school in rural areas. The increased dropout rate of girl children deprives them of their right to education and restrictions on all other activities is the hindrance in their all round development.

In urban areas also, girl children are discriminated against as they are not allowed to go outside to cinema, garden and for excursion; participation in sports activities in school is denied, punishment for mistake and public insult are common practices. Girls are discriminated in both areas due to their biological sex. This shows the negative attitude in our society towards girl children. This discriminatory treatment to girl children is an indicator of their low status in the family. Due to low status, they feel inferior, and due to lack of attention by the parents these girl children never find suitable atmosphere in their homes to share their problems. They feel insecure, as there is a lack of communication and existence of a tensed atmosphere in the family makes them sit silently without raising their voice against their sexual abuse. The abuser gives them special attention and makes them feel as if she is special to him and gains her trust and abuses her sexually. Thus, discrimination of girl child is an important causative factor in her sexual abuse.

Table 4.6 *Abusers of Girl Children at Home*

Year 2011

S. No.	*Abusers*	*Rural*		*Urban*	
		Frequency	*Percentage*	*Frequency*	*Percentage*
1	Maternal uncle	51	24.05	33	20.88
2	Paternal uncle	40	18.86	28	17.72
3	Male cousin	61	28.77	57	36.07
4	Father	10	4.71	06	3.79
5	Brother	02	0.94	01	0.63
6	Step-father	02	0.94	01	0.63
7	Step-brother	01	0.94	01	0.63
8	Grandfather	04	1.88	02	1.23
9	Brother-in-law	10	4.71	07	4.43
10	Maternal uncle, paternal uncle and male cousin	11	5.98	08	5.06
11	Father, grandfather, and brother	08	3.77	06	3.79
12	Brother-in-law and brother	09	4.24	06	3.79
13	Step-father and Step-brother	03	1.41	02	1.26
	Total	212	84.8	158	63.2
14	No complaint	38	15.2	92	36.8
	Total	250	100	250	100

Source: Primary Data

Table 4.6 shows the frequency of the abusers of girl children at her home. Among all abusers from both areas, the percentage of male cousin is higher, i.e. 28.77 per cent, in rural area and 36.07 per cent in urban area followed by the percentage of maternal uncle, 24.05 per cent, in rural area and 20.88 per cent in urban area. The percentage of paternal uncle is at the third position, i.e. 18.86 in rural area and 17.72 in urban area. The percentage of father as abuser is 4.71 in rural area and it is 3.79 in urban area. Quite a sizable number of girls from both the areas alleged sexual abuse by more than one member, while 15.2 per cent girls from rural area and 36.8 per cent girls from urban area did not complain of sexual abuse by family members. Also, 84.8 per cent girls from rural area interviewed by researcher have suffered sexual abuse by different members of the family; whereas the same is the complain of 63.2 per cent girls from urban area. These figures prove that there is rural and urban divide regarding girl sexual abuse and rural girls are suffering in large numbers. The figures from the table prove that the family, the home, which is the place of protection and security for every human being has become for the girl children an insecure place and the very persons who are her caretakers and protectors have turned into villains and destructors of her future. The percentage of male cousin as abuser is higher among all the abusers in both the areas, followed by cases of sexual abuse by maternal uncle and paternal uncle. The number of cases of sexual abuse by other relatives like brother-in-law, step-father, step-brother, own brother and father is also not negligible.

The table reveals that father is also an abuser of his own girl child and it reveals the fact that the sacred relationship of father and daughter that is considered as pure and trustworthy is being abused. These figures show that this sacred relationship of father and daughter has also become harmful and a protector is becoming a threat to a girl child. It also proves that this relationship is losing its value and strength, bringing down the man to the level of the beast. This table shows that the grandfather also is an abuser. The status of a grandfather is respectful. The girl child holds the grandfather in high esteem as she has seen her parents and other people in the family almost worshipping him. The girl child does not feel anything wrong when the loving grandfather caresses her. But the girl child is shocked and bewildered when the same old man makes the girl child an object of his lust.

Sexual abuse is prevalent in joint and nuclear families, in rural area though joint families are set-ups where family members come together to share the joys and sorrows of one another. Children enjoy such set-ups and the number of people having access to the child is greater in these families. Unfortunately, these people misused the opportunities by sexually abusing the children.

Brothers, step-brothers, and step-fathers are also abusing the girl children in their families. In Indian culture, brother and father (even step-father and brother) are considered as caretakers and protectors and they are known for their love and affection for family members. There are emotional bonds between one another in the family, but the above table reveals the fact that the elders in the family, who are most trustworthy caretakers of the girl child, instead of giving support to the girl child in difficult situation, they themselves, by their conduct, are putting a question mark on their relationship with children.

Marriages with male cousin (like son of father's sister, son of maternal uncle) are customary in some Indian communities and the children are made to think of themselves as life partners. Elders from both the families speak about this in jocular tone and the male cousin exploits the sentiment to sexually abuse the girl.

The table also shows that paternal uncle and maternal uncle who are trusted to be caring persons and protectors of girl child are also the abusers. Addiction of the father, tensed atmosphere in the family and presence of authoritative paternal or maternal uncle, makes the girl suffer sexual abuse by the maternal or paternal uncle. Family is a secure place, but sexual abuse of girl children occur in the family and the abuse are by none other than the nearest and dearest trusted members of the family.

The place of brother-in-law in Indian family is somewhat different. It is considered as trusted relationship. The girls are given freedom to make fun with their sister's husbands. Nobody takes objection and doubt about such fun with brother-in-law. But in many cases the man sexually abuses the girl child by misusing the values of the relationship. During the teenage period of the girl, attraction towards a man is only natural. The girl child loses faith in such relationships and it becomes very difficult for the child to trust any other person and the relationship.

Hence, about 85 per cent girls from rural area and 63 per cent girls from urban area have suffered sexual abuse by different members of the family. This shows the severity of the problem and how the girl child is losing her faith and trust in the family relationship. Indian culture taught her to respect and trust the elders in the family. This teaching did not allow her to speak about her sexual abuse by the different relations in the family. Lack of interaction in the family made her keep quiet. Keeping silent increases recurrence of the abuse of girl child within the family. Inadequate control of the family, neglect of the child's needs by the family and helplessness of the girl child, taken together, has resulted in the increase of such incidents.

Hence, sexual abuse by family members and close relatives is a fact of life for many girl children as it happens in all kinds of families and in all areas. It disturbs the girl child and makes the child self-blaming, feeling guilty, causes mistrust in her and in others.

Table 4.7 *Outside Abusers of Girl Child Victim*

Year 2011

S. No.	*Abusers*	*Frequency*	*Percentage*
1	Neighbour	55	11
2	Teacher	18	3.6
3	Boyfriend	11	2.2
4	Male family friend	11	2.2
5	Female family friend	03	0.6
6	School servant/lab assistant.	14	2.8
7	Strangers	228	5.6
8	Persons at work place	15	3
9	Neighbour, teacher and family friend	85	17
10	Boyfriend, male family friend and teacher	17	3.4
11	Persons at work place, house owner and neighbour	28	5.6
12	Conductor, school servant and stranger	15	3
	Total	500	100.00

Source: Primary Data

Table 4.7 shows the identity of abusers. Of all abusers, the percentage of 'neighbour' is higher, i.e. 11 per cent, followed by 'stranger' 5.6 per cent and 'teachers' 3.6 per cent. Respondents are abused by more than one abuser. The percentage of 'neighbour, teacher and family friends is higher, i.e. 17 per cent, and 'persons at work place, house owner and neighbour' is 5.6 per cent.

People in the contact of the girl children, like teacher, neighbour, family friends, school servants, watchmen, person at work place and house owner, etc. clearly form the majority of the abusers. It is significant that female family friends, though few in number, are also abusers.

This table reveals the fact that girls are sexually abused by known persons and also by strangers. 'Neighbours' in Indian culture are having special place as caretakers and well-wishers and helpers in needy situations and they are the persons who are supposed to follow 'Shejar-dharma' and so they are trusted and known persons. But this study reveals that 11 per cent neighbours are sexually abusing teenaged girls living next door. The behaviour of such a neighbour is disgusting and reprehensible. Another known person who is an abuser is 'teacher'. Teacher-student relationship is considered sacred in India and he is an idol for the student and they respect him. But the above table shows that the behaviour of the teacher with his student is immoral and he is unworthy of his profession. Family friends who are also considered as trusted persons are also violating the trust of the child. In such conditions, life of the victim becomes bewildering as the child finds it difficult to cope with the feeling of hurt and fear. When the known person, male and even female family friend, betrays the trust of the child, the child loses faith in such relations and it becomes very difficult for the child to believe in any person. School servants are considered as caretakers of children in schools and, hence, they are trustworthy persons whom girl children call 'manager kaka' and they believe in them. But such persons whom the girl children do not expect to behave in an indecent manner betray the trust of girl children of the school. Sexual abuse by teacher and servant in schools hurts the girl child most and it may lead to low academic achievement, poor concentration in studies and it also may affect the ability of the child to develop trustworthy and intimate relationship with adults. Hence, the girls should be taught to respect the behaviour instead of age and profession of people around her. Poverty, ignorance and illiteracy and teenage years of the girl makes the girl child an easy prey of abusers like owner of house and persons at work place. These persons take undue advantage of their position to sexually exploit the poor adolescent girl.

The above discussion proves that even the persons who are the most respected and trusted people are forgetting their moral values. Their behaviour disturbs the child and makes the child self-blaming, guilty and causes her to lose mistrust in herself and in others.

Table 4.8 *Nature of Help to Girl Children by Frequent Visitors*

Year 2011

S. No.	*Nature of Help*	*Relatives*		*Family friends*		*Neighbour*	
		Frequency	*Percentage*	*Frequency*	*Percentage*	*Frequency*	*Percentage*
1	Accompany to school	69	18.64	3	21	14	25.45
2	Going to market	71	19.18	2	14	8	14.54
3	Help in studies	84	22.7	3	21	16	29.09
4	Going on a trip	26	7.02	2	14	5	9.09
5	Any other	120	32.43	4	28.52	12	40.00
	Total	370	74.00	14	2.8	55	11.00

Source: Primary Data

Table 4.8 shows the nature of help to girl children extended by frequent visitors. Out of all kinds of helps by relatives 'any other' is 32.43 per cent, followed by 'help in studies', i.e. 22.7 per cent, 'going to market' is 19.18 per cent, 'accompany to school' is 18.64 per cent. Out of help by family friends 'any other' is 28.52 per cent, 'accompany to school' and 'help in studies' is same, i.e. 21 per cent, and co-incidentally 'going to market' and 'going on a trip' is same, i.e. 14 per cent, out of nature of help by neighbour, 'any other' is 40 per cent and 'accompany to school' is 25.45 per cent.

'Any other' option includes supplying school study materials, CDs, helping to prepare projects, use of computer and internet, helping in dance practice, drawing classes, competition or any other cultural programme. In such situations, the potential abusers take entry in the home by helping the child in studies or by meeting other needs and gain trust of parents and the girl children by their behaviour. Generally, parents do not send the girl children for trips, but girl children want to go in such situations such abusers help the girl children by convincing their parents to send them on a trip with them. Parents agree to send their girl child with such known and trusted persons. Accompanying the girl child to school, going to the market and arranging trips with the girl children are all the other nature of help used by the abuser to build intimacy with them and, thus, gain trust.

This type of help makes the abuser to initiate contact with the girl child, helping children provides opportunity to the abusers to come close to the girl child. Such abusers are just waiting for the right time to initiate contact. It involves a process of initially introducing the child to the idea of sex and then gradually engaging them in sexual activity.

Table 4.9 *Nature of Sexual Abuse of Girl Children by Frequent Visitors*

Year 2011

S. No.	*Nature of Abuse*	*Frequent Visitors*					
		Relatives		*Family friends*		*Neighbour*	
		Frequency	*Percentage*	*Frequency*	*Percentage*	*Frequency*	*Percentage*
1	Touching private parts	114	30.81	5	35.00	13	23.63
2	Making sexual comment	79	21.35	3	21.00	16	29.09
3	Hugging, kissing in sexual way	79	21.35	3	21.00	5	9.09
4	Intercourse	33	8.91	2	14.00	6	10.9
5	Any other (showing private parts, asking to show her private parts, showing dirty pictures)	65	17.56	1	7.14	15	27.27
	Total	370	74	14	2.8	55	11

Source: Primary Data

Table 4.9 shows the nature of sexual abuse of girl children by the frequent visitors, such as relatives, family friends, and neighbours. As many as 74 per cent girls reported sexual abuse by relatives, 11 per cent girls from neighbours and 2.8 per cent girls from family friends. This shows how the relatives, the trusted persons, are abusing the girl child by violating her and her parents' trust. Of the nature of abuse, touching private parts is higher. It is 30.81 per cent by relatives, 35 per cent by family friends and 23.63 per cent by neighbours. Making sexual comments and hugging, kissing in sexual way is same 29.09 per cent by neighbour, 21.35 per cent by relatives and 21 per cent by family friends. Demand of intercourse is 10.90 per cent by neighbour and 8.91 per cent by relatives and 14 per cent by family friends.

Exhibitionism, pornography and showing children obscene pictures, etc. is the form of sexual abuse resorted to by family friends and neighbours. The study reveals that many respondents were made to watch pornographic material by close relatives, family friends and neighbours. The source of such material is mobile phone, books, video CDs and internet. This indicates a horrifying picture of enormity of problem of sexual abuse of girl child in the society. The girl children are not having appropriate and accurate knowledge about sex and sexuality and this is an obstacle in the healthy development of adolescent girl. Due to her ignorance and teenage years, the potential abuser abuses her sexually. As described above, after gaining her trust, he starts gradually fondling the victim or having the victim fondle him, all the while rationalizing that having sex is alright. The girl is rewarded with gifts for her participation and this exchange makes it possible to slowly build up to the point to where the girl is made to agree to more serious sexual acts like intercourse. This is the modus operandi of the abusers. All this is planned by the abuser and it creates such a situation that even when the girl child speaks about her abuse to her parents they do not believe and they blame the girl child and this makes her to sit silently. This revelation in the study challenges the common misunderstanding that girl child sexual abuse is normally a 'western problem' and does not happen in Indian society and culture.

Table 4.10 shows the nature of sexual abuse and abusers of girl children during wedding ceremony in rural and urban area. The percentage of relatives as abusers is high in both rural (44.4%) and urban (46.4%) areas. Photo snapping without the consent of the girl is frequently resorted to by abuser compared to other forms of abuse. Looking at the girl child in a sexual way as a form of sexual abuse and touching private parts is about 30 per cent and 18 per cent, respectively, in both the areas. The abusers are relatives like maternal uncle, paternal uncle, male cousins and brother-in-law, neighbours, and family friends. These are known and trusted persons of the child.

In Indian culture, wedding is an important ceremony which is an occasion to get-together for all relatives, family friends, neighbours and

Table 4.10 *Nature of Sexual Abuse of Girl Child During Wedding Ceremony*

Year 2011

		Rural							
S. No.	*Nature of Abuse*	*Relatives*					*Neighbours*	*Family Friends*	*Stranger*
		Maternal Uncle	*Paternal Uncle*	*Male Cousin*	*Brother-in-Law*	*Total*			
		Frequency	*Frequency*	*Frequency*	*Frequency*	*Frequency*	*Frequency*	*Frequency*	*Frequency*
1	Looking at in a sexual way	6 (18.18)	8 (24.24)	15 (45.45)	4 (12.12)	33 (29.72)	05 (17.85)	05 (22.72)	10 (18.18)
2	Making sexual comments	4 (21.05)	3 (15.78)	5 (26.03)	7 (36.84)	19 (17.11)	05 (17.85)	05 (22.72)	22 (40)
3	Touching private parts	3 (15.00)	6 (30.00)	8 (40.00)	3 (15.00)	20 (18.01)	03 (10.71)	03 (13.63)	02 (03.63)
4	Photo snap	2 (13.33)	3 (20.00)	7 (46.66)	3 (20.00)	15 (13.51)	06 (21.42)	05 (22.72)	17 (30.10)
5	Rubbing	2 (15.38)	4 (30.76)	5 (38.46)	2 (15.38)	13 (11.71)	05 (17.85)	02 (09.09)	02 (3.63)
6	Fondling in sexual way	2 (18.18)	3 (27.27)	5 (45.45)	1 (9.09)	11 (09.90)	04 (14.28)	02 (09.09)	02 (3.63)
	Total	19 (17)	27(24.32)	45 (40.54)	20 (18.11)	111 (44.4)	28 (20.14)	22 (15.82)	55 (39.56)

Cont'd...

...Cont'd

S. No.	Nature of Abuse	Urban							
		Relatives					Neighbours	Family Friends	Stranger
		Maternal Uncle	Paternal Uncle	Male Cousin	Brother-in-law	Total			
		Frequency	Frequency	Frequency	Frequency	Frequency	Frequency	Frequency	Frequency
1	Looking at in a sexual way	6 (17.14)	7 (20.00)	17 (48.57)	5 (14.28)	35 (30.17)	06 (15)	06 (23.07)	11(18.33)
2	Making sexual comments	2 (10.00)	6 (30.00)	5 (25.00)	7 (35.00)	20 (17.24)	06 (15)	08 (30.76)	25 (41.66)
3	Touching private parts	5 (23.80)	6 (28.57)	8 (38.09)	2 (9.52)	21 (18.10)	09 (22.5)	12 (46.15)	03 (05)
4	Photo snap	1 (7.69)	2 (15.38)	9 (69.23)	1 (7.69)	13 (11.20)	10 (25)	03 (11.53)	15 (25)
5	Rubbing	1 (6.66)	2 (13.33)	8 (53.33)	4 (26.66)	15 (12.93)	04 (10)	04 (15.38)	03 (05)
6	Fondling in sexual way	2 (16.66)	3 (25.00)	6 (50.00)	1 (8.33)	12 (10.34)	05 (12.5)	03 (11.53)	03 (05)
	Total	17 (14.65)	26 (22.41)	53 (45.68)	20 (17.24)	116 (46.4)	40 (29.85)	26 (19.40)	60 (44.74)

invitees. Unfortunately, the occasion is misused by the abusers by sexually abusing the teenaged girls in the crowd. Table 4.10 reveals that among the relatives, the percentage of male cousins as abuser is high, i.e. 40.54 per cent, and paternal uncle is at second position, with 24.32 per cent in rural area. In urban area, it is 45.68 per cent and 22.41, respectively. Wedding ceremonies are special events and people gather to enjoy and feel happy. But unfortunately, the girls are harassed while attending functions like wedding ceremony. The girls are facing forms of sexual abuse like being looked at in a sexual way, making sexual comments, touching private parts, fondling in sexual way and photo snapping by both known and unknown persons. In addition to the forms of abuse girls generally have to face in a crowded place, being photographed without their consent in wedding ceremony is common. Camera in a mobile phone is very conveniently used by relatives and family friends. Strangers also take advantage of the situation and snap photos and misuse the photograph. Many a times the girls are embarrassed and shocked when they have to face defamation and blackmail due to misuse or abuse of their photographs. The special atmosphere and the crowd give greater opportunity to the abuser to get an access to the girls and the situation and the environment help the perpetrator. His activity is not considered objectionable even if noticed and the girl cannot complain about it for fear of being laughed at.

This table proves that the wedding ceremony is the place and occasion where girls are sexually abused in large number by mischievous relatives family friends, neighbours, invitees and even by strangers.

Table 4.11 *Nature of Sexual Abuse of Girl Children at Market Place*

Year 2011

S. No.	*Nature of Abuse*	*Rural*	*Urban*
		Frequency	*Frequency*
1	Whistling	33 (17.46)	26 (10.4)
2	Singing vulgar songs	38 (20.10)	41 (16.4)
3	Making sexual comments	44 (23.28)	60 (24)
4	Looking at in a sexual way	49 (25.92)	73 (29.2)
5	Touching Private Parts	25 (13.22)	50 (20)
	Total	189	250

Source: Primary Data

It is observed that 'looking at in a sexual way' as a form of sexual abuse is highest among all other forms in both the areas, It is 25.92 per cent in rural area and 29.2 per cent in urban area. This above statistics show the prevalence and nature of sexual harassment of girls in both rural and urban areas. It is found that the incidence of whistling is higher, i.e. 17.46 per cent in rural area compared to that in urban area, i.e. 10.4 per cent for the girls of both the age groups.

Whistling is used in different tunes to indicate one's identity and to attract the attention of the girl concerned. Tunes of song with different meanings, such as 'you are beautiful', 'I Love you', 'I am waiting for you', 'please come', etc. are frequently used in whistling. Different tunes are not commonly used in whistling in urban areas, perhaps because the music of the tunes is drowned in the noise. Shrill whistling is resorted to invite the attention of the girl. Percentage of nuisance of singing vulgar songs is also higher in rural areas as compared to that in urban areas. The girls are embarrassed and hurt as these songs invariably have 'sexual' meanings. The abuser follows the girl singing such songs and the poor girl is helpless as she cannot stop him from doing so. She cannot say she is the target of the abuser and the 'song' and the singing of it is meant for her.

It is observed that the other forms of abuse such as ogling or looking at the girl in a sexual way, making sexual comments, or touching with sexual motive is more common in urban areas because the abuser can take advantage of the surrounding crowd to go near the young girl to gain proximity and get the pleasure of satisfaction of his sexual desires. The girls have to suffer this more on 'bazaar day' in their village or when they visit market in the town for purchases or for selling agriculture produce. For girls living in urban area, this form of abuse is almost a daily occurrence. Girls from rural area are comparatively saved from this type of abuse as they are not normally in a crowd in their villages. Thus, it is seen that the girls are victims of sexual abuse only because people have no moral values and derive pleasure by resorting to sexual advances towards girls. A girl or even a woman for these people of perverted mentality is only an object of sexual satisfaction.

Table 4.12 *Sexual Abuse of Girl Child During Travel*

Year 2011

S. No.	*Nature of Abuse*	*Rural Frequency*	*Urban Frequency*
1	Touching private parts	75 (36.94)	98 (39.2)
2	Making sexual comments	37 (18.22)	47 (18.8)
3	Sitting very close	36 (17.73)	47 (18.8)
4	Looking at in a sexual way	32 (15.76)	41 (16.4)
5	Any other (asking phone number, asking address, personal information, showing pictures on mobile)	23 (11.33)	17 (6.8)
	Total	203	250

Source: Primary Data

Table 4.12 shows the extent of different forms of sexual abuse during travel. Among all forms of sexual abuse, the percentage of touching private part is higher in both urban and rural areas. It is 36.94 per cent in rural area and it is 39.2 per cent in urban area. Surprisingly making sexual comments and sitting very close, these forms of sexual abuse are same, i.e. 18.8 per cent in urban area and it is 18.22 per cent in rural area. Sitting very close is 17.73 per cent in rural area. Looking at in a sexual way is 15.76 per cent in rural area and 16.4 per cent in urban area.

This table shows the extent of different forms of sexual abuse during travel. If a girl is travelling alone, or even with family members, she has to face sexual abuse of various types. Ogling, i.e. looking at in a sexual way, making sexual comments, sitting very close, or even touching breasts and hips are the common forms of harassment. Showing obscene pictures on mobile, playing songs on mobile phone, trying to establish uncalled for intimacy by offering tea or food and asking for personal information are apparently innocent gestures but are with sexual overtones.

As revealed by the above table, it is found that the sexual abuse in the various forms is high in the urban area than in rural area. The girls are facing this problem while travelling in the crowded buses. If the girl is sitting in the aisle seat, the standing passenger even goes to the extent of rubbing his private part to the shoulder of a sitting girl. The same is the case when the girl is standing in the aisle while travelling. The girls complain that they are afraid of travelling as it is very embarrassing for the above said reason. The girls cannot complain to anybody when this kind of behaviour is from an elderly person. City buses are generally crowded and the crowd is an excuse for the mischievous adult. Such incidents make the girls angry, feel insecure and mentally disturbed. They cannot concentrate on their studies in school and college. Parents are reluctant to send the girls to school if they have to travel in a public transport.

Sitting very close is the form of sexual abuse faced by girls in both the areas, if they have to travel to school in private transport such as auto-rickshaw, six-seaters or private minibuses. The girls of tender age, if they are living in villages, have to go to a nearby town daily for their High school and college. Sexual abusers take advantage of this necessity of these girls and travel in these vehicles purposely to harass the girls by sitting close to them, by developing intimacy by various means. Paucity of public transport in rural area forces the girls to use this private transport. They do not even complain to their parents for the fear that they might be asked to discontinue their education.

As many as 47 girls from rural area reported that they have no bad experiences during travels but all the girls from urban area expressed that they have been facing bad experiences during travels. It shows that the exposure of travelling is higher to the girls of urban area than the girls of rural area.

Table 4.13 *Action Taken Against Sexual Abuse During Travel by Victims*

Year 2011

S. No.	*Action*	*Urban* (*Frequency*)	*Rural* (*Frequency*)
1	Opposed	15 (7.38)	21 (8.4)
2	Told to conductor	08 (3.94)	36 (14.4)
3	Told to co-passenger	11 (5.41)	31 (12.4)
4	Kept silent	169 (83.25)	162 (64.8)
	Total	203	250

Source: Primary Data

Table 4.13 shows the action taken by the girl children during travel. The 'keeping mum' option is higher in both the areas; it is found 83.25 per cent in rural area and 64.8 per cent in urban area. The percentage of 'opposed' is very less in both the areas it is 7.38 in rural area and 8.4 in urban area. There is a little difference in the percentage of opposed option in both the areas. It is shocking that even though there is exposure in urban area, the girls from urban areas are also hesitating to oppose the abuse like girls from rural area. This shows that girls from both the areas are treated as secondary due to their sex and secondary status and inferiority make them sit silently by not opposing to their abuse. 'Told to co-passenger' is 12.4 per cent in urban area where as it is 5.41 per cent in rural area. This table proves that even though the girls from both the areas are facing sexual abuse during travel, they are hesitating to oppose the abuser, even telling to conductor and co-passengers. The girl children are shocked when they find even elderly persons behaving in abhorrent manner. Their upbringing has taught them to respect the elders and such incidences are never discussed before others due to fear of defamation. For the sake of family, they are asked to keep mum. They learn to tolerate, thinking that it is an unavoidable evil and cannot be stopped. This makes the girl to keep quiet without opposing or without breaking their silence.

These girls feel that they themselves would be blamed for the trouble they have to face and the girl children are afraid that they would not be allowed to go outside if they disclose the matter and these girls also think that they might have to face more trouble from the abusers if they complain against them.

Table 4.14 shows the reasons for keeping mum about the abuse during travel. Fear about the blame is high among all reasons in both the areas. It is 53.25 per cent in rural area and 49.38 per cent in urban area.

Fear about not allowing to go outside is 24.69 per cent in urban area and 18.38 per cent in rural area. Fear about more trouble is 23.66 per cent in rural area and 21.60 per cent in urban area, the difference is very less. The percentage of fear about blame and fear about more trouble are alarming that how girl children are afraid to oppose the abuse due to the teaching of protecting the dignity of family.

Table 4.14 *Reasons for Keeping Mum About Abuse During Travel*

Year 2011

S. No.	*Reasons*	*Rural Frequency*	*Urban Frequency*
1	Fear about blame	90 (53.25)	80 (49.38)
2	Fear about not allowing to go outside	31 (18.38)	40 (24.69)
3	Fear about more trouble	40 (23.66)	35 (21.60)
4	Any other (became habitual, not use of opposing)	08 (4.73)	07 (4.32)
	Total	169	162

Source: Primary Data

As discussed in Table 4.14, the girls who have to face sexual abuse while travelling to school, etc. are keeping mum and are unwilling to disclose the matter. In fact, their silence only increases the nuisance and emboldens the abusers. Investigation into causes for their keeping quiet about the trouble revealed the disturbing fact that they have to lose much by telling people about the nuisance than by tolerating it. Girls from rural area are well aware of the fact that the first reaction of their parents and guardians would be stopping the girl from going to school also. The tendency is to blame the girl herself. Still the girl is afraid that if she complained, she herself would be accused of improper behaviour and would be scolded for no fault of her.

Even if the girl informs them and complains against the abuser, the parents would not believe their own child and try to keep strict watch on the girl and the girl is not allowed to visit her friends or to go out alone unless it is absolutely necessary. Girls from rural area have to travel long distances for school daily and are afraid that if they protest against the mischief, it would only add to their trouble. Nobody would sympathize with them. On the other hand, they would be laughed at and ridiculed. So they learn to get accustomed to the evil, accept and live with it. This state of affairs speaks a lot about the attitude of society towards girl children even in the 21st century. People are unmindful of their social responsibility towards girl children, their education and their proper upbringing. All these make the girl child keep silent and this results in recurrence of the incident.

In Indian society, family plays a vital role. It is a small social group consisting ordinarily of a father, mother, grandfather, grandmother, and children.[2] Peculiarity of Indian family is the emotional binding of family members and relationships.

Man is a social animal and cannot live alone in society. He is surrounded by a number of people, some of these people are his relatives, some are friends, some are neighbours and some are acquaintances. There are others who are strangers and unknown persons. He is bound to people who are related to him either on the basis of blood or marriage. The bond of blood or marriage which binds people together in a group is called kinship. Every relationship involves a particular type of behaviour.[3] In Indian society, each relationship is role performance, behaviour of a son-daughter towards father is one of love. The behaviour of a brother towards his sister is one of affection. Fathers and brothers are caretakers of family members, especially of girl children in the family. Father is head of the family, he has sole authority over his wife and children. Father and grandfather are loved by the children and children are taught to respect and obey them. These are trustworthy elderly persons in the family and brother is also supposed to be a protector of girl children in the family. There is an emotional binding between and among the family members as they are dependent on each other and feel secure in their home.

Relatives in Indian families constitute an important part. All the relatives like maternal uncle, paternal uncle, sister of mother, sister of father and their children gather at the ceremonies like weddings and even during festivals. These people are close to the family and children enjoy their company not only because they are affectionate but they also act as caretakers.

'Neighbourhood' is a peculiar characteristic of Indian culture. The neighbours are well-wishers and even caretakers. Most of the time they help the neighbourly families, by taking care of children because they are also trusted people. By helping each other they follow the principle of their neighbourhood. Family friends are also very important persons who participate in all activities of the family. All these relationships are valued in Indian culture. Every relationship has its own place in the life of an individual in society.

The tables analysed in this chapter reveal shocking facts that family and all the relationships are fast losing the strength of these values. The girl children are not secure in their own families and are abused by their own family members, known persons and family friends. Abusers constitute the persons who are participating in the socialization of child and who are caretakers and trustworthy person, i.e. father, grandfather, brother, step-brother, step-father, maternal uncle, paternal uncle, male cousin, brother-in-law, family friends, teachers, servants, persons at workplace, known person, etc. These persons are having opportunity to gain the trust and confidence of the child by developing relationship with the child over a period of time. The child knows them and trusts them. These people get authority over the child by close contact and association. Because of a relationship, these people are not suspected of being capable of behaving with the child in an abusive manner and, therefore, are in a position to make pre-planned insidious abuse of a relationship. Majority of the abusers are generally people known to the child.

The places of sexual abuse found in the study are homes, public places and crowded-places, while travelling, market place and functional halls. In a wedding ceremony, festival atmosphere and crowd gives greater opportunity to the abuser to get closer access to the girl and the situation and the environment helps the perpetrator, the abuser. Addiction of father, quarrels between parents, tensed atmosphere in the families are some of the factors that are responsible for girl child sexual abuse. The family is fast losing the values of love, affection, morality and the emotional bonds among the family members are breaking down. The punishment given to the girl child makes her to feel inferior, of low dignity and helpless. Poverty, teenage years and her unfulfilled demands make the girl child an easy prey of the abuser. Instead of giving psychological and emotional support to their child, parents create a tense atmosphere in the family. Such atmosphere makes the girl keep mum and she is scared to share her emotions. In response to all her exploitation, the only sound a sexually abused girl makes is silence, silence for manipulation, ignorance, fear, shame and guilt. While it is the moral obligation of adults and the community as a whole to ensure that children are protected, we remain silent and think that the reputation of the girl and her family is at stake. Silent vulnerable child and a silent non-protective environment are to the advantage of the abuser. Abusers tell the girl child to keep mum, as the best thing is to keep the secret between them.

Indian society is grappling with so many problems and one of the serious problems is that of girl child sexual abuse. Due to gender bias and patriarchy in the society, a male child is preferred to girl child in the family. The girl child is considered as a burden and a liability. Due to a particular type of social upbringing, sexually abused girls do not seek any help from inside and outside the families. Attitude of the family members makes and compels the abused girl child not to respond and to bear, adjust with and suffer in silence. The persons who are responsible for the socialization of child are indulging in sexual abuse of the girl child. Elderly persons in the family, who are being respected by the children due to their age and relationship, are found to have been sexually abusing the girl child from the family.

Above discussion proves that such elderly persons in the family, other family members and close relations have lost their moral values, trust and their role as caretakers and protectors is forgotten. The family is also losing its control on its family members. All this puts a question mark before our society and Indian culture, and also to a common misunderstanding that girl child sexual abuse is normally a 'western' problem and does not happen in India.

Notes

1. Panchal, Trupti (1997), Documentation of Police Cases of Sexually Abused Girls in Mumbai City between 1994–95, The Special Cell for Women and Children.
2. Sachdeva, D.R. and Bhushan, V. (1961), *An Introduction to Sociology,* Kitab Mahal, Allahabad, p. 291.
3. Ibid., p. 347.

5

Consequences of Sexual Abuse on Girl Child

In this chapter the reactions of the victims to the incident of sexual abuse, reactions of various people to whom the girl child tells about the incident and the consequences of such bad experience on the mind of the girl child are discussed.

In this study, it was found that girl child sexual abuse is a serious problem affecting a large number of girl children. Consequences of sexual abuse especially on girl children are far-reaching. Stigma and defamation around the subject make the girl child a silent sufferer. Due to secrecy and taboo, it remains undisclosed and under-reported.

Girl child sexual abuse has been known through ages. In the Indian society, sexual offence against girl children remains one of the most ignored and under-reported crime. Girls are sexually abused in the family as well as outside the family. Offenders are of all ages; they are adolescent youths, young boys, adults, middle-aged persons and even aged persons. They come from all classes, creed and professions. Girl child sexual abuse is horrific because of the psychological harm it causes to the victim. The effect on the mind of the girl child is all the more damaging when the child experiences incest, rape, or indecent behaviour in the family or from persons held by her in high esteem. The apathy and indifference of people near and dear to the girl child in the event of the girl child's sexual abuse alters the emotional world of the child causing irreparable damage to the psyche of the child, having far-reaching consequences on her life and people from her family also.

Hence, the researcher felt it necessary to understand the consequences and reactions of victims and her family members to suggest coping strategies and rehabilitative measures which can help them to come out from the trauma and to feel that sexual abuse is not their fault. The following tables show the consequences and reactions of girl children and their family members to girl child sexual abuse.

Graph 5.1 *Victim's Reactions towards Sexual Abuse*

Year 2011

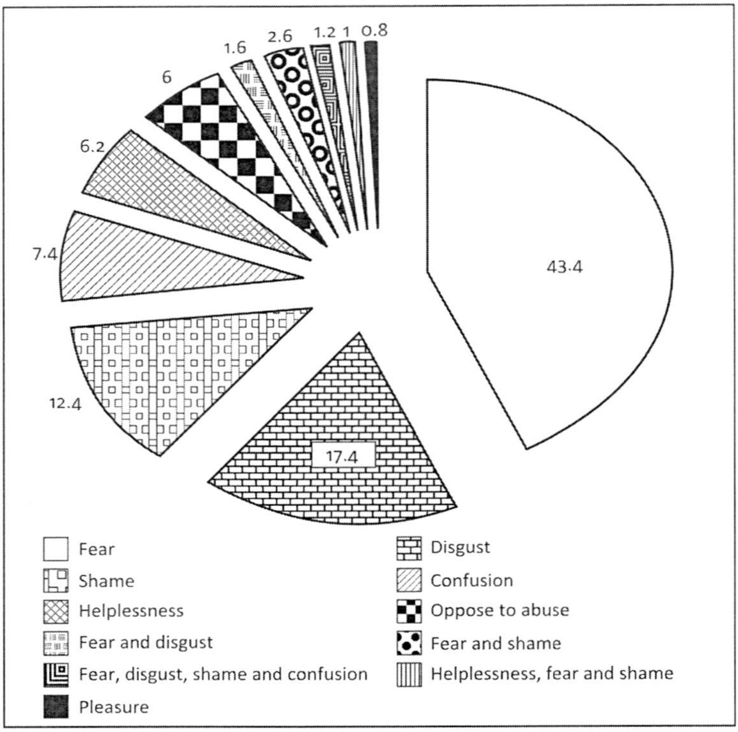

Table 5.1 *Victim's Reactions towards Sexual Abuse*

Year 2011

S. No.	*Reactions of Victims*	*Frequency*	*Percentage*
1	Fear	217	43.4
2	Disgust	87	17.4
3	Shame	62	12.4
4	Confusion	37	7.4
5	Helplessness	31	6.2
6	Oppose to abuse	30	6.0
7	Fear and disgust	08	1.6
8	Fear and shame	13	2.6
9	Fear, disgust, shame and confusion	06	1.2
10	Helplessness, fear and shame	05	1.0
11	Pleasure	04	0.8
	Total	500	100.00

Source: Primary Data

Graph 5.1 and Table 5.1 show the reactions of victims towards sexual abuse. The sexual abuse in childhood is an experience causing trauma. There are many negative reactions to the incident from the child concerned. These are reactions of fear, disgust, shame, helplessness and confusion of all these reactions. The percentage of 'fear' is the highest, i.e. 43.4 per cent, the percentage of feeling of disgust is 17.4 per cent. The percentage of 'shame' is 12.4 per cent, confusion is 7.4 per cent and helplessness is 6.2 per cent. A small number (0.8) of respondents admitted to have experienced a feeling of pleasure as the abuser showered them with gifts and money and met their demands of love and affection that were not fulfilled in the family.

A very little percentage of girls, i.e. 6 per cent, are actively opposing the abuse. The teenage girls do not know the consequences of sexual abuse and many a times they are not aware that they are being abused; as such matters are not spoken in the family due to the stigma attached to the subject. Most of the time, the abuser is a close relative or a known person and, moreover, he is a trusted person. The relationship and the status of the abuser in the family and his role as a caretaker and protector and her teenage does not allow the girl child to raise her voice against him. She does not know what is right and what is wrong, so the percentage of girls who oppose the abuse is very less.

The percentage of 'fear' is the highest among all reactions. The sense of 'fear' is largely due to non-interactive atmosphere in the family and the abuser is generally an elderly respected person in the family. The girls are in fear because the atmosphere in the family is tense due to addiction of the head of the family and frequent quarrels between parents. Parents have no time to interact with their children, and girl children are taught to keep silent and tolerate their exploitation for the sake of dignity of the family. Hence, the girl child is afraid to share her feelings with her parents. The girls are also in awe of the trusted relationship of abuser in the family. The abuser gains trust of family members, so the girl children are not believed by their family when they disclose their sexual abuse. Instead of giving support to her, they blame her, so she keeps silent. The upbringing of a girl child has taught her that it is her duty to protect the dignity of family so she keeps quiet. Due to social stigma attached to the sexual abuse, girl children are fearful of society also.

As the abuser is a family member or a person in close relation, the child is in utter confusion as to the incidence of abuse and is filled with a sense of shame and disgust. The child finds herself helpless and is forced to hide the 'family secret'. Their entire concept of family relationship gets distorted and they face problematic relationships in their future life. In that mental state, the child who has experienced sexual abuse in childhood loses her self-confidence and risks developing a number of psychological problems.

The sexually abused girl child loses her sense of curiosity, her urge to learn skills necessary to navigate social life in the outside world and fails to achieve her full intellectual potential.

Graph 5.2 *Consequences of Sexual Abuse on Victims*

Year 2011

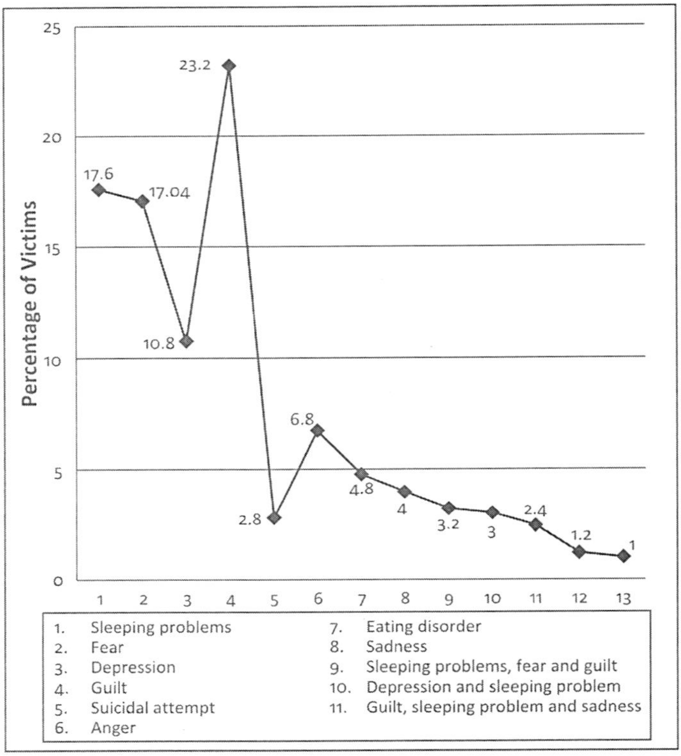

Table 5.2 *Consequences of Sexual Abuse on Victims*

Year 2011

S. No.	*Consequences*	*Frequency*	*Percentage*
1	Sleeping problems	88	17.6
2	Fear	87	17.04
3	Depression	54	10.8
4	Guilt	116	23.2
5	Suicidal attempt	14	2.8
6	Anger	34	6.8
7	Eating disorder	24	4.8
8	Sadness	20	4
9	Sleeping problems, fear and guilt	16	3.2
10	Depression and sleeping problem	15	3
11	Guilt, sleeping problem and sadness	12	2.4
12	Anger and eating disorders	6	1.2
13	Guilt and suicidal attempt	05	1
	Total	491	100.00

Source: Primary Data

Graph 5.2 and Table 5.2 reveal the consequences of sexual abuse on girl children. The consequences are depression (10.8%), guilt complex (23.2%), fear (17.04%), feeling of anger (6.8%), sleeping problems (17.6%) suicidal attempt (2.8%). Of all these consequences, 'guilt complex' is the highest at 23.2 per cent of the victims. Most of the respondents indicated more than one consequence. Feelings of guilt leads to self-pity, depression, anger and fear resulting into sleeping problems, eating disorders and sadness. Suicidal attempts are also noticed in many victims. Even if these children feel angry at the abuser, they are helpless and cannot do much in the matter.

The girl children who are victims of sexual abuse are made to feel that it was their fault and that they are responsible for what has happened or the abuse is something that they have brought upon themselves. This leads to self-loathing.

The feeling of shame and guilt makes it very difficult for the girl child to come forward and tell about the incident to others. They are worried that the people would not believe them and would be angry with them and that the family would be disturbed. For a girl child, sexual contact with an adult, especially a trusted elder, creates trauma which often has a long-lasting effect on the mind of the child.

Table 5.3 *Disclosure about Sexual Abuse by Victims to Other Persons*

Year 2011

S. No.	*Persons*	*Rural 250*	*Urban 250*
		Frequency	*Frequency*
1.	Mother	61 (48.41)	77 (43.01)
2.	Father	08 (6.03)	21 (11.73)
3.	Sister	24 (19.04)	18 (10.05)
4.	Brother	02 (1.58)	12 (6.70)
5.	Friends	09 (7.14)	15 (8.37)
6.	Concerned person (Conductor, Head Master)	04 (3.17)	06 (3.35)
7.	Police	02 (1.58)	08 (4.46)
8.	Parents (Father and Mother)	10 (7.93)	17 (9.49)
9.	Sister and Mother	06 (4.76)	15 (8.37)
	Total	126	179

Note : Figure in parenthesis is percentage.

Source: Primary Data

It is found that many victims suffer from more than one effect of harrowing experience. The tender age of the girl child, lack of understanding of sexual relationship, makes the sexual encounter, howsoever tender it might be, mentally destructive to the child. The fact that the offender appeared harmless is very disturbing aspect of the abuse and leaves a strong legacy of self-blame, guilt and mistrust of close relatives. The child loses self-confidence and cannot live a happy life in future.

Table 5.3 shows the number of people to whom the victims have disclosed their abuse. The highest single category of persons to whom the girl child speaks about her sexual abuse is the mother; 48.4 per cent girls from rural area and 43 per cent from urban area have told to their mother about the sexual abuse experienced by them. Sister is taken in confidence by about 19 per cent girls from rural and 10 per cent girls from urban area. Not more the 6 per cent respondents from rural area and 12 per cent from urban area dared to tell their father about their experience of sexual abuse. That of 'friends' is the other category of people with whom the children find rather free to discuss things regarding sexual abuse they face (7 to 8%).

Highest percentage of girls in both rural and urban area is that of disclosing the matter of abuse to their mother. The mother is close to the girl children in the family even though most of the mothers are busy with their occupation (as breadwinner). The girls preferred mothers for disclosing the matter. Majority of fathers of girl children are addicted and the tense family atmosphere never allowed for an interaction between father and daughter; they are afraid of the father. Rarely is there a dialogue between father and daughters. Hence, the girls disclose the matter to their mothers.

But in a patriarchal Indian family, the male-dominated atmosphere in the house and the authoritative father or grandfather prevents, the mother of the victim from telling others about sexual abuse of her girl child. The mother finds herself powerless and helpless and as a result keeps mum and also asks her child to keep quiet about the ugly incidence. The child is not protected, the offender is not exposed and the abuse in many cases continues. Disclosure to parents, i.e. father, is a little more in urban area, perhaps, because the victim feels that the father would do something to prevent the abuse. There is more interaction between the father and the daughter in urban area compared to rural area. Considering the insidious and manipulative nature of abuse, proximity to the abuser because of a relationship and fear of stigmatization, the abused girl child finds it very difficult to disclose the fact of abuse. The upbringing process of a girl child in a family has only taught her to respect the adults, to never find fault with them and to keep silent and to tolerate their behaviour towards her. The atmosphere in the family is not quite friendly and the child is afraid that she would not be believed. There is possibility of her being blamed and punished for no fault of hers. The high percentage of non-disclosure in rural area is 49.06 and that it is 24.4 per cent in urban area is shocking as it leads to increase and recurrence of abuse which the girl children have to bear without raising their voice against their exploitation in the society.

Graph 5.4 *Reactions of Parents about Sexual Abuse of Girl Child*

Year 2011

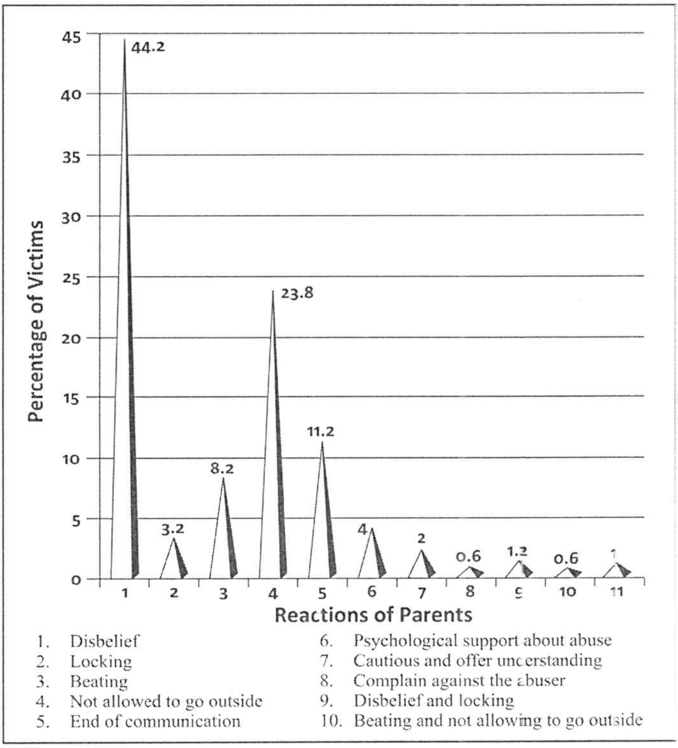

Table 5.4 *Reactions of Parents about Sexual Abuse of Girl Child*

Year 2011

S. No.	*Reactions of Parents*	*Frequency*	*Percentage*
1	Disbelief	221	44.2
2	Locking	16	3.2
3	Beating	41	8.2
4	Not allowed to go outside	119	23.8
5	End of communication	56	11.2
6	Psychological support about abuse	20	4
7	Cautious and offer understanding	10	2
8	Complain against the abuser	3	0.6
9	Disbelief and locking	06	1.2
10	Beating and not allowing to go outside	03	0.6
11	Disbelief and end of communication	05	1
	Total	500	100 00

Source: Primary Data

It is important to know the need of children to be provided with age-appropriate information so that they can take care and participate in their protection from sexual abuse. They should also be made aware of their rights so that they will know to whom and where to approach for help. They should feel confident to break the silence, bring the incidence to the notice of the people concerned and expose the culprits to be held guilty and punished appropriately.

Graph 5.4 and Table 5.4 show the reactions of parents about sexual abuse of their girl child. The percentage of 'disbelief' is the highest, i.e. 44.2 per cent, the percentage of 'not allowed to go outside' is 23.8 per cent. 'Complain against abuser' is very less, it is 0.6 per cent.

The data shows that parents in such a situation reveal the negative attitude of looking at the phenomenon. The first reaction of the parents is to disbelieve their own child and even if it is found that the child is telling the truth, the tendency is to hold the child, who is a victim, guilty and blame her for her misfortune. They go even to the extreme of punishing her though she is not at all at fault and it is their negligence and ignorance of warning signs that had made the child undergo the shame and humiliation of sexual abuse.

Not believing the girl child is the most common reaction. The parents think that it is simply not possible that the girl child is sexually abused and that too by a person named by her. Many parents believe that the sexual abuse of children is generally found in society under western influences and culture and just not probable in Indian society. But at the same time these parents live under fear that their girl children are always in danger of sexual assault and are careful enough to keep them under watchful eye. In rural area, the girls are rarely allowed to go out alone, they're going to school is not thought necessary, and to give away the daughter in marriage is the priority. Child marriages are not uncommon and an adolescent girl is considered always a burden on and a cause of anxiety to the parents.

Lack of acceptance of sexual abuse of girl children by her family members, not believing the girl child when she speaks about the incidence, believing the abuser and blaming the girl for what happened and not disclosing the matter results in low percentage of complaints against the abuser and allows the recurrence of the abuse.

The girl is discouraged from speaking about the incidence of abuse for fear of defamation and disrepute. The girl feels helpless and powerless to teach a lesson to the offender. The abuser cherishes a feeling of immunity and the abuse continues to the utter disgust and torture of the victim.

The community structure and traditional conservative family system do not allow the members even to speak about sex and sexuality at all, let alone making the growing children aware of the lurking danger in their life. There is a conspiracy of silence and the behavioural and psychological changes in the victim are ignored. The girl child feels insecure in her own family and lives under constant fear of being blamed and punished for her plight.

Not allowing the girl to continue her education, not allowing her to mix with other girls of her own age, preventing her from participating in outdoor games and discouraging her from going for shopping, etc. are the means adopted to save the girl child from prospective abusers. This results into the stunted growth of the personality of the girl. She loses her self-confidence and may not mature into a healthy and happy human being.

The unfortunate girl child is confused as to what is right and what is wrong and this confusion pervades in all aspects of her development. She isolates herself from company of others, does not share her sorrows, grief or joys with others and learns to adjust with the situation as her fate.

There is a need to enlighten the parents, guardians and caretakers of girl children about the strategies to cope with the situation and to adopt proper rehabilitative measures in dealing with these sexually abused girls.

Table 5.5 *Reactions of Outsiders about Sexual Abuse of Girl Child*

Year 2011

S. No.	*Reactions of outsiders*	*Frequency*	*Percentage*
1	Sympathy	51	10.2
2	Told to oppose	23	4.6
3	To be cautious	15	3
4	Dismissal	52	10.4
5	Told to neglect	91	18.2
6	Denial	39	7.8
7	Disbelief	229	45.08
	Total	500	100.00

Source: Primary Data

Graph 5.5 and Table 5.5 show the reactions of the outsiders (other than family members, relatives and family friends) to the incidence of sexual abuse of a girl in their knowledge.

In this table disbelief is the highest, i.e. 45.08 per cent, followed by 'told to neglect' the incident at 18.2 per cent, and then dismissal at 10.4 per cent and denial at 7.8 per cent, while 10.2 per cent people showed sympathy towards the victims.

The attitude of persons in the above category is not to accept that such incident has taken place. Though the people know that no girl would speak

Graph 5.5 *Reactions of Outsiders about Sexual Abuse of Girl Child*

Year 2011

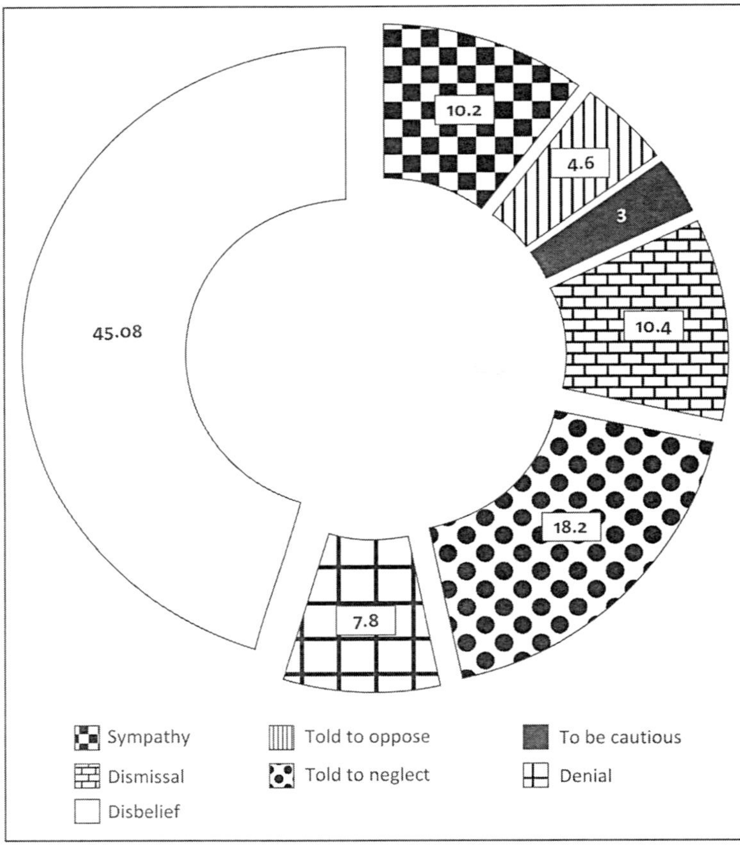

about it unless it is absolutely true, these people derive satisfaction from telling themselves that the girl might be lying and not telling the whole truth. They feel safe by making themselves believe that such incidences normally do not happen in their society and they and their own children are safe. At the same time these people are afraid that their feeling of safety is unfounded and they show sympathy and pity for the unfortunate girl child. They just advice the girl and her parents to neglect as they know that had they been in the position of parents of the girl, they would have found themselves helpless and in a dilemma. The fear of defamation and the stigma attached to the issue make them to keep quiet.

Such incidences bring a bad name to the girl child who already is suffering. Some show courage and ask the parents to oppose and complain against the abuser, knowing full well that they would not have done any such thing had they been the victim of such a nasty episode. On the one hand, they dismiss the incidence as a lie, but at the same time they advice the girl and her parents to be cautious in future. It is found that some people come forward and give moral support to the girl and her family to overcome the grief. At the same time, many people are indifferent to the suffering of the family. Sometimes they also blame the girl and family and find faults with their lifestyle. These peoples' sincerity is put to test and the girl and her parents are disappointed when they find no support of any kind is being given by the society when they are in need of it. The insensitivity of the members of surrounding society adds insult to injury, as far as the unfortunate family is concerned. The girl and her family's belief in keeping quiet and to suffer in silence only strengthens aggravating the problem of sexual abuse of girl children in the society. They find to their horror that they have not gained anything from the disclosure, but have lost much. The family had faced damage to its reputation creating problems for the future of the girl. This attitude of indifference on the part of the people is badly needed to be corrected for avoiding and curtailing the disease of sexual abuse of girl children from society.

Table 5.6 *Consequences of Sexual Abuse on Family of the Victims*

Year 2011

S. No.	*Consequences on Victims Family*	*Rural 250*		*Urban 250*	
		Frequency	*Percentage*	*Frequency*	*Percentage*
1	Quarrel between parents	51	20.4	41	16.4
2	Tension in the family	55	22	44	17.6
3	Parents become sick	07	2.8	03	1.2
4	Raised doubt in parent's mind	31	12.4	26	10.4
5	Opposed to send to school	21	8.4	16	6.4
6	Oppose to go outside	31	12.4	20	10.8
7	In company of somebody while going outside	31	12.4	40	16
8	Quarrel between parents and tension in the family	10	4	31	12.4
9	Tension in the family and raised doubt in the minds of parents	06	2.4	15	6
10	Opposed to send to school or outside	05	2	05	2
11	Any other	03	0.8	09	3.6
	Total	250	100	250	100

Source: Primary Data

Table 5.6 throws light on the consequences of sexual abuse on girl child on the immediate family of the child. Among all consequences the percentage of 'tension in the family' is higher in both the areas. It is 22 per cent in rural area and 17.6 per cent in urban area. 'Quarrel between the parent's is in second higher percentage in both the areas, i.e. 20.4 per cent in rural area and 16.4 per cent in urban area. Lowest percentage is 'parent becomes sick' in both areas, it is 2.8 per cent in rural area and 1.2 in urban area. 'Any other' option's percentage is 3.6 in urban area and it is 0.8 per cent in rural area. 'Depression, stress was found in parents', some of the 'mothers become silent', 'ill-treatment was given to other girl children in the family', all these are included in 'any other' option. This shows the severity of the problem as above-mentioned consequences are seen among the parents.

The family which has experienced girl child sexual abuse finds itself in an unenviable situation. The atmosphere in the family is no friendlier. The peace in the family is lost. Members of the family live in a tensed atmosphere and suffer anxiety about the future of the girl. They feel that the girl is spoiled and they are ruined. Parents blame each other for neglecting the child. Mother is accused of pampering the children. They frequently quarrel on small matters. They doubt their own capacity to raise their children. They are angry at themselves and also at other innocent siblings and deprive them of love and affection that is necessary for their proper upbringing. They do not allow the unfortunate girl to go outside even for genuine reasons. In some cases, the girl is asked to discontinue her education and she is not allowed to meet friends. She cannot even think of outdoor games and entertainment. If she is sent outside, she is to be accompanied by any family member like brother, grandfather grandmother or any other near relative.

The above numerated consequences show that the family fails to come to terms with the sad incident. Life in the family is seldom the same as before. Sexual abuse of the child makes them depressed, avoid people, and on the whole the family is unable to cope with the problem. They feel that their reputation in the society has suffered an irreparable damage and the future of their girl has been forever ruined.

Being unable to overcome grief, they suffer from depression, anxiety disorder or some other psychological problems. They become sick and fail to give support to their dear, unfortunate girl to win over her suffering.

A girl child who is victim of sexual abuse first tells her mother about the incident. The mother for various reasons keeps quiet and asks the unfortunate girl child also not to speak about the incident with anybody. Mother is afraid that even the father of the girl would not show any sympathy for his daughter. On the other hand, there is every possibility that the girl would be held responsible for what had happened and she would be made to feel she had brought it upon herself. Elder brother also blames the girl and tries to put more restrictions on her movements when he learns about the repulsive incident. The general tendency is either to disbelieve the complaining girl or to ignore her grievance. An elder sister or a girlfriend also expresses helplessness though she is sympathetic to her. In such situation, the girl finds it difficult to come forward and protest against the abuse. People around her think that the reputation of the family and the future of the girl would be ruined if the incident is known by one and all. This thinking also prevents them from taking any action against the abuser. So the girl keeps quiet or is made to keep mum. Enforced secrecy and fear of losing the security of the family are powerful obstacles in the way of disclosure. This peculiar dilemma makes the crime of girl child sexual abuse difficult to be checked and controlled. Non-disclosure only results into increase and recurrence of this evil in the society.

In her tender age, the girl child believes in the goodness of family relationship. She reposes her trust, love and attraction in the family members around her. She looks upon the elders in the family with respect and thinks of them as her caretakers and protectors. When an outsider sexually abuses the girl child, she turns to the family for support even though she rarely gets it, but if the abuser happens to be a close relative, she is all the more shocked to find that the person who is supposed to love her and protect her is also the person who hurts her. She is confused about the values of relationship and a feeling of disgust, hostility and depression fills her mind. She is inclined to dissociate herself from the company of family members resulting into stunted growth of her personality. The horrible experience affects her emotionally and psychologically influencing her future decisions and choices. Consequences of sexual abuse in the childhood are far-reaching. She is tormented by shame and guilt and loses her inquisitiveness and fails to realize her full potential in life and, therefore, might not mature into a healthy citizen contributing to the well-being of the society. The girl child who is the victim of sexual abuse suffers from low self-esteem, poor social functioning, and inability to trust, isolation and trauma. The impact of sexual abuse in childhood is in psychological, behavioural and also societal terms. It leads to poor concentration in studies resulting in low academic achievements. It affects her ability to develop trust and intimate relationship with peers and adults if an elderly family member is involved in the abuse.

The consequences found in this study are: these girl children frequently experience feelings of shame, guilt, isolation, powerlessness, embarrassment, and inadequacy. They blame themselves by accepting the responsibility for the abuse and think that something is wrong with them or the abuse is their fault. Sometimes they are reluctant to answer and they are not disclosing the abuse because of fear that disclosure will bring about consequences even worse than being victimized, and because these girl children face irreparable loss and long-term effects as an abused girl child. Early pregnancy and injury to reproductive organs are physical harms. Self-blaming, self-destructive behaviour, anxiety, depression, feeling of isolation are serious psychological problems; also stigma, substance abuse, recurrence of the incident, make her to think that being a girl child is a 'curse'.

The consequences of girl child sexual abuse from the family also affect the life of people who love her. Their mental peace and equilibrium is disturbed and they are also tormented by feeling of hurt and helplessness. Social stigma attached to the victim and the fear of being maligned forces the victim and her parents to keep silent and they find it is very difficult to disclose the fact of sexual abuse of the girl child from the family. In order to expose the offender before the society and to have him held guilty and punished, it is necessary that the victim and her family members break the silence and bring the incidence to the knowledge of concerned people, so that the victim can get strength to disclose the matter and can get timely help.

The silent rage takes a toll on their physical health and mental poise. Their behaviour with other family members and people outside is no more cordial and affectionate. The fabric of social relations is torn and their life is no more the same as it was before the sad incident in their beloved child's life. The attitude of society is not reassuring and instead of adopting strategies to rehabilitate the psychologically disturbed victim and her family, tolerance is preached as virtue. Girl child sexual abuse is a harsh reality of life and this disease of the society cannot be curtailed unless the point of view of the society is changed.

6

Rehabilitation of Victims of Sexual Abuse

This chapter deals with the rehabilitation programmes for victims of sexual abuse by the government and the NGOs. Girl child sexual abuse is still considered as the issue of secrecy. In India, it is exclusively undisclosed and under-reported due to number of factors which make the victim keep quiet with a feeling of shame, guilt, isolation, powerlessness and helplessness. The victims feel that they are responsible for the abuse and such feeling makes them highly vulnerable to further sexual abuse within and outside the family.

The children who are victims of abuse may show a number of physical, emotional and behavioural changes. They may be withdrawn or unusually aggressive. They may refuse to attend school or have difficulty in concentrating so that their school work is affected. They show unexpected fear, disgust, guilt, anxiety, anger about particular adult, or they refuse to continue with their usual social activities.

Sexually abused girl children suffer from psychological symptoms and risk of harm is greater if the abuser is a relative and the abuse involves intercourse or attempted intercourse, or if threat or force is used. The level of harm may also be aggravated because of various factors such as penetration, duration and frequency of abuse. Abuser may act alone or as part of an organized group. After the abuse, they put the child under great pressure not to tell anyone about it. They also go to great lengths to get close to girl children and to gain their trust. The child may speak about receiving special attention from a particular adult, or refer to a new 'secret' friendship with an adult or a young person.

Rehabilitation is a process of making the victim physically, mentally, emotionally, socially, educationally and economically empowered. This process also includes the treatment plans that include protecting the child by stopping abuse, providing support during the resulting crises and being handled carefully to avoid magnifying children's negative definitions of situations and help them to regain their confidence of 'self'.

A successful rehabilitative programme is one which includes an effective prevention programme because the dynamics of girl child sexual abuse is complex, so intervention strategies need to be well planned and carried out with appropriate skills. Rehabilitation is a process which involves several tasks, planning and it also aims to reach out to all the victims who disclosed the matter and even to those girls who failed to disclose the occurrence because of fear that disclosure will bring consequences even worse than being victimized again. This results in recurrence.

Keeping child in such a condition means giving her punishment for not doing any mistake. In this concern, rehabilitation of victims of sexual abuse is very essential. So it is the duty of the guardian to make the child feel better and give her the strength to regain her confidence. One should help the child to shed her shame and guilt by telling the child that it is the abuser's fault and not that of the child. It will help the child to respect herself and live as a normal human being.

So, it is very important that anyone who gives birth to a child has to take the full care of her. It's not only important to feed and bathe a child, it's also important to discipline her. A girl child is neglected in our families. She should be brought up with love and affection equal to what is given to a male child in the families so that she can gain confidence and dignity of a human being.

The girl children who are victims of sexual abuse are facing irreparable loss due to their sex. Sometimes sexual abuse results in early pregnancy and injury to her reproductive organs after incident of abuse. The whole life of the girl child becomes aimless; her future is dark due to defamation. Pregnancy from rape is a mental agony and could impact her mental health. There is no social status to such girls in our society. Upbringing of girl child teaches her to keep quiet without asking questions of elders and is made to feel that she should bear the responsibility of protecting the dignity of family and its honour. Such teaching makes her to remain silent. The notion of shame and defamation are the largest culprits in keeping the girl silent about sexual abuse in our country. Moreover, girl children in Indian families find that adults often exercise a natural hold over their children, demanding complete and unquestioned obedience and the girls are taught that by obeying elders they are protecting the dignity of family. Boys are not compelled to do such things, but girls in Indian families are discriminated against in this respect.

Sexual abuse has in it a pronounced psychological and emotional element and such abuse negatively impacts girl child's physical, emotional and mental well-being, leading to severe behavioural and psychiatric disorders and the girl child may even attempt suicide because she, who is a victim of sexual abuse, rarely finds any support from the family and society. Instead, she is blamed and she is made to think that it is her fault and there is a fear of victimization. The abuse of girl child is highly stigmatized in Indian society. Due to the male dominated patriarchal nature of Indian society, and abuse usually being associated with loss of virginity and with notions of family honour or dignity, abused girls are often disbelieved or blamed for their abuse. Sex and sexuality are taboos in Indian society. More so for girls than boys, all these factors are hindrances in disclosure of the incident by girl victim. The irreparable loss suffered by the girl child is the worst consequence of sexual abuse. Timely rehabilitation is very important to come out of the trauma. Proper rehabilitation can minimize the occurrence of sexual abuse and it will also help to control and prevent the problem, whereas improper rehabilitation gives way to recurrence of the incident. So, proper and specific rehabilitation of victim is badly needed.

The governments and many NGOs at national and international levels are working through their own rehabilitative programmes for sexually abused girls to overcome this problem and help the abused children to live happily which is their right as human beings.

Rehabilitative Programmes at International Level

In Western countries, the issue of child sexual abuse came to the forefront in 1970. Before that, the issue was considered as a secret but later the issue came to be regarded as a serious crime against children. So government and NGOs have done a lot and still are working with enthusiasm to prevent the problem and for the healing of victims.

USA

Today, the United States has more children living in poverty than any other industrialized nation. More than a quarter of all children grow up in poverty. The poverty rates for African American and Latin American children exceed 40 per cent. Furthermore, the United States, a country which once pioneered strategies to prevent child abuse and which now spends more money fighting the child abuse than any other industrialized country, has the highest rate of child abuse in the industrialized world.

By 1968, 44 out of 50 US states had enacted mandatory laws that required physicians to report cases of suspicious child abuse. Legal action became more prevalent in the 1970s with enactment of The Child Abuse Prevention and Treatment Act in 1974 in conjunction with the creation of the National Centre for Child Abuse and Neglect. Since the creation of The Child Abuse and Treatment Act, reported child abuse cases have increased dramatically. Finally, the national abuse coalition was created in 1979 to create pressure in Congress to create more prevention of sexual abuse laws.

In 1986, Congress passed the Child Abuse Victims Rights Act, giving children a civil claim in sexual abuse cases. The number of laws created in the 1980s and 1990s began to result into greater prosecution and detection of child sexual abusers. During 1970s, a large transition began in the legislature related to child sexual abuse. Megan's Law which was enacted in 2004, gives the public access to knowledge of sex offenders nationwide.

Anne Hastings described these changes in attitude towards child sexual abuse as the beginning of one of history's largest social revolution.

United Kingdom

The United Kingdom has a comprehensive child welfare system according to which local authorities have duties and responsibilities towards children in need, in their area. This covers provisions for advice and services, accommodation and care of children who are uncared for, and also the capacity to initiate proceedings. The criterion for the latter is 'significant harm' which covers physical, sexual and emotional abuse and neglect. In appropriate cases, the Care Plan before the court will be of adoption.

The role of Independent Visitor, a voluntary post, created in the United Kingdom under the 1989 Children Act is to befriend and assist children that need care.[1]

In England, Wales and Scotland, despite the Children Act, there never has been a statutory obligation to report alleged child abuse to the police. Northern Ireland was the exception to this legislative omission. In 2007, the Department for Children, Schools and Families created the Local Authority Designated Officer (LADO) to whom alleged abuse should be reported. The appointee is designated to act as an independent set of eyes and ears to assess the situation prior to contacting any other Agency. However, there is no statutory obligation to report alleged abuse to this officer, and no sanction on any setting or organization for failing to report.[2]

Child sexual abuse is outlawed nearly everywhere in the world, generally with severe penalties, including in some cases, life imprisonment or even capital punishment. An adult's sexual intercourse with a child not capable of consent is defined as 'rape', based on the principle that a child is not capable of consent and that any apparent consent by a child is not considered to be a legal consent.

Interpol: The International Criminal Police Organization in 1971 was recognized as an international governmental organization. It acts as an information exchange and a liaison body between police forces of different countries.

ILO: International Labour Organization has sponsored some studies and conferences on child labour and child protection.

Child Protection and Rights

The International Convention on the Rights of the Child (1989)

The convention calls to protect children from all forms of sexual exploitation and abuse, including exploitative use in prostitution and pornography (Article 34).

The optional protocol to the convention on the rights of the child, on the sale of children, child prostitution and child pornography (2000) further refines the UN CRC provisions. It insists on the criminalization of child prostitution and pornography (Article 3.1)

The International Labour Organization's Convention 182 (1999) defines sexual exploitation as one of the worst forms of child labour.

The Convention on the Elimination of all Forms of Discrimination against Women (CEDAW), (1979)

The countries that have ratified this convention are legally bound to take appropriate measures against the commercial sexual exploitation of women and applies also consequently to the girl child.

The South Asian Association for Regional Cooperation (SAARC) Convention on Prevention and Combating the Trafficking in Women and Children for Prostitution

The convention aims at promoting cooperation amongst member states to effectively deal with various aspects of prevention, prohibition and suppression of trafficking of girl and children, repatriation and rehabilitation of victims of trafficking and preventing the use of girl and boy children in international prostitution network, particularly where the South Asian Association for Regional Cooperation (SAARC) member countries are the countries of origin, transit and destination.

International Law

The United Nations Convention on the Rights of the Child (CRC) is an International Treaty that legally obliges states to protect children's rights. Article 34 and 35 of the CRC require states to protect children from all forms of sexual exploitation and sexual abuse. This includes outlawing the coercion of a child to perform sexual activity, the prostitution of children and the exploitation of children in creating pornography. States are also required to prevent the abduction, sale or trafficking of children. As of November 2008, 193 countries are bound by the CRC including every member of the United Nations except the United States and Somalia. India has acceded to the convention on 11 December 1992, and accordingly a Bill was passes in Parliament of India in 2012.

Role of NGOs in Healing and in Prevention of Child Sexual Abuse at International Level

In the early 21st century, the issue of girl child sexual abuse was considered a serious crime which cast a lifelong shadow on girl child and became a hindrance in her development. So a number of voluntary organizations in the world considering the severity of the problem started work for the rehabilitation of victims and prevention of child sexual abuse.

Child Help, USA's National Child Abuse Hotline 1-800-422 -4453 (1-800-4 A child)

Child Help USA is a nonprofit organization dedicated to meeting the physical, emotional, educational and spiritual needs of the abused and neglected children. Its programmes and services include this hotline, which children can call with complete anonymity and confidentiality.

Rape Abuse and Incest National Network (RAINN) 1-800-656-4673 (HOPE)

Rape Abuse and Incest National Network (RAINN) has a 24-hour National Sexual Assault Online Hotline (Chat), staffed with trained volunteers and paid staff members who also have knowledge of sexual abuse issues and services. All calls are confidential and callers may remain anonymous if they wish.

National Domestic Violence/Abuse Hotline
1-800-799-SAFE
1-800-799-7233
1-800-787-3224 TDD

This is a 24-hour hotline, staffed by trained volunteers who are ready to connect people during emergency, help in their own communities, including emergency services and shelters. The staff also provides information and referrals for a variety of non-emergency services, including counsellor for adults and children and assistance in reporting abuse.

Child Line (UK)
0800 1111

Child Line is the free helpline for children and young people in the UK. Children and young people can call on No. 0801111 to talk about any problem to get help from counsellor.

CARI

An NGO provides a professional child-centred therapy and counselling services to children and families that have been affected by child sexual abuse. It provides services in Ireland.

CPHCSA

Centre for Prevention and Healing of Child Sexual Abuse is working in Philippines, Malaysia, and Vietnam.

ISPCAN

'International Society for Prevention of Child Abuse And Neglect', Denmark, details child protection activities. Founded in 1977 by international pioneer and visionary, Dr C. Henry Kempe, ISPCAN works to prevent cruelty to children in every nation, in every form, physical abuse, sexual abuse, neglect, child fatalities, child prostitution, emotional abuse, children of war, child labour and street children.

As the premier international network of child protection professional ISPCAN has expanded its work tirelessly to make an impact worldwide. Participating in crafting the UN's general comment is on Article 19 of the convention of the rights of the child, working with partners to develop the ground breaking ISPCAN child abuse screening tools translated into several languages, impacting the work of practitioners and policy-makers in over 175 countries, with multidisciplinary teams trained in well over 30 countries with emerging economics, is ISPCAN's mission to support individuals and organizations working to protect children from abuse and neglect worldwide.[3]

ECPAT

End Child Prostitution and Trafficking, an agency in France/Germany, is working for prevention of child trafficking with an offshoot against child sexual abuse.

Stop-it-Now

'Stop-it-now' in UK and Ireland is a major national and local campaign that aims to stop child sexual abuse by encouraging abusers and potential abusers to seek help and by giving adults the information they need to protect children effectively. It tries to prevent the sexual abuse of children by mobilizing adults, families and communities to take action that can protect children before they are harmed.

Vision

Encourages adults to be respectful, show caring behaviour towards children and help other adults to create safe, stable and nurturing relationships for all children. Children grow up free of trauma from any form of violence, including sexual abuse and exploitation.

Guiding Principles

Children have right to safety and well-being. Children have right to freedom from sexual harm. Public health framework programmes are developed that view child sexual abuse as a preventable social problem.

Focus on Adults and Communities

Programmes focus on adults and communities, challenging them to take responsibility for preventing the preparation of sexual abuse of children.

Balance Accountability with Understanding

'Stop-it-now' NGO, in its work with those who have been sexually abused, now supports media approaches, programmes and public policies that effectively balance accountability for the crime with an understanding of the need for treatment to prevent further sexual abuse.

A centralized telephone helpline supports the local projects and offers confidential advice and support to adults who suspect that someone they know, presents a risk to a child and to those seeking help to stop their own abusive thoughts and behaviour. 'Stop-it-now' is also working with politicians and policy-makers at national level to promote a wider understanding of child sexual abuse as a preventable public health issue and to increase the services available to the victims and survivors of abuse and to abusers.

EMDR Institute

Eye Movement Desensitization and Reprocessing (EMDR) has proved to be an effective and efficient treatment for Post-Traumatic Stress Disorder (PTSD), which is an effect of child abuse. It can be particularly helpful in transforming intrusive and upsetting memories of abuse, does not require one to talk about what happened in detail in recent years. The therapists have learned how to use EMDR with children, the EMDR Institute provides referrals to EMDR trained therapists around the country and around the world.

Faith Trust Institute

Faith Trust Institute is an international, multi-faith organization working to end sexual and domestic violence. Faith Trust Institute works with many communities, including Asian and Pacific Islander, Buddhist, Jewish, Latin, Muslim, Black, and Indigenous, Protestants, Roman Catholic. Thus, these western NGOs are working for the problem of child sexual abuse.

Rehabilitative Programmes by Government of India

Girl child sexual abuse is really a horrible face of Indian society and a problem for the human growth and creativity. Despite its ethos of non-violence, tolerance, spirituality, India hosts the world's largest number of sexually abused children, at a far higher rate than any other country. According to the World Health Organization (WHO), one in every four girls and one in every seven boys in the world are sexually abused. So government of India is trying to overcome this problem in the following way.

The Indian Penal Code considers certain acts like kidnapping or maiming the child for the purposes of begging (Section 363-A) and exposure and abandonment of child under 12 years by parents or persons having care of the child (Section 317) as serious offences, the children Acts in particular, have provisions for punishment for cruelty to children. There are provisions for care, protection and rehabilitation of the neglected and abused children. The new Juvenile Justice Act 2000, considers it necessary to provide protection and care for children who are likely to be explcited and abused. Provision of child protection will be a key intervention in the Eleventh Five-Year Plan. 'Child protection' refers to protection from violence, exploitation, abuse and neglect.

There are a considerable number of central and state laws which have direct or indirect bearing on different aspects of child abuse like exploitation, cruelty and neglect. Every child has a right to protection, even if he/she is not in difficult circumstances. The Eleventh Five-Year Plan intervention for child protection takes both a preventive and a protective approach. In the Eleventh Plan, Child Line 1098 will be extended to rural areas and to all districts of the country.

With the recent reported cases of child sexual abuse and incest, we have focused on what is an unfortunate reality. Child sexual abuse (CSA) and incest are widely prevalent in India cutting across gender, class, caste, cultures, religions, occupational and economic backgrounds.

The Legal Protection to the Victims of Sexual Abuse by Indian Government

According to the Convention on the Rights of the Child, Article 1 defines 'the child' as 'every human being below the age of 18 years, unless under the law applicable to the child, majority is attained earlier'.

There are very few Sections under the Indian Penal Code that deal with child sexual abuse. Some terrible home truths are:

- The laws for women are extended to include children.
- The major weakness of these laws is that only penile penetration is considered a grave sexual offence. The crime is considered lesser when it is oral, or through penetration with an object.
- Although Section 377, dealing with unnatural offences, prescribes seven to 10 years of imprisonment, such cases are tried in a magistrate's court, which can impose maximum punishment of only three years.
- If the abuse is repeated several times, it affects children more severely; however, as yet there is no law for repeated offenses against the one child.

How do we apply Section 354, on outraging the modesty of girl, with respect to children? How do we define modesty? These are some of the intriguing questions inadequately answered by the Penal Code.

The gravity of the offence under Section 509, dealing with obscene gestures, is less, though even in such cases, the child's psyche may be affected as severely as in a rape.

With the aid of public interest lawyers across the country, Maharukh Adenwala, a senior lawyer practising in child protection laws in the High Court, has initiated the National Campaign on Law for Child Sexual Abuse. This group will help draft a new law and circulate it among child rights groups. Once the legal work is complete, Maharukh will take the draft to a standing committee within the Parliament to gain support for the new law. In addition to a book she has written on Child Sexual Abuse and Law, Maharukh is working with other lawyers on a white paper on child sexual abuse that will serve as the starting point of her work countrywide.

(The Protection of Children from Sexual Offences Bill, 2012 has been recently passed by the Parliament)

National Framework

The law in India only recognizes certain kinds of sexual abuse as an offence. The forms of child sexual abuse recognized by the Indian Penal Code are: outraging the modesty of a woman or a girl (Section 354), rape, which (Section 376) is defined in the IPC as an act when a man has sexual intercourse with a woman against her will or without her consent and with or without her consent if she is under 16 years of age, or when she is his wife and is under 15 years of age, sodomy or unnatural offences (Section 377).

The maximum punishment for rape is 7 years of imprisonment but when the girl is under 12 or where the rapist is a person in authority (from a hospital, children's home, a police station, etc.), the punishment is greater.

The Immoral Traffic (Prevention) Act, 1956

This Act covers both the sexes exploited sexually for commercial purposes and provides enhanced penalties for offences involving children and minors.

Section 3: Stringent action and punishment for keeping a brothel or allowing premises to be used as a brothel.

Section 4: Living on the earnings of prostitution.

Section 5: Procuring, inducing or taking a person for the sake of prostitution.

Section 67: If any person is found with a child in a brothel it shall be presumed, unless the contrary is proved, that he has committed an offence of detaining a person in premises where prostitution is carried on.

Section 6 (1B): The punishment consists of imprisonment of either description for a term which shall not be less than 7 years, but which may be for life or for a term, which may extend to 10 years and shall also be liable to fine, with a provision for less than 7 years under special circumstances.

Section 6 (2A): A girl child or minor found in a brothel, on medical examination, detected to have been sexually abused, it shall be presumed, unless the contrary is proved, that the child or minor has been detained for purposes of prostitution or as the case may be, has been sexually exploited for commercial purposes,

Section 21: Establishment of protective homes by the state government.

The Section 23 of the Juvenile Justice Act 2000, deals with child abuse. The Section provides for punishment (imprisonment up to six months) for cruelty to child if a person having the charge of or control over a child causes or procures him/her to be assaulted, or exposed in any manner likely to cause such child unnecessary mental or physical suffering (The Goa Children's Act, 2003).

The Protection of Children from Sexual Offences Bill, 2012

The Protection of Children from Sexual Offences Bill, 2012 has been passed by the Parliament. This Act is made to strengthen the legal provision for the protection of children from sexual abuse and exploitation. At present sexual offences are covered under different Sections of Indian Penal Code (IPC). However, the penal code did not treat a child who is a victim of sexual abuse as a class by itself and did not differentiate between adult and child victim. The Act seeks to protect children from sexual offences and, therefore, provides for harsh punishment for various types of sexual abuse of children and is gender neutral.

The term 'sexual offence' has been defined as a sex made with a person below 18 years, as an offence. Sex with minor (below 18 years) is 'rape' as per this new law. Burden of proof is shifted to the accused in cases of sexual assault, aggravated sexual assault, penetrative sexual assault and aggravated penetrative sexual assault keeping in view the innocence and vulnerability of the child. The Act provides for the establishment of special court to try the offences of sexual abuse of children, and child's right to privacy and confidentiality is tried to be respected and protected during the judicial process in the trial of the accused of sexual offence in respect of a child. Various forms of sexual abuse of children, other than penetrative sexual abuse, are being covered in the Act under definition of sexual abuse and exploitation such as, inducement and coercion of a child in any unlawful sexual activity, the exploitative use of a child in prostitution or other unlawful sexual practices and, remarkably, the exploitative use of child in a pornographic material and performances. The definition of penetrative sexual assault is wide and expansive. Penetration of sex organ to any extent is an offence. Oral sex is also covered by this definition. The definition is vague when it says that manipulation of 'any part of the body' so as to cause penetration into any part of the body is a penetrative sexual assault.

Sexual assault by a person of the armed forces or police personnel, by a person being on the management or staff of place of custody, care or protection of children; hospital; an educational institution; a public servant; staff of a jail, etc. is an aggravated sexual assault. So the persons who are on the management of remand home, protection home or observation home and commit a sexual assault of the inmate child, it will be treated as aggravated assault, inviting heavy punishment of not less than 10 years rigorous imprisonment. Use of weapon, fire, heated substance or corrosive substance while sexually assaulting the child is also an aggravated sexual assault. Touching body part with sexual intent which involves physical contact without penetration is also a sexual assault as defined in the Act. Sexual intent is a question of fact.

As per Section 11 of the Act, 'sexual harassment' is an offence when a person with sexual intent:

1. utters any word or makes any sound, makes any gesture or exhibits any object or part of the body with an intention that the word or sound should be heard by the child, or the gesture, object or part of the body be seen by the child,
2. makes the child exhibit its body or any part of the body or,
3. shows any object to a child in any form or media for pornographic purposes, or,
4. repeatedly or constantly follows or watches or contacts a child either directly or through any means, or,
5. threatens to use in any form of media, a real or fabricated depiction through electronic, film or digital or any other mode, of any part of the body of the child or the involvement of the child in a sexual act.

This definition of sexual harassment tries to cover almost all forms of sexual abuse of child found in the society.

Section 13 of the Act defines the offence of use of child for pornographic purposes. It provides that use of a child in any form of media, for the purposes of sexual gratification including indecent or obscene representation of a child is an offence of 'use of child' for pornographic purposes. The expression 'use of a child' shall include involving child in various manners in production and distribution of pornographic material.

Section 15 of the Act provides for punishment for even storage of pornographic material involving child. As per the Penal Code, if any act is an offence, the abetment of such act is also an offence. It further provides that an abetment of an offence being an offence, an abetment of such an abetment is also an offence. Section 16 of this Act provides that a person commits an offence of abetment if he instigates any person to do that offence, or engages with others in any conspiracy for doing that offence. If an act or illegal omission takes place in pursuance of the conspiracy, or intentionally aids by any act or illegal omission, he is an offender. What amounts to instigation and also what is meant by aid and facilitate an offence is also defined. Section 18 provides punishment for attempt to commit an offence. Section 19 makes provision for reporting of offences. Every person shall have to report to special Juvenile Police Unit or local police if he knows that offence has been committed or likely to be committed. It there is a need of protection or care for the victim of child sexual abuse; it shall be the duty of police to provide such care and protection to the child. Section 20 casts duties on the media, studio and photographic facilities to report cases. It further provides that a person being in charge of a company or institution happens to know that his subordinate is involved in offence under this Act and fails to report the same to police will also be punished.

The Act provides for non disclosure of the identity of the child victim. It also bars media from making report on any child either as an accused or as victim in a case of sexual offence, as the disclosure may have the effect of lowering its character or infringing upon its privacy. Section 24 provides for recording the statement of a child before a magistrate and makes it mandatory to record the statement of a child in the presence of parents or any other person in whom the child has trust or confidence. Assistance of an interpreter or special educator or an expert may be taken while recording the statement, if a child has a mental or physical disability. If the statement of a child is recorded by audio-video electronic means then also the presence of parent is necessary. There is a provision in the Act that the police officer present at the time of recording the statement of the child should not be in uniform. Section 26 provides for the accused not be in contact with the child. The police officer investigating the offence must ensure that at no point of time the child comes in contact with the accused in any way. Section 27 provides for medical examination of the child to be conducted in accordance with Section 164 (A) of the Criminal Procedure Code, 1973, whether or not FIR or complaint is registered for the offence. Section 28 provides for Special Court, speedy trial by Sessions Court. Section 29 says that where a person prosecuted under offence of sexual assault, aggravated sexual assault, penetrative sexual assault and or aggravated penetrative sexual assault and the victim is a child below 16 years of age, the Special Court shall presume that such person has committed the offence, unless the contrary is proved. Section 30 provides for presumption of culpable mental state. Any offence which requires a culpable mental state on the part of the accused, the court shall presume the existence of such mental state and it is for the accused to prove that he had no such mental state in respect of the act charged as an offence in that prosecution. However, the existence of mental state on the part of accused should be beyond reasonable doubt and not only a probability. There is a provision in the Act for the appointment of special public prosecutors and further provides that the special public prosecutor or the counsel for the accused while recording the examination in chief, cross-examination or re-examination of the child, communicate the questions to be put to the child to the Special Court. The Special Court shall create child friendly atmosphere by allowing a family member, guardian, or a friend or relative in whom the child reposes confidence, to be present in the court. The court shall also ensure that the child is not called repeatedly to testify in the court. The Act also provides that the court shall not permit aggressive questioning or character assassination of the child and ensure the dignity of the child is maintained at all times, and the identity of the child is not disclosed at any time during the course of investigation or trial. The identity of the child includes the identity of the family, relative, school, neighbourhood or any other information by which the identity of the child is revealed. In appropriate cases, the court has power to award compensation to a child for any physical or mental trauma caused to the child or for immediate rehabilitation of such child. The Act expects the court to record the evidence within 30 days, and complete the trial within a period of one year from the date of taking cognizance of the offence. Section 36 of the Act casts upon the court a duty to ensure that the child is not exposed in any way to the accused at the time of recording the evidence while at the same time ensuring that the accused is in a position to hear the statement of the child.

Most important of all, the Act makes it mandatory to try the offence 'in camera' and in the presence of parents of the child or any other person in whom the child has trust or confidence. The child may be examined by appointment of commission also at any other place than Court Hall. Assistance of an interpreter or expert may be taken while recording the statement of the child. There is provision to the effect that the state government shall prepare guidelines for use of non-governmental organizations, professionals and experts or persons having knowledge of psychology, social work, physical as well as mental health and child development to be associated with the pre-trial stage to assist the child.

So the Act tries to meet the problem of sexual abuse of children to a great extent. How to allow sexual activity between children below 18 years of age without being criminalized was a problem before the framers of the statute. The age of consent is lowered to 16 but concept of consent is made so complicated that any such consent can easily be said to be no-consent making the children involved being labeled as guilty.

At first there was wide criticism for increasing the age of consent to 18. As per added proviso, it will be taken into consideration whether the consent obtained by using means of deceit, force or inducement, if the child is between 16 and 18 years of age. This is an attempt to decriminalize consensual sex of a child above 16, even if it is a minor. The Act further provides that nonresistance is not necessarily consent. Cases would not be rare where the parents of a girl between 16 and 18 years would force the girl to complain against the offender of sexual assault and the burden to prove that it was a consensual sex would be heavy on the accused to discharge. So the age of consent is reduced to 16 from proposed 18 but unequivocal voluntary consent is made very difficult to prove as consent, keeping a hanging sword on the head of the young lovers almost making premarital sex a taboo.

The difficulties of law are better revealed when the law is implemented. Let us wait and watch.

NGOs Working for Girl Child Sexual Abuse in India

ARPAN

Arpan is a registered organization based in Mumbai with a mission to prevent the occurrence of child sexual abuse and heal those who have been affected by it. Founded by Pooja Taparia, Mumbai, it began in year 2003, with passion and conviction and a trained team of dedicated professionals, clinical and counselling psychologists. Arpan began working on the issue of child sexual abuse (CSA) in year 2006. Today, Arpan works in a focused manner only on CSA.

The impact of child sexual abuse stays with the child for a long time beyond the immediate trauma. Intervention is needed to prevent child sexual abuse and heal its ill effects in the lives of the victims and survivors.

Interventions Undertaken by Arpan

Prevention: Empowering adults and children with skills to protect children from sexual abuse and healing – Enabling victims and survivors of abuse to heal and live beyond the trauma of their abuse.

Core Activities of Arpan

- Spreading awareness amongst various stakeholders of children, parents, teachers, NGO professionals and staff to provide them with prevention and intervention skills.
- Teach personal safety skills to children in schools so that they can protect themselves from sexual abuse.
- Heal child victims and adult survivors through counselling and therapy so that they are able to get healed and live beyond the trauma of their abuse and have a right to life with dignity.
- Build practitioner capability to deal with child sexual abuse cases to facilitate better healing of victims and survivors.
- Training mental health professionals, counsellors, B.Ed, D.Ed and social work students.

Arpan also addresses various stakeholders in a child's life to inform and train them on child sexual abuse. Prevention and intervention skills are imparted through awareness and training sessions customized as per the target audience. Arpan also constantly tries to bring forth the reality of child sexual abuse, its ill effects, myths surrounding it, prevention methods in society through newspapers and magazines.

Teaching Children Personal Safety Skills in Schools

This is a comprehensive programme that trains parents, teachers, and school counsellors on prevention and intervention skills with the main focus on teaching children personal safety skills through role play, oral and written material.

Healing Programmes

Counselling for victims, adult survivors, family members and abusers themselves along with helping the victims to get healed. It is important to extend help to the abuser as well. It is seen that therapeutic intervention can help abusers stop abusing children in future. As a method of prevention, healing services are offered for abusers also.

Building Practitioner Capability

While there are numerous counsellors, very few really have the ability to deal with cases of trauma. Most often children and adults are traumatized due to being sexually abused and need specific therapeutic skills to help get healed. Arpan conducts a study group on trauma for practitioners in the field of mental health and social workers to gain skills on dealing with cases of trauma.

Activity-based therapy for sexually abused and trafficked minors. It is seen that alternative therapies like yoga, dance, art and craft help to heal traumatized victims and survivors. Arpan extends its healing programmes to sponsor therapeutic activities like yoga to victims of sexual abuse.

Thus Arpan, an NGO, is working in Mumbai with a mission to prevent the occurrence of child sexual abuse and heal those who have been affected by it.[4]

RECOVERING AND HEALING FROM INCEST (RAHI)

RAHI is another NGO working towards prevention and intervention in the area of incest and child sexual abuse (CSA) in New Delhi. It functions as a counselling and support centre as well as education, training, research and communication centre in the field. It was set up in 1996 on the basis of a MacArthur's Foundation Fellowship.

Anuja Gupta, founder of RAHI, started her NGO to help overcome the torment of incest. She has rehabilitated thousands of victims of incest, a social evil that has been swept under the carpet by middle and upper class South Asian households.

For all those who scoffed at the hint of incest in an upper class Indian family in Mira Nair's film *Monsoon Wedding* here are some sobering statistics. Social scientists are now coming to believe that sexual abuse of children in India is far more prevalent than most people realize. This and many more factors inspired Anuja Gupta to set up an NGO called RAHI for recovering and healing from incest.

Focus Area

- Student community education
- Capacity building
- Support services: healing connections
- Research and communication

Vision and Mission

Vision

To build an India without child sexual abuse.

Mission

RAHI's mission is to visualize the issue of incest and child sexual abuse, build resources within the country for effective prevention and intervention and provide girl survivors quality support and therapeutic services.

Goals

RAHI's main goals are to:

- Facilitate the recovery of girl survivors of incest/child sexual abuse.
- Reduce the risk of incest/child sexual abuse in the country.
- Equip individuals and groups to be effective incest/child sexual abuse interventionists.
- Build a body of incest/child sexual abuse literature in the Indian context.

To achieve these goals, RAHI uses combined strategy of awareness raising, capacity building and individual healing.

Programmes

Ever since its inception, RAHI is working closely for communities which are relevant to its mission. These are mental health, social work, student and survivor communities.

Student Community Education

RAHI's Peer Education Programme (PEP) is a unique student-peer intervention strategy aimed at building resources within the student community for incest/CSA prevention and healing. It works with young girls on college campuses to bring about change at grassroot level. These girls are selected and trained as peer educators on the subject of incest/CSA. The PEP seeks to effectively utilize that which comes to young girls most naturally, learning from, confiding in and supporting each other.

Capacity Building

RAHI's capacity building work aims at equipping social workers and mental health professionals with skills in the area of incest/CSA that will help them to be more effective in their work with girls and children.

NGOs

An important segment of RAHI's activities has been its training work with NGOs and mental health professionals over the last 10 years using its own skills as well as those of international experts. With NGOs so far, its work has focused on helping them to have an in-depth understanding of the issue and draw links between incest/CSA and the impact such violence has on a girl's sexual, reproductive, mental and emotional healing. RAHI reaches to both grassroot and urban NGOs in India.

Incest Course

This is offered to counselling students, practicing psychologists, counsellors and social workers in Delhi and other cities. This is a one-three days course entitled Incest/Child Sexual Abuse: Occurrence, Impact and Treatment. It provides a theoretical framework for the understanding of incest/CSA and its traumatic factors and presents different perspectives on its immediate and long-term effects.

Support Services: Healing Connections

Healing connections is RAHI's series of individual and group services designed to meet the unique needs of girl survivors. They combine eclectic psychotherapeutic approaches and experimental techniques with traditional healing methods to include psychodrama, bodywork, art and craft, meditation and massage.

Support Group

Circle of strength is RAHI's 12-week facilitated support group offering 36 hours of therapeutic work. In this group, girls explore together the effects of abuse on their lives and honour and what they did to survive. Through this process girls are able to develop inner strengths, build, heal their relationships, feel a greater sense of self and engage with their environment with renewed confidence, mastery and responsibility.

Individual Counselling

RAHI provides one-to-one counselling for girl-survivors to talk about their abuse and related issues to an experienced counsellor. The clients are girls from age 17 onwards, including college students.

Consultation and Supervision

RAHI offers its consultation and supervision to other individuals and groups working with incest survivors. It works closely with individuals and organizations interested in starting survivor groups in other parts of the country. It is involved in conceptualizing and planning stages and offers clinical supervision and guidance for the running of the groups. RAHI also provides individual supervision to mental health practitioners and other NGOs on their incest/child sexual abuse cases.

Research and Communication

A significant work has been done in research and communication. The research work focuses on providing evidence of the problem of incest/CSA in the Indian context. It gathers such evidences from survivors who avail their support services as well as through generating research project.

The communication work focuses on mainstreaming the issue of incest/CSA and bringing it out in the larger public domain. It is aimed to draw and sustain public attention on the issue through using a variety of communication means that are acceptable to the audience. This range from posters, postcards, brochures and ribbons to public events films, publications and theatre.

RAHI also organizes workshops on incest and sexual abuse and provides training for counsellors, individuals and organizations working with girl children.[5]

FORUM AGAINST CHILD SEXUAL EXPLOITATION (FACSE)

This forum is a 12-year-old network of individuals, professionals and organizations working to eliminate sexual exploitation and abuse of children. The forum is a direct outcome of the consensus that emerged from a Maharashtra-level brainstorming meeting on the issue in April 1996 in Mumbai. With this understanding and background, FACSE was started with two broad objectives:

1. To create awareness about the issue of child sexual abuse among different target groups, as well as the general public.
2. To lobby for necessary changes in the law.
3. To handle individual cases of child sexual abuse.

Vision

- To create awareness about the issue of child sexual abuse among different target groups as well as the general public.
- To lobby for necessary changes in the law.

Mission

Networking and mass awareness.

Services Offered

Trainings, workshops on issue of child sexual abuse, generation of information, education and communication (IEC) material on the same.

Brief Project and Achievement

- Creating Awareness: through IEC (Information Education and Communication) materials like brochures, posters, leaflets, translation of booklets and articles to be published in regional languages like Hindi and Marathi.
- Compilation of all the efforts activities of FACSE since its inception.
- Taking part in campaigns against child trafficking, prevention of child abuse and neglect in India.
- Being part of other larger forums working on the issue of child rights.
- Making a pathway into the legal perspective of existing laws of CSA by conducting extensive workshops where participants were city/civil court judges, public prosecutors and other lawyers and professionals.
- Dealing with a few of child sexual abuse cases as an outcome of preventive work.

The forum members are NGO representatives, professionals such as doctors, lawyers, counsellors, psychiatrists, psychologists, media persons and other concerned individuals from varied fields. The intention is to involve more and more people from different professions and backgrounds to broad base the forum as issues cut across all sectors of society, caste and religions.[6]

TULIR-CPHCSA

Centre for the Prevention and Healing of Child Sexual Abuse (CPHCSA) is a registered, non-governmental organization/committee to work against child sexual abuse in India.

Tulir, in Tamil, means the first tender leaves of a plant; leaves suggesting a period symbolizing children and the belief in the resistance and resurgence of the human spirit.

Mission/Objectives

- To support and participate in local, national and international efforts to promote and protect the rights of children.

- To raise awareness on child sexual abuse.
- To work towards improving policy and advancing practice to prevent and address cases of child sexual abuse with special emphasis on the psycho-social well-being of children.
- To provide direct intervention services in the areas of prevention and healing of child sexual abuse.
- To undertake research, documentation and dissemination of information on child sexual abuse.

Services and Programmes of Tulir-CPHCSA

Personal safety education is a school-based curriculum that empowers children to participate on their own in three integral components of the methodology of providing age-appropriate information, developing decision-making skills and promoting self-esteem to translate learning into practice. Besides, it strengthens those that are professionally, socially and morally responsible for the protection of children, i.e. the government schools and the larger community.

Training and Consultancy

Tulir-CPHCSA training programmes are designed to meet the requirements and needs of various professions, professional sectors and include sensitization and skill building programmes for teachers, social workers and other multi-disciplinary stakeholders crucial to an effective response.

Training workshops are also extended to organizations working on varied issues. Child labour, child rights, HIV/AIDS Preventive institutions-equipping them with the skills and knowledge required to effectively respond to the sexual abuse.

Tulir-CPHCSA believes in sharing its knowledge, resources, expertise with other organizations for better relief of child sexual abuse, by providing consultancy in research and practice areas for other organizations working on issues.

A multidisciplinary approach is the basis of therapeutic services for abused children and is premised on the holy healing and teaching model along with socio legal assistance.

Research and Documentation

Research and documentation projects are undertaken with an aim to expand knowledge base, advance practical and better strategy within the Indian context to combat child sexual abuse.

To assist other researchers and practitioners, Tulir-CPHCSA has resource library of a collection of books, studies and multimedia resources, focused on child sexual abuse.

Advocacy and Networking

Since attitudinal change is only possible with information, creating and raising awareness and sensitization is the work of Tulir-CPHCSA. It works towards achieving this goal by periodically organizing public awareness, sensitization and campaigns, and by making use of different platforms to bring the issue to the forefront of public consciousness and includes joining with individuals, groups and organizations, and networking with different professional sectors enforcement, judiciary, health care and education.

Partnering with media and writing on the issue to provide and sensitize visibility to the issue is a constant 'Awaaz', the quarterly newsletter of Tulir-CPHCA, another vehicle of advocacy and networking of spreading awareness.

Thus, Tulir is a registered, non-government, non-profit organization committed to working against child sexual abuse in India.[7]

MUSKAAN, Pune

Muskaan is a campaign formed by the coming together of some Pune-based organizations and individuals who feel strongly about the issue of child sexual abuse. These include child rights and girls groups as well as activities, social workers, counsellors, doctors, media people, lawyers, teachers and parents.

In the last two-and-half years, Muskaan has conducted approximately 30 child sexual abuse awareness workshops and training programmes at various schools, colleges and NGOs in Pune. During this period, Muskaan has also organized discussion forums with counsellors, psychiatrists and NGO activists who have had the experience of dealing with CSA cases and with educationist who are involved in sexuality education to adolescents.

Aims and Objectives

- To network and continue advocacy with organizations working on similar issues.
- To work towards holding the abuser accountable for violating the child's rights.
- To lobby for changes in the legal system with reference to CSA.
- To undertake research and documentation on the issue.

Above discussion indicates that prevalence of child sexual abuse is accepted in the Western countries and it became a public issue in 1970s and 1980s. The government and NGOs of various Western countries have taken steps to protect the children from sexual abuse by enacting laws.

The NGOs in Western countries are also working for the prevention and healing of child sexual abuse. Their mission, their objectives and guiding principles, and the services rendered by them are really appreciable.

Their innovative ideas of diagnosis, treatment and giving help are really helping the victims, survivors and even abusers. The workshop, awareness camps and counselling work done by them will definitely be helpful in the problem. Hence, the rehabilitative work of the NGOs in Western countries is a commitment work for the issue as they realized that 'no violence against children is preventable. There should be no more excuses' (Paolo Sergio Pinheiro, author of *World Report on Violence against Children*).

In India, the issue of child sexual abuse is still secretive and socially unspeakable. It is a hidden fact in Indian society, even though some studies show the prevalence of child sexual abuse in India. Taboos and traditions in Indian culture hide the issue.

But the research work of some NGOs found that the abuse of children in India is far more prevalent than most people realize. It is prevalent in all societies from poor to so-called respectable families (RAHI).

The studies by NGOs also found that:

- Sexual abuse can result in both short-term and long-term harm, including psychopathology in later life. Psychological, emotional, physical, and social effects include depression, post-traumatic stress disorder, anxiety, eating disorders, poor self-esteem, dissociative and anxiety disorders, general psychological distress and disorders such as somatization, neurosis, chronic pain, sexualized behaviour, school/learning problems, and behavioural problems, including substance abuse.
- *Physical Harm*: Depending on the age and size of the child, and the degree of force used, child sexual abuse may cause internal lacerations and bleeding. In severe cases, damage to internal organs may occur, which in some cases, may cause death.
- *Infections*: Child sexual abuse may cause infections and sexually transmitted diseases. Depending on the age of the child, due to lack of sufficient vaginal fluid, chances of infection are higher.

Even though sexual abuse is a subject of social issue, most people would rather not think or talk about and it has continued to be shrouded in myth, secrecy and taboos, but despite its invisibility, it is prevalent in India.

Dealing with the victims of sexual abuse requires a multidisciplinary approach. Their treatment includes protection of child by stopping the abuse, providing support during his/her need, helping the family and intervention. It needs to be handled carefully to avoid magnifying children's negative attitudes.

Louise Arbor, former UN High Commissioner on Human Rights has rightly stated: 'A veil of silence covers violence against children, yet abuses are so pervasive that no country can ignore them and no society can claim to be immune from them'.

R. Mukherjee, in his book *Democracy – A Failure, Shefocracy – The Solution, for Human Welfare* (2000) stated that 'The Government should take all responsibility of economical and social rehabilitation of such victims not merely by giving service or the like, but by encouraging the man who would like to marry her. Similarly from society's end, she should not be looked down upon. On the contrary, she should not be talked about or sympathized with but should be given normal treatment to enable her in doing her duties and obligations in society in normal way'. He calls it 'operational rehabilitation'.[8]

Hence, this is the time for proper rehabilitation of victims of sexual abuse which would help to control and prevent the issue of girl child sexual abuse. So rehabilitation work by NGOs and government is an urgent need of the victims to feel free in their homes and in society where they break their silence and live without pressure. Early treatment is essential to counter the consequences.

Notes

1. Singh, K.K. and Singh, R.S. (2010), *Encyclopedia of Social Work in 21st Century*, ABD Publishers, New Delhi, p. 166.
2. Ibid., p. 167.
3. www.ispcan.org
4. www:/arpancsa.blogspot.com
5. www:/http:/rahi.org
6. http://www.karmayog.org/ngo/facse
7. http://www.tulir.org
8. Mukherjee, R.N. (2000), *Democracy – A Failure, Shefocracy – The Solution, for Human Welfare*, United Press of America, Lanham, Md.

7

Conclusions and Recommendations

The present research was undertaken on the topic *A Study of Sexual Abuse of Girl Children with Special Reference to Beed District*. The subject is studied with the help of multi source data collection, i.e. 500 school-going girl children, 30 case studies (reported and unreported cases) and interviews of 40 key informants who are working on the issue. The findings derived from analysis of this data are presented in this chapter. The extent, nature, causes and consequences of girl child sexual abuse are studied and coping strategies are also suggested in the present study. The issue was selected due to its severity and the need for immediate action. Girl child sexual abuse is not an individual problem. It is emerging as one of the most heinous offences and is gaining more and more momentum as a social issue.

It is very necessary that the issues like girl child sexual abuse are not neglected by the government and social activists. Majority of the human rights groups in India, so far, have focused chiefly on the rights of adults. This mindset and approach has to be changed. There is an urgent need to appeal to all concerned to treat violation of rights of the children with equal importance. While punishing the guilty is important, concerted action to make the people aware of the problem is also urgently needed. The emergence of this issue as a global problem needs to be given special attention. The researcher, therefore, selected this subject for study and also to suggest some coping strategies and tackling measures.

For the present study, some objectives were set and for testing the validity of hypothesis, the analysis of data was undertaken and the conclusions were drawn.

To Study the Socio-Economic Background of the Victims of Sexual Abuse was the Objective of the Present Study

In this regard it was found that the school-going girls in the age group of 11 to 18 years, who had suffered sexual abuse, were mostly from lower income group of the society: 28 per cent victim's fathers were daily wage earners in rural area and 24.40 per cent were daily wage earners in urban areas, 21.20 per cent fathers of the victims in rural area and 16 per cent in urban area were unemployed.

The number of victims whose fathers are government servants earning salary is very less in both the areas. Persons other than government servants had no certainty of job and did not have fixed income. Unemployment exists in large scale in both rural and urban areas and the data shows that the percentage of victims whose fathers are unemployed is very high in both the areas. The unemployment of father gives him more leisure time and that leisure time makes him an addict and addiction leads to tension and quarrel in the family. Such families are not having healthy environment and interactions with their children. Most of the girl children are having their mother working as wage earner, domestic worker or engaged in agricultural work. Only few, 1.20 per cent in rural area and 4.40 per cent in urban area, are government servants. The mother of victim bears the responsibility of working to earn for the family and this work keeps her away from home and she has no time to interact with her child.

These girls are, most of the time, alone in the home as the parents are away for earning; 97 per cent victims from the rural area and 76 per cent victims from urban area had to give considerable time for household work and responsibility of their siblings. This results in the girls irregular schooling and school drop-out and deprives the girls from education and recreation. This situation is misused by the male family members and the relatives who visit the home to misuse the trust of the girl child by sexually abusing her. Women in the family are sometimes aware of this fact, but they are unable to protect the girl children from abuse as they cannot afford to abandon their work outside, due to poverty and are forced to keep mum because of fear of social stigma and male authoritarian atmosphere in the family.

Television is the only medium of entertainment for 62.8 per cent victims. These girls were rarely allowed to go outside for cinema, on a trip, to a garden or even to chitchat with friends. So the television is the only medium of entertainment for girl children in both rural and urban areas. These girls are deprived of healthy means of recreation such as reading, playing games and mixing with peer groups.

This study also reveals the fact that even though sexual abuse is prevalent in all income group families, girls belonging to lower income group are at a high risk. Beed District, which is the universe of this study, is known for its migration, poverty and low literacy level of girls and for female foeticide. The poverty renders the family unable to fulfil the needs of their girl children and the teenage girls are generally tempted by the gifts, money and items of luxury and by false promises offered to them by the abuser and these girls become victims of sexual abuse.

Thus, the main factors that contribute to the magnitude of the problem of girl child sexual abuse are gender discrimination, poverty, illiteracy and unhealthy family environment. Hence, a girl child who is a future mother, with such socio-economic background, runs a greater risk of being victimized.

From this study the hypothesis that the lower the economic condition, the more is the vulnerability of a girl child to sexual abuse, is proved.

To Find out the Nature and Causes of Girl Child Sexual Abuse was another Objective of the Present Study

For the proper understanding of the problem, the nature and causes of girl child sexual abuse were studied in the present study. The various kinds of girl child sexual abuses found in the study included rape, sodomy, prostitution, molestation, abduction, incest, intercourse, touching private parts of the child, fondling of child genitals, making the child fondle an adult genitals, exhibitionisms and pornography.

Abusers of girl children found in the study were father, brother, grandfather, family members, frequent visitors like relatives, family friends, male cousins, maternal uncle, paternal uncle, step-father, step-brother, brother-in-law, neighbours, etc. The study revealed that many victims were made to watch pornographic material by the frequent visitors and the sources of such material is mobile phone, books, videos, CDs and internet. Among all these abusers from both urban and rural areas, the percentage of male cousin is higher (28.77% in rural area and 36.07% in urban area) followed by maternal uncle (24.30% in rural area and 20.88% in urban area). The percentage of paternal uncle is at the third position, i.e. 18.86 in rural area and 17.72 in urban area. The percentage of father as abuser is 4.71 in rural area and it is 3.79 in urban areas is quite distressing. Quite a sizeable number of girl children are abused by more than one abuser, 84.8 per cent girls from rural area have suffered sexual abuse by different members of family, whereas the same is reported by 63.2 per cent victims from urban area.

These figures prove that there is rural and urban divide about girl child sexual abuse and girl from rural area in large number suffers sexual abuse.

The girls have adjustment problem in reconstituted families. Ill-treatment at the hands of step-father and cousin is common. Thus, the causes leading to sexual abuse of girl child within a family are found to be lack of communication among parents, no or little interaction with parents, deprivation of teenage needs of love and affection, breaking of values about brother-sister and other close relationships. Because of this, victims loose faith in relationship and family system.

This shows that 'the family', which is a place of protection and security for every human being, has become for the girl children the most insecure place and the persons who are the known, the trusted persons and are expected to be the caretakers and protectors have turned into villains and destructors of the future of girl children. Such people are almost just waiting for the right opportunity to initiate contact with the girl and then gradually to engage her in sexual activity. The girl child is losing her faith and trust in members of her family and family relationship. Indian culture had taught her to respect and trust the elders in the family. This teaching does not allow her to speak about her sexual abuse by incest.

The study also reveals the fact that the abusers from outside the family are generally the persons known to the child such as neighbour, teacher, boyfriends, male and female family friends, school servants, watchmen, persons at work place and house owners: Neighbours and family friends who have special place in Indian society as caretakers and well-wishers are found to be sexually abusing the girl children. Around 11 per cent girls reported sexual abuse by neighbours, 2.8 per cent by family friends and 3.6 per cent by teachers. The behaviour of such neighbours and family friends is disgusting and reprehensible. Teacher-student relationship is considered sacred in India but it was found that in many cases the behaviour of teacher with his student is immoral and unworthy of this profession. This shows how these known and trusted persons are abusing the girl child, violating her by betraying their and their parent's trust.

The present study reveals the fact that the problem of girl child sexual abuse is prevalent in secured place like home and also in neighbour's house, and public places like market, while travelling and also in the joyful ceremony of weddings, etc.

Wedding ceremonies are special events where people gather to enjoy and feel happy. But it was found that, unfortunately, the girl children are harassed at such functions. The nature of sexual abuse faced by the girls in the wedding ceremony was: looking at them in a sexual way, making of sexual comments, touching private parts, fondling in sexual way and photo snapping by both known and unknown persons. Camera in mobile phone is very conveniently used by relatives and family friends. Many a times the girls are embarrassed and shocked when they have to face defamation and blackmail due to misuse or abuse of their photographs. In this study it was found that during the marriage ceremony the percentage of relatives as abusers is high in both rural and urban area (47.93). Among the relatives, percentage of male cousins (51.38) as abusers is high in both areas, i.e. 45.45 in rural and 48.57 in urban area followed by paternal uncle which is 24.24 per cent in rural area and 20 per cent in urban area.

In market place, nature of sexual abuse of girl children is: looking at them in a sexual way, whistling, singing vulgar songs, making sexual comments and touching private parts. It was observed that looking at in a sexual ways is highest among all other forms of abuse in both the areas. It is 19.6 per cent in rural area and 29.2 in urban area. It was found that whistling is higher in rural area. It is 13 per cent in rural area and 10.4 per cent per cent in urban area. Whistling is used in different tunes to indicate one's identity and to attract the attention of the girl concerned. It was observed that the other forms of abuse such as ogling or looking at the girl with sexual intention is more common in urban area because the abuser can take advantage of the surrounding crowd to go near the young girl to gain proximity to satisfy his sexual desire. But the girls from rural area have suffered this more on 'bazaar day' in villages. For girls living in urban area this form of abuse is of almost a daily occurrence. Girls from rural area are comparatively saved from this type of abuse as they are not normally in the crowd in their villages.

During travel, the nature of sexual abuse faced by the girls is, touching private parts, making sexual comments, sitting very close and 'looking at in a sexual way'. It is found that the sexual abuse in various forms is high in the urban area than in rural area. The girls complain that they are afraid of travelling as it is very embarrassing. The standing passenger even goes to the extent of rubbing his private part to the shoulder of a sitting girl. Parents are reluctant to send the girl to school if she complained of such things. The girls of tender age who are living in the rural area have to go to nearby town daily for their high school. Sexual abusers take advantage of this necessity of these girls and travel in these vehicles purposely to harass the girls by sitting very close and try to develop intimacy by means of various ways. The girls do not even complain to their parents for fear that they might be asked to discontinue their education.

The girls who have to face sexual abuse during travel to school are keeping mum and are unwilling to disclose the matter. In fact, their silence increases the nuisance and emboldens the abusers. Investigation into causes for their keeping mum about trouble at public places revealed the disturbing fact that they have to lose much by telling people about the nuisance than by tolerating it. Among the reasons for keeping mum, the highest is the fear about being blamed, it is 53.25 per cent in rural area and 49.38 per cent in urban area. Nobody is caring for their complaint so they learn to get accustomed to the evil, to accept and to live with it. It was found that abusers take advantage of crowd in the market place, in marriage ceremony and while travelling to go near the young girl to gain proximity and the pleasure of satisfaction of his sexual activities.

In this study, the various causes of girl child sexual abuse were noted. Among them the family atmosphere is prominent. Tense atmosphere in the family is higher in rural area, i.e. 52.40 per cent whereas it is 48.46 per cent in urban area. Only 10 per cent families are having friendly atmosphere in the rural area, whereas it is 16 per cent in urban area. This shows the severity of the problem and the difference between urban and rural families.

About 82.61 per cent families having the head of the family addicted is quite a distressful situation as this results into disharmony, frequent quarrels between parents and tension affecting the childhood of the girl child in the family. Tensed atmosphere at home makes the child feel inferior, lose her self-confidence, makes her keep quiet and, therefore, vulnerable to abuse, Due to the silence of the girl children, they are easily carried away by allurements and become an easy prey of the abusers who exploit them for their personal sexual gratification. Around 68.10 per cent victims reported that their parents always quarrel, 31.89 per cent victims reported that their parents quarrel frequently and 7.2 per cent girl children did not respond. It is clear that quarrel between parents leads to tension in the family. This study reveals that the sexual abuse that occurs in the context of granting of special privileges may be as traumatic and bewildering to the child as a violent molestation. If the home and surrounding are not congenial enough and basic needs of food, clothing, education and hobby are not met, the child is likely to fall prey to sexual abuse.

Nature of punishment for mistakes committed by victims is also a causative factor in abuse. Nature of punishment 'scolding' is higher in both the areas, i.e. 63.20 per cent in rural area and 59.60 per cent in urban area. In rural area, forms of punishment for girl children, such as giving food late, giving more work, asking to do agricultural and household work, and not purchasing new clothes during festivals, etc. are very common. In urban area, the 'other punishments' include, not allowing to go outside, insulting in front of the friends, beating, locking, etc. not talking are inhuman punishments given by the parents to girl child. Such punishments make the girl upset and it leads to mental strain and makes her keep mum. It creates distance and lack of rapport between the parents and child and makes the girl child feel insecure in her home. In such a situation, potential abuser gets a chance to give the child emotional support and an opportunity to win the trust of the girl. He not only abuses the girl once or twice but frequently, because her silence emboldens him.

Gender discrimination is also prevalent in both the areas. It is an important causative factor in girl child sexual abuse. This shows the negative attitude towards girl child in our society. This discriminatory treatment to girl children is an indicator of their low status in the family. Due to low status, girls feel inferior and due to lack of attention by parents these girl children never find a suitable atmosphere in their homes to share their problems. They feel insecure as there is lack of communication and the tense atmosphere in the family makes them suffer silently without raising their voice against their sexual abuse.

In rural families, economic discrimination is the highest, i.e. 97 per cent, whereas it is 86 per cent in urban area households. Even though gender inequality is there in both the areas, the discrimination is very profound for girls from rural area. Indicators of discrimination in the present study show that the girls from rural area are more discriminated against than urban area in the familial level and also in economic, educational and cultural level.

These girl children are not having appropriate and accurate knowledge about sex and sexuality and this becomes an obstacle in the healthy development of adolescent girls. They cannot differentiate between right and wrong. The media, TV with its serials, film song items, reality shows and movies have the negative effect on their mind. The 'make-believe world' of this mode of entertainment, accompanied by lack of proper education and neglect by parents, makes these innocent girls vulnerable to deceit and exploitation. The potential abuser abuses her sexually due to her ignorance and teenage. By gaining her trust, he gradually starts fondling the victim or having the victim fondle him, all the while rationalizing that sex is alright. She is rewarded by gifts for her participation and slowly this situation makes the girl child to agree to more serious sexual acts like intercourse. Abuser is a trusted person in the family so even when the girl child speaks about her sexual abuse, nobody believes her. On the other hand, they blame her and this makes her suffer silently.

A girl child is at high risk when she is neglected. If parents are suffering financial problems, if there is no communication between parent and children, between husband and wife, the abuser lays the trap taking advantage of the situation, attracts the child towards him by giving things and by giving emotional support and with the trust, thus gained, sexually abuses the girl child. Poverty, ignorance, illiteracy, the tense atmosphere in the family and teenage years of a girl tempts her to believe the person who has sexually abused her. A girl child, especially if she is poor, is considered as a commodity devoid of any personal choice and desire.

It is found in the study that instead of reporting the case to the police, her guardian scolds and beats the girl child calling her a 'girl of bad character'. Instead of giving her any emotional support they insist on her even to leave her home. The girl has nowhere to go and, therefore, is depressed. For no fault of her she is blamed. In fact, the girl is a victim of deceit.

The girl child in such a family lives with tensions and would not share her feelings with others. The child keeps mum even when she is sexually abused in the family itself. This silence works actively because it is the main perpetrator as it puts a curtain before the eyes of the parents and they do not see the reality. Recurrence of the abuse of girl child in a family is possible because of this silence on the part of the girl and her parents. Investigation into causes for their keeping mum about trouble, revealed the disturbing fact that they have to lose much by telling about the nuisance than by tolerating it.

The study reveals that 'no disclosure' is there because the victim and her family members feel that disclosure of the incident causes too many problems such as difficulties in victim's marriage, the family is isolated from the social relationships, the girl is 'labelled' as 'damaged goods'. This 'labelling' of the victim gives an easy access to the abuser to abuse the girl child again and again or even expose her to be abused by more than one abuser. All the potential abusers find it easy to abuse the victim and it leads to recurrence of abuse. Thus, 'disclosure' gives rise to disrepute and stigma instead of solving the problem. Hence, the parents keep silent and they tell their girl child also to keep quiet and ask her to tolerate her abuse, as unfortunately she is a 'girl child'. She is asked to keep quiet to protect the dignity of the family. If the culture teaches her to bear this responsibility of protecting the dignity of the family being a 'girl child', of what is such 'dignity of family' which ends her childhood and even her happy life. This destroys the life of the girl child as she suffers from long lasting consequences.

Lack of interaction in the family makes her keep quiet. Keeping mum only adds to recurrence of the abuse of the girl child. Inadequate control exerted by the family, neglect of the child's needs by the family and helplessness of the girl child, taken together, has resulted in the increase of incidents. Sexual abuse within kinship is a fact of life for many girls as it happens in all kinds of families and in both, the rural as well as urban area. It disturbs the girl child and makes the child self-blaming, feel guilty, causes her to mistrust herself and others.

The results of the study reveal that sexual abuse of girl children is caused by number of situations like lack of communication between parents and children, little or no interaction with mother, no respect for relationship, tense atmosphere in the family, addiction of father, migration of parents, ignorance, illiteracy, poverty and deterioration of value system and morality in the family and society, inadequate control of the family over children, presence of an authoritative person in the family who thinks it to be his privilege to exploit the girl children in the family, the lust of the elders, an easy access to the girl child and helplessness of the girl child, neglect of girl children by parents because of separation of parents or because of reconstituted family. These are some of situations that are taken advantage of by neighbours and other people to sexually abuse the lonely children. Lacunae in the criminal justice system and negative attitude of society towards abused girl children compel such children not to disclose their abuse and suffer in silence.

Thus, it is seen that the girls are victims of sexual abuse only because people have no moral values and derive pleasure by resorting to sexual advances towards girls. A girl, for these people of perverted mentality, is only an object of sexual satisfaction. Temptation, immaturity of age and not knowing the consequences of sexual behaviour on the part of girl children, deterioration of value system and mortality are some of the important factors that are found responsible for this phenomenon of sexual abuse of girl children in the Indian society.

From this study the hypothesis, (1) urban and rural divide exists about girl child sexual abuse, (2) girl child sexual abuse occurs mainly within kinship and (3) deterioration of morality and value system leads to higher incidence of girl child sexual abuse, are proved.

To Study the Consequences of Sexual Abuse on Victims was Another Objective of the Study

In this study it was found that the consequences of sexual abuse especially on girl children are far-reaching. Stigma and fear of defamation around the subject makes the girl child a silent sufferer. Due to secrecy and taboo, sexual abuse remains undisclosed and under-reported.

The study shows many reactions to the incident from the concerned child, such as fear, disgust, shame, helplessness and confusion. Of all these reactions, the percentage of 'fear' is the highest, i.e. 43.4 per cent and the percentage of 'feeling of disgust' is 17.4.

A very little percentage of girls, i.e. 6 per cent, actively oppose the abuse. These teenage girls do not know the consequences of sexual abuse and many a times they are not even aware of the fact that they are being abused. Such matters are not spoken in the family due to secrecy around the subject. Most of the time the abuser is a family member or a person in close relation of the child and, therefore, she is in utter confusion as to the incidence of abuse and her mind filled with sense of shame and disgust. The girl child finds herself helpless and is forced to hide the family secret. The entire concept of family relationship gets distorted and such girls face problematic relationship in their future life. In this mental state the girl child who had experienced sexual abuse loses her self-confidence, and is at risk of developing a number of psychological problems.

The study also reveals some other consequences of sexual abuse on girl children. Of all these consequences, guilt complex is the highest, i.e. 23.2 per cent. Feelings of guilt leads to self-pity, depression, anger and fear resulting into sleeping problem, eating disorders and sadness. Suicidal tendency is also noticed in many victims. Even if these girl children feel angry at the abuser, they are helpless and cannot do much in the matter.

It is also found that many victims suffer from more than one effect of the harrowing experience. The tender age of girl child and lack of understanding of sexual relationships, the sexual encounter, howsoever minor it might be, is mentally destructive to the child. The sexual abuse leaves strong legacy of self-blame, guilt feeling, and mistrust of close relatives. The child loses self-confidence and cannot live a happy life in future.

In their tender age, the girl children are unaware of the consequences of sexual abuse. Due to the abuse these girls suffer from inferiority complex, devoid of self-confidence and self-respect and lose the capacity to communicate with outside world.

Analysis of case studies in the present research reveals that sexual abuse by close relative leaves the girl child confused about the values of relationship and a feeling of disgust, hostility and depression fills her mind. She is inclined to dissociate herself from the company of family members resulting into stunted growth of her personality.

It was found that consequences of sexual abuse in childhood are far-reaching. She is tormented by shame and guilt and loses her inquisitiveness and fails to realize her full potential in future life. The girl child who is the victim of sexual abuse suffers from low self-esteem, poor social functioning, and inability to trust, isolation and trauma. The impact of sexual abuse in childhood is in psychological, behavioural and also in societal terms.

In the study of reported cases to police station in Beed District during 2006–10, it was found that 10 per cent victims are suffering from damage to internal organs, internal lacerations and bleeding and the children are not getting any treatment. The parents say 'she is not the only child of us, from where should we bring money for treatment as we are dependent on wages, have no guarantee of work and have to give food for other four or five children, What can we do?'

It was found that the victims of sexual abuse blame themselves by accepting the responsibility for the abuse and think that something is wrong with them or that the 'abuse' was their fault. These girl children face long-term effects and irreparable loss as an abused girl child. Early pregnancy and injury to reproductive organs are physical harms. Self-blaming, anxiety, depression, feeling of isolation are serious psychological problems, and stigma and recurrence of the incident, make her think that being a girl child is a 'curse'.

The study shows that absence of normal family life adversely affects the physical and emotional well-being of the child. The girl suffers from lack of trust in family adults, fear of men, and wants to be alone. Dreamy age of the girl is changed into an age of fear and depression.

Thus, in accordance with the fourth objective of the study, the above stated findings were identified in context of consequences of sexual abuse. This also confirms the hypothesis that sexual abuse leads to mental and physical disorder in victims.

To Assess the Attitude of Family Members towards the Victims was another Objective of the Study.

Disclosure about sexual abuse by victims to other persons is to mother, father, sister, brother, friends and persons in whom the child reposes confidence. The highest single category of persons to whom the girl child speaks about her sexual abuse is mother: 48.4 per cent girls from rural area and 43 per cent from urban area have told their mother about the sexual abuse experienced by them. Even though most of the girls are disclosing the matter to the mother, in the patriarchal Indian family, the mother finds herself powerless due to male dominated atmosphere in the house and secondary status given to mother and girl, and asks her girl child to silently tolerate the abuse. This shows the negative attitude of family members towards the girl child.

It was found in the study that 44.2 per cent parent's reaction is one of 'disbelief' in the sexual abuse of their girl child. The first reaction of the parents is to disbelieve their own child and even if it is found that the child is telling truth, the tendency is to hold the child, who is a victim, guilty and blame her for her misfortune. They even punish her though she is not at all at fault. This high percentage of 'disbelief' shows the negative attitude of family members towards the phenomenon. This negative attitude and disbelief of parents makes the child undergo the shame and humiliation of sexual abuse.

It was found in the present study that lack of acceptance of the fact of sexual abuse of girl children by her family members, not to believe her even if the girl child speaks about the incidence, believe the abuser and blame the girl child saying she is telling lie, and not disclosing the matter due to conspiracy of silence surrounding the phenomenon, results in low percentage of complaints against the abuser and allows the recurrence of the abuse.

The action of the parents not allowing the girl to continue her education, not allowing her to mix with other girls of her own age, preventing her from participating in outdoor games and discouraging her from going for shopping, etc. shows the negative attitude towards girl children. The parents say that the above actions are the means to protect her from sexual abuse. This attitude results into the stunted growth of the personality of the girl. She loses her self-confidence and may not mature into a healthy and happy human being.

About 22 per cent of families of girl children in the study were found to have 'tension' in the family due to sexual abuse of their girl child. They feel that sexual abuse is the fault of their girl child and they think this causes disreputation of family. So the parents do not allow the unfortunate girl to go outside even for genuine reasons. In some cases girl children are asked to discontinue their education and are not allowed to meet even friends. They cannot even think of outdoor games and entertainment. If they are sent outside, they are accompanied by some family member like brother, grand-father, grandmother or any other near relation.

These girls are always considered as burden and a cause of anxiety to the parents. They feel that the family reputation in the society has suffered an irreparable damage and the future of their girl child is forever ruined due to stigma attached to the issue. This results in non-disclosure which leads to increase and recurrence of this evil in the society.

The study reveals that the girl child sexual abuse is a harsh reality of life and the negative attitude towards girl child which results in disbelief, tendency to believe the abuser but not their own girl child makes the girl child a silent sufferer of sexual abuse.

In the present study of 500 school-going girl children, it was found that just 10 per cent victims got psychological support, only 4 per cent victims have parents who filed complaint with the police station, almost nobody met the counsellor due to lack of awareness of 'counselling' and again 'due to fear of defamation, they feel this matter should not be disclosed'. The parents feel that their girl children should tolerate the sexual abuse by keeping mum because they think that it is the responsibility of girl child to protect the dignity of family. She should keep silent because she is a 'girl child'. This shows the severity of the problem and negative attitude of parents towards girl children.

The present study also found gender discrimination, increasing school dropout rate, girls shouldering the responsibility of household work and of siblings, and not meeting the demands of teenage years is the outcome of negative attitude towards girl children.

Thus, negative attitude and not giving support to the girl child by parents, results in more trauma and continuing abuse for longer period. From this study the hypothesis that attitude of family members is negative towards the victims of sexual abuse is proved.

Conclusions drawn from the present study other than the above-mentioned hypothesis are as follows:

- It was found that girl child sexual abuse is not the problem of any particular country, but it is a rapidly increasing global problem. According to a study conducted by UN Population Fund, titled as International Statistics on Child Sexual Abuse, at least two out of four girls are victims of sexual abuse.
- A multi-country study by WHO, including both developed and developing countries, showed that between 1 to 21 per cent of women have reported to have been sexually abused before the age of 15, in most cases by male family members other than the father or step-father (WHO, 2005).
- In the present study of 500 school-going girl children, only 30 per cent victims found to have knowledge of sex relations. Remaining 70 per cent victims were unaware of it. This proves how the subject is kept under covers in Indian families, this secrecy is a cause of sexual abuse of girl child as they are not aware of the consequences of sexual abuse and, therefore, they become easy prey of the abuser.
- It was also found that 95 per cent girls were unaware of legal provisions. Only 5 per cent girls were aware of the laws preventing sexual abuse of children and were of the opinion that if there is law regarding sexual abuse, it must be implemented effectively so that the accused is punished. Around 8 per cent girls were eager to get self-protection training to protect them against the sexual assault. About 62 per cent girls wished to change the mindset of the society regarding girl child sexual abuse. These girls want to get equal treatment without discrimination as human beings. This will help them to build their confidence to face the problem.

- In the present study, when asked about getting help from the police in case of sexual abuse, 59 per cent girls were of the opinion that there is no surety of any help from the police, 61 per cent respondents replied that the police do not help and 62 per cent victims told that they are afraid of the police. This shows how the police personnel have lost faith and trust of the common man. This should make the police ponder over their image in society.
- About 90 per cent girls needed psychological support and trust of their parents and society as sexual abuse is not 'girl child's fault'. This will help for more disclosure and for breaking the silence.
- It was also found in the case studies in the present research that sexual abuse hurts the psyche of the child and it leads to low academic achievements, poor concentration and it also affects the ability of the child to develop trustworthy and intimate relationship with adults. Due to the age of the elderly abuser, the girl did not expect him to behave inhumanly by misusing her trust. So, these girls should be taught to respect the behaviour instead of age of a person.
- The conclusion drawn from interviews of the key informants in the concerned field is that the crime is on increase because the offender is rarely punished for the offence. One of the factors for this is the reluctance of the family of the victim to report the matter to the police in time.
- According to key informants, hardly 5 per cent cases of sexual abuse of girl children are reported and then also the police is reluctant to take cognizance of the offence, and to bring the accused to book.
- It was found in the interviews with key informants that poverty of the victim's family tempts the family to compromise and settle the matter outside the court for money. Witness, if there is any, is unwilling to testify before the court. There is inordinate delay in reporting the matter affecting the availability of medical and other clinching evidence.
- In the present study, key informants have revealed that the accused often gets acquitted for want of sufficient evidence to prove the offence. The general tendency is to push the matter under the carpet as the affected child's parents feel that a court case leads to defamation and girl child's future is in jeopardy.
- In the present study, key informants were of the opinion that the parents approach the doctors only when the girl is pregnant. They insist on abortion to avoid disrepute. Doctors are persuaded to terminate the pregnancy even if there are no medical grounds for it. The possibility of the girl committing suicide or being killed in such a situation is not rare. Therefore, the doctors agree to do so for money or on humanitarian grounds.

- It was found that among the reactions of outsiders about sexual abuse of girl child, 'disbelief' is the highest, i.e. 45.08 per cent followed by 'told to neglect the incident' at 7.8 per cent; 10.2 per cent people showed sympathy towards the victims. The attitude of the persons is generally not to accept that such incident has, in fact, taken place.
- Because of social stigma and shame attached to the victims, sexual offence remains one of the most misunderstood and under-reported crime which gives strength to the abusers to abuse innocent girls. Thus, girl child sexual abuse is really an ugly face of Indian society and a problem for the human growth and creativity.

Children are real social capital of our future, so we must take steps to solve this problem, by avoiding inadequate care, negative disciplining and, above all, faulty socialization, and by controlling abnormal behaviour; then only we can save our girl children.

Theoretical Presentation

'Integrated model' and 'systems theory' has been adopted for the present research as a theoretical framework.

Integrated Model of Child Abuse

Kewalramani's study (1991) of child abuse focused on the major premise of this model and the interdependence between parent, child and situation. This model focuses on four factors in child abuse. (1) Family environment, (2) Structural stresses, (3) Individual characteristics of parents and (4) Sub-cultural learning.

The model requires knowledge in five different areas: (1) Child development, (2) Socialization processes, (3) Family interactions, (4) Learning principles and (5) Sources of arousing anger, aggression, hatred and so forth.

These areas point out that:

> Child abuse can be viewed in terms of the degree to which a parent uses negative or inappropriate control strategies with her/his child. Employing 'normal' methods (meeting all the child's needs, adequate control, positive disciplining and clear communication) contributes to a child's social, emotional and intellectual development, whereas taking recourse to 'abnormal' methods (neglecting child's needs, inadequate control, negative disciplining, conflict between parents, addiction of father, unclear communication, negligent parenting, being indifferent and unresponsive and not paying due attention and over-reliance on coercion) in child rearing inhibits a child's development and causes child abuse. Factors like unemployment and dissatisfaction with job affects an individual's behaviour which leads to child abuse.

Individual characteristics of parents like lack of parenting skill and lack of resources (low prestige, little education and low income) also causes the child to be victim of abuse. The sub-cultural learning that is socialization in a violent home is another cause of the child being vulnerable to abuse. The factors in the integrated model of child abuse are found in the present research. They are:

1. *Family Environment*: The analysis of family environment, i.e. low socio-economic status of family which creates economic crises, lack of adequate control on children, lack of accountability, conflict between parents and weakening of inhibitions leading to neglect of the children, absence of affectionate relationship between parent and child, gender discrimination, unfulfilled desires, no interactions between parents, parents and children, deprivation from emotional bonds which creates favourable situation to abusers to enter in the family.
2. *Structural Stresses*: Illicit relationship of father and mother, dominance of step-father, brother, cousin reconstituted families, single parent families, migration of the family, migration of the parents, divorce, separation of parents and dissatisfaction with job of parents, lack of resources like low prestige, little education and low income, deteriorating relationships, bitterness and unhappiness in the family. These are the circumstances that lead to sexual abuse of children in the family.
3. *The Sub-Cultural Learning*: Socialization in a violent home is another cause, neglecting child's needs, inadequate control, negative disciplining, unclear communication and over reliance on coercion, negligent parenting being indifferent and unresponsive and not paying attention to child, gender discrimination, no interaction with children and asking the girl child to suffer in silence under pretext of the responsibility of protecting dignity of the family causes reoccurrence of abuse.
4. *Individual Characteristics*: Of parents like self-centredness, deteriorating relationships, strained marriage, poverty, lack of parenting skills, illiteracy and ignorance of the teenage victim about abusing, depression and helplessness that she cannot escape from abuse are also some of the causes of child falling prey to abuse. All these findings support the Integrated Model of Abuse.

Systems Theory (Fouche and Oliphant, 1977)

According to Fouche and Oliphant, there is a link between basic principles of system theory and sexual abuse. The focus is not only on the victim as a child who has been sexually abused but also on the context of abuse.

The abuse forms part of a larger pattern of dysfunction such as marriage problems, financial problems or other dysfunctional behaviour.

The family system forms pattern of behaviour, which acts as the basis of family functioning. When these patterns of behaviour are operating to maintain the abusive relationship, they can be seen as dysfunctional and not to the benefit of the child.

Behaviour in the system (including the behaviour regarding the sexual abuse) – the sexual abuses are circular in nature. The system is constantly in a state of stability and change, indicating that the family tries to cope with the abuse by means of certain patterns of behaviour, for instance, family may decide to cope with the sexual abuse by means of secrecy.

In the present study, it was found that 97 per cent girls are belonging to lower-income group and these families are facing financial problems and dysfunctional behaviour in their families. As most of the respondents reported that their parents always quarrel and there were no cordial relationship which leads to no interaction between children and parents

It is also found in the study that the sexual abuse of girl children is more prevalent in lower income group families. The poverty of the family renders it unable to fulfil the need of their girl children and the teenage girls are tempted by the gifts, money and items of luxury by the abuser and the girl became victims of sexual abuse. These victims are facing marriage problems due to defamation and stigma attached to the incident. The principle of social system, the abuse forms part of larger pattern of dysfunction such as marriage problems, financial problems or other dysfunctional behaviour supports the above findings of this research.

It was found in the present study that almost all (100%) victims were asked to keep quiet about their sexual abuse due to their gender, and maintain the dignity of the family with the fear of defame, due to stigma attached with the problem. The problem of sexual abuse is kept in secrecy by asking all the family members and especially the victims to keep quiet without raising her voice thus the family provides the context for continuation of abuse which emboldens the abuser for recurrence.

Draucker (1991–92) indicates that it is essential to acknowledge that sexual abuse occurs within a larger context, often important factors of sexual abuse according to him are family composition, for example the loss of a parent through divorce, death, separation, and the role of the other significant caretakers, the survivor's birth order and the number of siblings in the family.

In the present study, 74 per cent victims reported that they are sexually abused within their families and most of victims were having single parent due to divorce, death or separation and these families are large families having five to six siblings.

Draucker explains the social factors of socio-economic class. Other significant family is pathology or stresses, parental alcoholism, emotional or physical abuse, mental illness, criminal behaviour and extra family resource.

He further explains the characteristics of abusing families. These elements are denial, inconsistency and unpredictability, lack of empathy, lack of clear boundaries, role reversal, closed family system, incongruent communication, conflict, deterioration in relationships and strained marriage relationships.

In the present research, it was found that 82.61 per cent families with the head of the family being addicted is quite a distressful situation, as this results in disharmony, conflict, strained marriage life, stress, emotional and physical abuse of children. Tension in the family leads to incongruent communication between parents, parents and children; it results in closed family system and deteriorating relationship. This unhappy and unhealthy environment in the family results in sexual abuse of girl child in her family.

It is clear from the above discussion that the symptom of sexual abuse explained by Draucker in 'system theory' has been found in the present study which supports this theory.

Recommendations

Above discussion indicates the severity of the problem. Even though sexual abuse is a subject of social issue, most people would rather not think or talk about it. It continued to be shrouded in secrecy and taboos. Despite its invisibility, the problem is prevalent in India.

The following recommendations are made by the researcher which can be helpful to cope with and to help policy makers to take measures to tackle the problem of 'Girl Child Sexual Abuse':

- It is unfortunate that even though various studies in India proved the prevalence of girl child sexual abuse, still the Government of India has never thought about the rehabilitation of sexually abused girls. Around 42 per cent of India's population is children and, children are the future of emerging and developing countries like India. Children are still deprived of their rights as human beings.
- All the victims studied in the present study revealed that they have not got any rehabilitative services. Poverty of the parents does not allow them to meet any counsellor or even to give their children any medical treatment and they are unable to give any vocational training to make their child self-dependent. Hence, it is recommended that the government should provide rehabilitation services for the victims of sexual abuse at its level.
- The goal of rehabilitation is obviously to prevent sexual abuse of girl child, to ensure her safety in future and to help the victims of sexual abuse to come out from their feelings of guilt and self-blame and reduce their suffering. Enhancement of psychological development and healthier adult-functioning and also help to liberate these girl children

from their prison of secrecy and pain is the goal of rehabilitation programme. Special rehabilitative programmes for sexually abused girls are urgently needed, because the consequences of sexual abuse are for-reaching and devastating on these girls, who will be future mothers.

At Government Level

- Government should start rehabilitation centres that provide psychological, economic, medical, social and educational support to sexually abused girls. It was found in the present study that sexual abuse sometime leads to early pregnancy, injury to reproductive organs and this result in psychological trauma. Again, stigma attached to the subject makes her a silent sufferer, so the rehabilitative programmes should be prepared especially for girl children taking into consideration their irreparable loss. It should include healing child victims through counselling and therapy so that they are able to get healed and live with the dignity and have a right to life beyond trauma of their abuse. The present study reveals the fact that 90 per cent victims needed psychological support and trust of their parents and society. This study also reveals the fact that victim's family is isolated from the social relationships; the girl child is labelled as victim by facing default in her marriage. This labelling of the victim gives an easy access to the abuser to abuse the girl child again and again. It should include proper counselling to cope with the situation, to give knowledge about short-term and long-term treatments, about prevention of recurrence, training of yoga and encouragement for regular schooling, some vocational training like dance, art and craft which will help heal traumatized victims.
- Rehabilitation programmes are needed for the victims to make them available supportive and timely intervention, to raise public awareness regarding the issue of girl child sexual abuse, preventive programmes and the programmes which help in increasing the number of disclosures. It also should include treatment programmes which are essential for not only to treat current mental health but also to prevent future effects. Treatment goals may be carefully considered and made realistic and the treatment process should support the family's adaptive behaviour.
- Free physical and psychological treatment of victims should be made available by the concerned government, because most of the parents in the present study were of the opinion that due to poverty it was not possible for them to give proper treatment to their sexually abused girls (victims). Government should take not only the responsibility of economic and social rehabilitation of such victims but also encourage the man who would like to marry her. In the society, she should not be looked down upon. She should not only be given sympathy but also be

given normal treatment to enable her to do her duties and carry out obligations in a society in a normal way.

- All the agencies that children come in contact with like family, schools, hostels, observation homes, orphanages, rehabilitative centres should arrange workshop on what is sexual abuse and how it can be prevented, what can be done after the abuse, how the child would not be a victim of recurrence, how to control it, the consequences of sexual abuse. All these things will make the children aware of the problem and they can be mentally prepared for saying 'no' to the abuser. To organize frequent workshops on the issue are necessary at family level by the government.

Workshops

At Family Level

- It was found in the present study that most of parents were unaware of the sexual abuse of their girl child. Even though some parents knew about the incidents they keep quiet due to the stigma attached to the subject and fear of defamation. So it is found necessary to give orientation to them about the incident and about how to protect their child from this heinous crime and about how the parents should not feel ashamed but should support the victim to overcome the trauma. Parents should get orientation that they will not think that the disclosure gives them disrepute and stigma instead of solving the problem.
- In most sections of society, children's views are not given much importance. They are not normally listened to especially, when the child is a girl, she is more neglected due to gender discrimination. These girls are given low status in the family. This low status makes her feel inferior and she stays silent, tolerating her exploitation because her parents stop her from disclosing the incident by disbelieving her or by asking her to keep quiet as she is a 'girl child'. Thus, the imposition of restrictive norms is especially true for girl children.
- The parents should allow the girl child to speak and should listen to her and believe in what they hear from her. The girls should be given information about what is sexual abuse, its nature, about the possible abuser, about what can be done after the abuse, about proper and improper touch, about consequences of sexual abuse and how to prevent it. Parents should make her believe that they are her protectors and should create such atmosphere in the family that she is not afraid and share her feelings with the parents without hesitation. Parents should give psychological support to the victim and give her such confidence that she does not feel guilty, and also does not feel that something is wrong with her. The girl child should not feel that the abuse is her fault. If the parents are made aware of the consequences of

sexual abuse and if they give psychological support to girl child and build her confidence that it is not her fault, this gives her strength to say 'no' to the abuser.

- Orientation of parents should also include discussion about family atmosphere because in the present study, 82.61 per cent families were having the head of the family as an addict and 68 per cent victims reported that their parents quarrel always and there is no interaction between parents and children. So, the family atmosphere should be friendly and positive towards girl child and there should be interaction between parents and children. Family relations must be cordial, healthy and supportive so that the child feels secure and shares her feelings without hesitation. This can prevent the occurrence of sexual abuse and from among the near and dear ones, an abuser may not dare to make entry in the home. The girl child should feel secure and safe in her family and get emotional, psychological, social and economical support from the family and society. For the healthy development of the child who is the victim of sexual abuse it will be the real rehabilitation.
- It is also important to orient the parents about the process of socialization. The upbringing should teach the girl child how to keep away from temptation of luxury and she should not be attracted by the valuable gifts given by the abuser which may spoil her life, she should be made aware about the consequences of sexual abuse by parents and caretakers, then only would she be safe from occurrence and recurrence of sexual abuse. They should teach the girl child to respect the conduct and not the age of a person. The parents are also helped to adopt different coping skills and alternative values about child rearing.
- Parents should also be made aware about the newly passed Bill about sexual abuse and the procedure of reporting the cases in police station without any fear. This will be helpful in punishing the guilty.

At School Level

- School is an important unit in the socialization of child after its home. Teachers are the respected and ideal persons for the children, so it is the responsibility of the school to protect and create an atmosphere in the school which should be healthy, supportive and child friendly enabling the girl child to disclose the incident to the concerned person.
- There should be no gender discrimination at school level because it was found in the present study that gender discrimination is an important factor for sexual abuse of girl children. So the school should give equal treatment to the girls and boys that may give the girl confidence and she would disclose the incidence without hesitation. So, efforts should be made to increase the enrolment of the girl children and retention of

these children in school by adopting innovative, child friendly methods of teaching.

- Frequent workshops on the issue of girl child sexual abuse be made compulsory at school level by the government, especially for girl children and their parents. Orientation to teachers is also necessary, not only to train the students and parents but also to teachers themselves because in the present study some case studies revealed the fact that the teachers also sexually abuse their students.
- Workshop for teachers should include the message: abusing is a matter of guilt, shame and defamation for the abuser and not for the victim. Teacher-student relationship is considered sacred in Indian society, but in the present study, it was found that some teachers are behaving inhumanly with the students, not keeping in mind their relationship. The workshop should focus to make them realize their fault; they should feel the shame and guilt for their atrocious crime and try to change their mindset.
- Orientation of teachers should also give them training to tell the students and parents about sexual abuse and should include the issues like age, appropriate and right-based information on sexual abuse. This will help the girl children to act in their own protection. Workshop should focus on the issues like personal safety, knowledge about proper and improper touch, introduction of private body parts, and knowledge about sexual abuse, consequences of sexual abuse which will make the girl children conscious to prevent the occurrence of the incident. Awareness about newly passed Bill about sexual abuse, the procedure of report to police station for its proper implementation to record the cases in police station without fear should be made because it was found in the present study that 95 per cent victims were unaware about the Law.
- Lectures by police personal, doctors, advocates be arranged in the schools on the issue as these persons may act as protectors and helping hands for the parents and children in their difficult situation.

Police Personnel

- It was found in the present study that 59 per cent victims were of the opinion that there is no surety of any help from the police, 61 per cent victims replied that the police do not help and 62 per cent victims told that they are afraid of the police. This shows how the police personnel have lost faith and trust of the common man. So it is an urgent need for the police personnel to be given orientation for 'child friendly' behaviour in the workshop. So that the child can dare to disclose the matter without any fear and this is helpful in increasing the number of disclosures and the culprit is punished. It acts as a deterrent to the abusers from doing such heinous crime against girl children.

- *Child Help Line* centres should be started immediately at grassroot level (in each taluka) which may cover all the villages under its jurisdiction because the problem of sexual abuse is prevalent everywhere. Information about child help line and its telephone number should be given to the child. The child should be made to believe that the confidentiality of communication is maintained and disclosure of the identity is prevented so the child can open up freely about her problem. All the schools should be informed about the telephone number of help line so they can make their students aware of the number to be used in the difficult circumstances.
- Counselling Centres in Anganwadis be started by the government as Integrated Child Development Service (ICDS) includes adolescent girls as its beneficiaries. Anganwadi Tai is familiar with all the families from the locality and should be given training about the issue of Girl Child Sexual Abuse, about its nature, causes and preventive measures so that she can give proper counselling to the adolescent girls in the village to protect themselves from the problem.
- School counsellor should be appointed by State Government in each primary, middle and high school. This school counsellor should be an expert person who has the training about prevention and intervention skills with the main focus on teaching children about personal safety-skills through role play, poster exhibition, oral and written material, and he may show 'documentary film' on the issue of girl child sexual abuse.
- It is very important that all the persons related to and dealing with the child allow her to speak and listen to her and believe in what they hear from her. The child has to be protected from further abuse and the child should know that the horrible thing will not happen again.
- From the present study, it was found that some NGOs are working for the victims of sexual abuse in India. To make their work more wide they should help the government and be helped by the government in implementing schemes at grassroot level.
- Awareness programmes by the government and NGOs be arranged nationwide to promote a wider understanding of child sexual abuse as a preventable public health issue and to increase the services available to the victims.

At Academic Level

- A multi disciplinary approach is necessary in dealing with the case of girl child sexual abuse.
- The Ministry of Women and Child Development should launch the projects and action research programmes on the issue of girl child sexual abuse for the fuller understanding of the problem and prepare

action plans with the help of key informants who are working in the concerned field to prevent the occurrence of the problem. The ministry also should initiate preparation of documentaries on the issue by the experts and with the help of NGOs to create awareness about the problem at all levels.

- Government and NGOs should arrange programmes spreading awareness amongst various stakeholders like parents, teachers, caretakers, mental health professionals, staff in NGOs, B.Ed, D.Ed and Social Work students by giving training about prevention and intervention skills and to bring forth the reality of child sexual abuse, its ill effects, and false beliefs surrounding it.
- The issue of child sexual abuse should be included in the curriculum of Administrative Institutes, Social Work Institutes, Police Training, Academics, law colleges, medical colleges, teacher training schools, etc. so that the professionals passing out of these institutions have both the sensitivity and the knowledge to deal with these issues.

Awareness Through Media

- Media publicity should be made available so that it would help solve the problem by showing programmes on the subject of girl child sexual abuse and publishing the articles enabling the people an awareness of the issue. Thus, electronic media should be used to spread awareness to enhance people's knowledge and sensitivity upon this issue.

At Community Level

- The children have the right to live in safety and dignity in a protective and nurturing environment, both at home and in a community.
- It is not the responsibility of the government and NGOs alone to protect girl children from sexual abuse but it is also the responsibility of citizen and society to do so. Each citizen should contribute his/her might to prevent this heinous crime. Social patrolling and social control is necessary in this regard. Participation of people by performing their role as a responsible citizen in this respect will help to control the occurrence of sexual abuse of the girl child. So, it is the responsibility of all citizens to allow the girl child who is a victim of sexual abuse to speak, to listen her, to believe her and to give her psychological support to come out of the trauma and free herself from the 'culture of silence'. It is necessary to make her a trustworthy 'girl child' and not to label her as 'bad girl'.

Appendix

The Protection of Children from Sexual Offences Act, 2012

To protect children from offences of sexual assault, sexual harassment and pornography and provide for establishment of Special Courts for trial of such offences and for matters connected therewith or incidental thereto.

Whereas clause (3) of Article 15 of the Constitution, inter alia, empowers the State to make special provisions for children; and whereas, the Government of India has acceded on 11 December 1992 to the Convention on the Rights of the Child, adopted by the General Assembly of the United Nations, which has prescribed a set of standards to be followed by all State parties in securing the best interests of the child.

And whereas it is necessary for the proper development of the child that his or her right to privacy and confidentiality be protected and respected by every person by all means and through all stages of a judicial process involving the child;

And whereas it is imperative that the law operates in a manner that the best interest and well-being of the child are regarded as being of paramount importance at every stage, to ensure the healthy physical, emotional, intellectual and social development of the child;

And whereas the State Parties to the Convention on the Rights of the Child are required to undertake all appropriate national, bilateral and multilateral measures to prevent:

(a) the inducement or coercion of a child to engage in any unlawful sexual activity;
(b) the exploitative use of children in prostitution or other unlawful sexual practices;
(c) the exploitative use of children in pornographic performances and materials.

Chapter I
Preliminary

Short Title, Extent and Commencement

1. (1) This Act may be called the Protection of Children from Sexual Offences Act, 2011.
   (2) It extends to the whole of India, except the State of Jammu and Kashmir.

(3) It shall come into force on such date as the Central Government may, by notification in the Official Gazette, appoint.

Chapter II
Sexual Offences Against Children

A – Penetrative Sexual Assault and Punishment Therefore

3. A person is said to commit 'penetrative sexual assault' if

(a) he penetrates his penis, to any extent, into the vagina, mouth, urethra or anus of a child or makes the child to do so with him or any other person; or

(b) he inserts, to any extent, any object or a part of the body, not being the penis, into the vagina, the urethra or anus of the child or makes the child to do so with him or any other person; or

(c) he manipulates any part of the body of the child so as to cause penetration into the vagina, anus or any part of the child or makes the child to do so with him or any other person; or

(d) he applies his mouth to the penis, vagina, anus, urethra of the child or makes the child to do so to such person or any other person:

C – Sexual Assault and Punishment Therefore

Sexual Assault

7. Whoever, with sexual intent touches the vagina, penis, anus or breast of the child or makes the child touch the vagina, penis, anus or breast of such person or any other person, or does any other act with sexual intent which involves physical contact without penetration is said to commit sexual assault:

Provided that where such penetrative sexual assault is committed against a child between 16 to 18 years of age, it shall be considered whether the consent for such act has been obtained against the will of the child or the consent has been obtained by use of violence, force, threat to use force, intoxicants, drugs, impersonation, fraud, deceit, coercion, undue influence, threats, when the child is sleeping or unconscious, or where the child does not have the capacity to understand the nature of the act or to resist it.

E – Sexual Harassment and Punishment Therefore

Sexual Harassment

11. A person is said to commit sexual harassment upon a child when such person with sexual intent–

(i) utter any word or makes any sound, or makes any gesture or exhibits any object or part of body with the intention that such word or sound shall heard, or such gesture or object or part of body shall be seen by the child; or

(ii) makes a child exhibit his body or any part of his body so as it is seen by such person or any other person; or

Chapter III
Using Child for Pornographic Purposes and Punishment Therefore

Use of Child for Pornographic Purposes

13. Whoever uses a child in any form of media (including programme or advertisement telecast by television channels or internet or any other electronic form or printed form, whether or not such programme or advertisement is intended for personal use or for distribution), for the purposes of sexual gratification, which includes –

(a) representation of the sexual organs of a child;

(b) usage of a child engaged in real or simulated sexual acts (with or without penetration);

(c) the indecent or obscene representation of a child, shall be guilty of the offence of using a child for pornographic purposes.

Chapter IV
Abetment of and Attempt to Commit an Offence

16. A person abets an offence, who–

First – Instigates any person to do that offence; or

Secondly – Engages with one or more other person or persons in any conspiracy for the doing of that offence, if an act or illegal omission takes place in pursuance of that conspiracy, and in order to the doing of that offence.

Thirdly – Intentionally aids, by any act or illegal omission, the doing of that offence.

Chapter V
Procedure for Reporting of Cases

19. (1) Not withstanding anything contained in the Code of Criminal Procedure, 1973, any person (including the child), who apprehends that an offence under this Act is likely to be committed or has knowledge that such an offence has been committed, he shall provide such information to,

(a) the Special Juvenile Police Unit; or

(b) the local police.

Chapter VI
Procedures for Recording Statement of the Child

24. (1) For the purposes of recording the statement of the child, the provisions of section 157 of the Code of Criminal Procedure, 1973 shall apply

(2) If the statement of the child is being recorded under section 164 of the Code of Criminal Procedure, 1973, the Magistrate recording such statement shall, notwithstanding anything contained therein, record the statement as spoken by the child in the presence of the parents of the child or any other person in whom the child has trust or confidence

Chapter VII
Special Courts

28. (1) For the purposes of providing a speedy trial, the State Government shall in consultation with the Chief Justice of the High Court, by notification in the Official Gazette, designate for each district, a Court of Session to be a Special Court to try the offences under the Act.

(2) While trying an offence under this Act, a Special Court shall also try an offence [other than the offence referred to in sub-section *(1)*, with which the accused may, under the Code of Criminal Procedure, 1973, be charged at the same trial.

(3) The Special Court constituted under this Act, notwithstanding anything in the Information Technology Act, 2000, shall have jurisdiction to try offences under section 67B of that Act in so far as it relates to publication or transmission of sexually explicit material depicting children in any act, or conduct or manner or facilitates abuse of children online.

Chapter VIII
Procedure and Powers of Special Courts and Recording of Evidence

Procedure and Powers of Special Court

33. (1) A Special Court may take cognizance of any offence, without the accused being committed to it for trial, upon receiving a complaint of facts which constitute such offence, or upon a police report of such facts.

(2) The Special Public Prosecutor, or as the case may be, the counsel appearing for the accused shall, while recording the examination-in-chief, cross-examination or re-examination of the child, communicate the questions to be put to the child to the Special Court which shall in turn pout those questions to the child.

(3) The Special Court may, if it considers necessary, permit frequent breaks for the child during the trial.

(4) The Special Court shall create a child-friendly atmosphere by allowing a family member, a guardian, a friend or a relative, in whom the child has trust or confidence, to be present in the court.

(5) The Special Court shall ensure that the child is not called repeatedly to testify in the court.

(6) The Special Court shall not permit aggressive questioning or character assassination of the child and ensure that dignity of the child is maintained at all times during the trial.

(7) The Special Court shall ensure that the identity of the child is not disclosed at any time during the course of investigation or trial, except with the consent of the child or his parents or guardian. *Explanation*: For the purposes of this sub-section, the identity of the child shall include the identity of the child's family, school, relatives, neighbourhood or any other information by which the identity of the child may be revealed.

(8) In appropriate cases, the Special Court may, in addition to the punishment, direct payment of compensation to the child for nay physical or mental trauma caused to him or for immediate rehabilitation of such child.

(9) Subject to the provisions of this Act, a Special Court shall, for the purpose of the trial of any offence under this Act, have all the powers of a Court of Session and shall try such offence as if it were a Court of Session, and as far as may be, in accordance with the procedure specified in the Code of Criminal Procedure, 1973 for trial before a Court of Session.

Chapter IX
Miscellaneous

Guidelines for Child to take Assistance of Experts, etc

39. Subject to such rules as may be made in this behalf, the State Government shall prepare guidelines for use of non-governmental organizations, professionals and experts or persons having knowledge of psychology, social work, physical health, mental health and child development to be associated with the pre-trial and trial stage to assist the child.

Power to Remove Difficulties

44. (1) If any difficulty arises in giving effect to the provisions of this Act, the Central Government may, by order published in the Official Gazette, make such provisions not inconsistent with the provisions of this Act as may appear to it to be necessary or expedient for removal of the difficulty:

Provided that no order shall be made under this section after the expiry of the period of two years from the commencement of this Act

(2) Every order made under this section shall be laid, as soon as may be after it is made, before each House of Parliament.

Bibliography

Ahuja, Ram (2000), *Criminology*, Rawat, Jaipur.

Bajpai, Asha (2007), 'Who is Child', *Info Changes News and Features*, p. 5.

Benjamin, F. Crabtree and Miller, W.L. (eds.)(1999), *Doing Qualitative Research*, Sage, California, USA.

Buchanan, Michael F.G. (1986), *Sexual Abuse of Children*, DVD Video. The University of Leeds, Audio Visual Service, Leeds.

Burgess, R.L. (1979), 'Child Abuse: A Social Interactional Analysis', in Laney, B.B. and Kazdin, A. (eds), *Advances in Clinical Child Psychology*, Vol. II, Plenum Press, New York.

Castelino, C.T. (1985), Child Sexual Abuse: A Retrospective Study, TISS, Bombay.

Chaudhary, Renuka (2007), *A Study on Child Abuse in India*, Ministry of Women and Child Development, New Delhi.

Children's Bureau (2011), *Child Maltreatment Report*, US Department of Health and Human Services, USA.

Crawford, Karin (2006), *Social Work and Human Development*, Bell and Bain Ltd., Glasgow, Great Britain.

Cunningham, S. and Cunningham, J. (2009), *Sociology and Social Work*, Bell and Bain Ltd., Glasgow, Great Britain.

Desai, Murli (1994), *Family and Interventions*, Tata Institute of Social Sciences, Bombay.

Devi, Ranjana (2009), *Social Welfare Models: Concepts and Theories*, Omega Publications, New Delhi.

Draucker, C.B., W. Lewandowski, R. Morris and J. Risko (2007), 'Chronic Pain and the Family: Theory-Driven Treatment Approaches', *Issues in Mental Health Nursing*, 28 (9), pp. 1019–44.

DuBois, Brenda and Miley, Karla Krogsrud (1999), *Social Work: An Empowering Profession*, Allyn and Bacon, London.

Finkelhor, D. (1979), 'What is Wrong with Sex between Adults and Children? Ethics and the Problems of Sexual Abuse', *American Journal of Orthopsychiatry*, 49(4), pp. 692–697.

Fouche, C.B. and Oliphant, E. (1997), *Child Sexual Abuse with the Basic Principles of System Theory*, Johannesburg, McGraw-Hill Book Co.

Gavhane, Shubhangi (1997), *Female Criminality and Sociological Theories*, South Asian Social Research Publications, Aurangabad.

Gil, D.C. (1970), *Violence Against Children: Physical Child Abuse in United States*, Harvard University Press, Cambridge, Mass.

Goode, W.J. and Hatt, P.K. (1952), *Methods in Social Research,* MCGraw-Hill Book Co., New York.

Hastings, A.S. (1998), *Treating Sexual Shame: A New Map for Overcoming Dysfunction, Abuse and Addiction*, Jason Aronson, Northvale, NJ.

Hayward, Ruth Finney (2000), *Breaking the Earthenware Jar: Lessons from South Asia to End Violence Against Women and Girls*, UNICEF, New York.

Herman, J.L. (1992), *Trauma and Recovery*, Basic Books, New York.

Hini, Robert (2012), 'Sex Abuse a Big Problem for All of Us', *The Record*, Perth, Australia.

Hopper, J. (2010), 'Child Abuse: Statistics, Research, and Resources'. www.jimhopper.com.

Human Touch Bureau (2004), Child Abuse: A Priority Issue for Immediate Action, New Delhi.

Human Touch Bureau (2011), *The Children of India: Victims of Malnutrition*, Vol. VIII, New Delhi, p. 31.

Hurlock, E.B. (1981), *Developmental Psychology*, Tata McGraw-Hill Publishing Company Ltd., New Delhi.

Ingleby, Ewan (2006), *Applied Psychology for Social Work*, Learning Matters Ltd., Great Britain.

Kerlinger, F.N. (1964), *Foundations of Behavioral Research: Educational and Psychological Inquiry*, Holt, Rinehart and Winston, Inc., New York.

Kewalramani, G.S. (1991), *Child Abuse*, Rawat, Jaipur.

Khandela, Manchand (2006), *Adhunikta aur Mahila Utpidan*, Pointer Publishers, Jaipur.

Kumar, Aman (2011), *Social Work: An Introduction*, Aadi Publications, Jaipur.

Lal Das, D.K. and Bhaskaran, Vanila (eds.) (2008), *Research Methods for Social Work*, Rawat, Jaipur.

Lawrence, Abigail (2010), *Invisible Tears*, Author House, Bloomington, USA.

Lawson, L. and Chaffin, M. (1992), 'False Negatives in Sexual Abuse Disclosure Interviews'. *Journal of Interpersonal Violence*, 7, pp. 532–542.

Leclerc-Madlala, S., et al. (2009), 'The Socio-cultural Aspects of HIV/AIDS in South Africa', in Poul Rohdeder, L. Swartz, Seth Kalichaman, L. Simbayi (eds), *HIV/AIDS in South Africa: 25 Years On*. Springer, New York

Mehta, M.N., Liokeshwar, M.R., Bhat, S., Athavale, V.B. and Kulkarni, B.S. (1979), 'Rape in Children', *Child Abuse and Neglect*, 3 (3–4), pp. 671—677.

Mrazek, P.B., M. Lynch and A. Bentovim (1981), 'Recognition of Child Sexual Abuse in the United Kingdom' in Mrazek, P.B. and C. Henry Kemp (eds) *Sexually Abused Children and Their Families*. Pergamon Press, Oxford.

Mukherjee, R.N. (2009), *Democracy – A Failure, Shefocracy – The Solution, for Human Welfare*, University Press of America, Lanham, Md.

Munde, V. (2011), 'Beed Zhilyat Chaar Mahinayat 11 Balatkar', *Loksatta*, 29 April.

Nagla, B.K. (2008), *Indian Sociological Thought*, Rawat, Jaipur.

National Crime Record Bureau (1993), Crime in India, National Crime Record Bureau Report, New Delhi.

National Crime Record Bureau (2000), Crime in India, Report of National Crime Record Bureau, New Delhi.

National Society for Prevention of Cruelty to Children (2007), The NSPCC Annual Report, UK.

NIPCCD (2010), *Statistics on Women in India*, NIPCCD, New Delhi.

Panchal, Trupti (1997), 'Documentation of Police Cases of Sexually Abused Girls in Mumbai City between 1994–95', The Special Cell for Women and Children, Bombay.

Pande, Bharati (2010), *Somali Mom*, Mehta Publishing, Delhi.

Paranjape, N.V. (2000), *Criminology and Penology*, Central Law Publications, Allahabad.

Patel, A.K. and Dubey, M.V. (2010), *Social Work and Social Welfare*, Crescent Publishing Corporation, New Delhi.

Patricia, Uberoi (ed) (1993), *Family, Kinship and Marriage in India*, Oxford University Press, New Delhi.

Poffenberger, T. (1981), 'Child Rearing and Social Structure in Rural India', in J. Korbin (ed), *Child Abuse and Neglect*, University of California Press, Berkeley.

Porter, Ruth (ed) (1990), CIBA Foundation, *Child Sexual Abuse Within the Family*, Tavistock, London.

RAHI (1998), *Voices from the Silent Zone: Women's Experiences of Incest and Childhood Sexual Abuse*, RAHI, New Delhi.

Rane, Asha J. (1991), 'Research on Child Abuse in Families', in Rane, J. Asha (ed.), *Research on Families with Problems in India*, Vol. II, TISS, Bombay.

Rane, Asha J. (1994), 'Dynamics of Child Abuse and Interventions', in Desai, Murli (ed.), *Family and Intervention*, TISS, Bombay.

Rath, S. (1991), 'Dynamics of Child Abuse: Role of Parenting Behaivour', in *Research on Families with Problems in India: Issues and Implications*, Vol. II, Unit for Family Studies (eds.), TISS, Bombay.

Reza, A. et al. (2009), 'Sexual Violence and its Health Consequences for Female Children in Swaziland: A Cluster Survey Study', *Lancet*, 373 (9679).

Rodney, H. (2009), Ending Sexual Violence Against Girls, Report by Together for Girls, Swaziland.

Russell, D. (1983), 'The Incidence and Prevalance of Intrafamilial and Extrafamilial Sexual Abuse of Female Children', *Child Abuse and Neglect*, Vol. 7(2), pp 133–146. Elsevier.

SAATHI (1997), A Situational Analysis of Violence Against Women and Girls in Nepal, Kathmandu.

Sachdeva, D.R. and Bhushan, Vidya (1961), *An Introduction to Sociology*, Kitab Mahal, Allahabad.

SAKSHI Foundation (2007), 'Child Sexual Abuse', Draft Manual, New Delhi.

Sardar, N.K. (2011), *Social Work in Mental and Substance Abuse*, Manglam Publications, Delhi.

Sharan, M.B. (1990), 'Child Abuse and Neglect in Indian Families', Paper Presented at the 52nd Annual Conference of the National Council on Family Relations, USA.

Shivkumar, A.K. (2007), 'Why Children are Neglected?', *Seminar*, New Delhi.

Shrivastava, Nidhi (2010), 'Children at Risk of Developing Unstable Personality in Modern Society', in Nidhi Shrivastava (ed.), *Family in Modern Society*, Ritu Publications, Jaipur.

Singh, A.K. (2010), 'Child Abuse', *Human Touch*, Vol. VII, New Delhi.

Singh, K. (1991), *Criminology and Social Disorganization*, Prakash Kendra, Lucknow.

Singh, K.K. and Singh, R.S. (2010), *Encyclopedia of Social Work in 21st Century*, ABD Publishers, New Delhi.

Sinha, P.K. (2011), 'Higher Education in India', *Human Touch*, Vol. VIII, New Delhi.

Sirohi, Anand (2005), *Modern Perspectives on Social Work*, Vol. III, Dominant Publishers and Distributors, New Delhi.

Sirsat, J. (2012), 'Nati Pisatlali', *Lokmat*, 20 May.

Srivastava, S.S. (1996), *Criminology and Criminal Administration*, Central Law Agency, Allahabad.

Stake, R.E. (1988), 'Case Study Methods in Educational Research: Seeking Sweet Water', in R.M. Jaeger (ed), *Complementary Methods for Research in Education*, American Educational Research Association, Washington D.C., pp. 253–300.

Stanely, J., Adam M. Tonlison and J. Pocock (2003), *Child Abuse and Neglect in Indigenous Australian Communities*, Child Abuse Prevention, 19, Australian Institute of Family Studies, Melbourne, Australia.

Sutherland, Edwin H. (1924), *Principles of Criminology*, J.B. Lippincott Co., Chicago.

Tardieu, A.A. (1857), *Medical-Legal Studies of Sexual Assault France*, J.B. Bailliere, Paris.

The Indian Penal Code (2011), Professional Book Publishers, New Delhi.

Thukral, G.E. and Abbasi, I.R. (2007), 'Ensuring Child Protection', *Seminar*, New Delhi.

TULIR-CHCSA (2006), *Prevalence and Dynamics of Child Sexual Abuse Among School Going Children in Chennai*, Tulir-CHCSA, Chennai.

UNICEF (2003), *Child Protection: Child Trafficking Statistics*, New York.

United Nations (2011), *Millennium Development Goals Report*, 2011, United Nations, New York.

Vijayalakshmi, B. (2008), 'Case Study Method in Social Work Research', in D.K. Lal Das and Vanila Bhaskaran (eds), *Research Methods for Social Work*, Rawat, Jaipur.

Virani, Pinki (2000), *Bitter Chocolate: Child Sexual Abuse in India*, Penguin, India.

Webster's II (1984), *New Riverside University Dictionary*, Houghton Mifflin, New York.

Wild and Wynne (1986), 'Analysis of Child Sex Rings in Leeds' in *Handbook on Prisons*, Yvonne Jewkes (ed), Wilan, Devon.

World Health Organization (2005), *The World Health Report, 2005: Make Every Mother and Child Count*, WHO, Geneva.

World Health Organization (2007), *Report on Sexual Violence and Health*, WHO, Geneva.

World Health Organization (2012), *World Report on Violence and Health*, WHO, Geneva.

www.aspancsa.blogspot.com

www.indianchild.com

www.ispcan.com

www.karmayog.org/ngo/facse

www.rahi.com

www.tulir.org

Young, P.V. (1956), *Scientific Social Surveys and Research: An Introduction to the Background, Contents, Methods and Analysis of Social Studies*, Prentice Hall, New York.

Index